Aug. 31, 2010

Pearl Harbor

To: Richard Kingson

Thanks Richard, for your service in the U.S. Air Force during the Vietnam war.

Semper Fidelis

Jerome T. Hagen

B-Gen. USMC

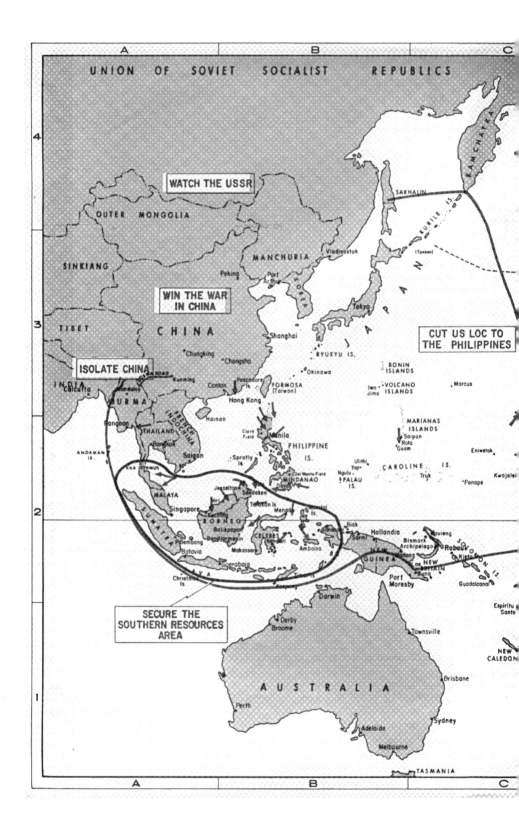

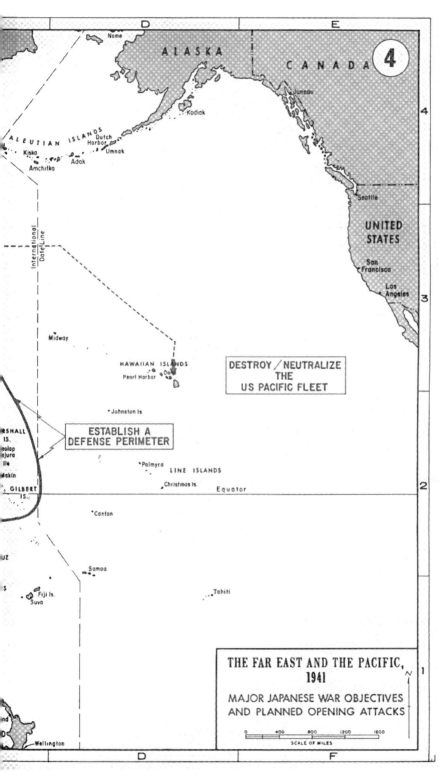

THE FAR EAST AND THE PACIFIC,
1941

MAJOR JAPANESE WAR OBJECTIVES
AND PLANNED OPENING ATTACKS

0   400   800   1200   1600
SCALE OF MILES

DESTROY / NEUTRALIZE
THE
US PACIFIC FLEET

ESTABLISH A
DEFENSE PERIMETER

Photo credit: frontispiece - Map of the Far East and Pacific 1941, from ATLAS FOR THE SECOND WORLD WAR: ASIA AND THE PACIFIC, ed. Thomas E. Greiss. Garden City, New York: Avery Publishing Group. Reprinted by permission.

太平洋戦争

WAR IN THE PACIFIC

Jerome T. Hagen

Volume I

HAWAII PACIFIC UNIVERSITY
Honolulu

Originally published in 1996 by Hawaii Pacific University

Printing history: 13th printing 2004. Copies of the book are available from the author at 47-446 Lulani St., Kaneohe, HI, 96744 (Fax: 808-239-1053)

Printed in the United States of America by Malloy, Inc.
Ann Arbor, Michigan 48103

Library of Congress Cataloging in Publication Data

Hagen, Jerome T.
    War in the Pacific / Jerome T. Hagen.—1st ed.
        p. cm.
    Bibliography:
    Includes index
    ISBN: 0-9762669-3-8
    1. World War, 1939-1945-Campaigns-Pacific Ocean.
    2. Islands of the Pacific. 1. Title.

    D767.H34 1996   96-77738
    940.54'26-dc   CIP

Photo credit: cover- Task Group 38.3 entering Ulithi anchorage near Palau after conducting air strikes against Japanese positions in the Philippines. Leading are carriers *Langley*, and *Ticonderoga*. Following are battleships *Washington*, *North Carolina*, *South Dakota*, and cruisers *Santa Fe*, *Biloxi*, *Mobile*, and *Oakland*. The photograph was taken in December 1944, and is reprinted with permission of the National Archives.

frontispiece- Map of the Far East and Pacific 1941, from *ATLAS FOR THE SECOND WORLD WAR: ASIA AND THE PACIFIC*, ed. Thomas E. Greiss. Garden City, New York: Avery Publishing Group. Reprinted by permission.

PREFACE

My purpose in writing this book is perhaps best expressed in this quote from Eleanor Roosevelt.

We have to remember that in the future we will want to keep before our children what this war was really like. It is so easy to forget; and then, for the younger generation, the hardships, the horror of war and the sorrow fade somewhat from their consciousness.

In a similar vein, in 1978, Saburo Ienaga wrote *The Pacific War* to remind a new generation that its peace and prosperity have roots in the fascism and aggression of the 1930s. In Ienaga's judgement, that could best be done by describing the horrors of war: "Otherwise, a generation raised on sugar-coated (revisionist) history would be likely to repeat the errors of the past."

Another goal was to write *War in the Pacific* as a story, not just a litany of dates, facts, and events that have little meaning in our lives. As a story, the book has heroes to emulate and villains to despise. As a story, the book provides each of us the opportunity to revisit, at least in our mind, the thrilling adventures of men and women who helped shape the world we live in today.

The contents of this book first appeared as a series of articles in *The Honolulu Advertiser* during August 1995. Material that was edited by *The Advertiser* to meet space constraints was reintroduced in a softback book published by Hawaii Pacific University in 1996. Additional material, including four more chapters and numerous graphics, have been completed and are included in this edition.

Japanese names appear in the Western style: i.e., personal name followed by family or surname.

ACKNOWLEDGEMENTS

I want to thank the readers for the calls, letters, and materials you shared with me during the series of articles on "The War in the Pacific." Especially appreciated were your comments concerning the quality and objectivity of the articles. A writer can hope for no more.

Special thanks to Executive Editor John Hollon and to the fine staff of *The Honolulu Advertiser* who assisted so much with the original series. Thanks also to President Chatt G. Wright, Senior Vice President Jim Hochberg, Dr. Helen Chapin, Barbara Benson, and George Moyer of Hawaii Pacific University. President Wright encouraged me to do the original series of articles and the subsequent book. He also provided extensive university support. George proof-read the articles for *The Advertiser* series and provided much needed editing and comments. Vice President Hochberg provided the support of the Special Programs department which included the excellent work of Barbara Benson, Joe Shrestha, and Akira Okada. Joe did the layout and graphics for this edition, and Akira did the Japanese calligraphy in the front of the book.

I am especially indebted to Dr. Helen Chapin and Vice President Rick Stepien of Hawaii Pacific University. Dr. Chapin encouraged me to put the articles in book form and did the final editing of the softback edition. Rick did the final editing for this edition.

Finally, I must thank the students of several "War in the Pacific" history courses. They suffered through several earlier editions of the book and provided valuable feedback which helped reduce errors and inconsistencies.

CONTENTS
VOLUME I

ILLUSTRATIONS

Photographs

Maps

1

JAPANESE COLONIALISM: 1874-1931

For many Americans, the war in the Pacific began on December 7, 1941. For millions of people, especially the Chinese, the war began much earlier.

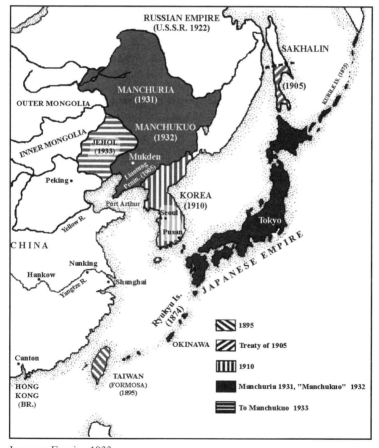

Japanese Empire, 1933.

HPU graphics

During the late 1800s, Western nations were seizing territory in Asia, Africa, and Oceania to add to their empires. Japan, now a major power, was quick to join the colonization race. In 1874, Japan sent a punitive expedition to Formosa and forced China to pay an indemnity, which, in effect, recognized Japan's claims to the Ryukyus.

The way Japan acquired the Ryukyus, or Liu-Ch'iu, as the Chinese referred to the islands, is most interesting. In 1873, 54 shipwrecked Ryukyuan sailors went ashore on Formosa where they were slaughtered by the aborigines. Japan adopted the exclusive right to represent the Ryukyuans, whose status had been one of ambivalence for several centuries even though Liu-Ch'iu had paid tribute to China since 1372.

Japanese foreign minister Soejima visited Peking and demanded compensation for the deaths of the sailors. The Tsungli Yamen, China's office that conducted foreign relations, scoffed at the demand, responding that Liu-Ch'iu was a Chinese tributary and Formosa was a part of China. Therefore, the killing of Liu-Ch'iu sailors on Formosa was no business of Japan.

Soejima countered that, since China was not able to effectively control either Ryukyu or Formosa, any action by Japan would not violate Chinese jurisdiction. Soejima, in a move that illustrates Japan's colonial motivation, obtained Tokyo's approval to send a military expedition to Formosa. Japan's military seized control of the government and constructed permanent occupation facilities. When neither side was willing to concede, Great Britain mediated the dispute and awarded compensation to Japan. China was also forced to recognize Japan's sovereignty over Ryukyu. The British minister in Japan correctly described the incident, whereby China was forced to pay for being invaded, as a clear invitation to further encroachment on the part of Japan.[1]

Next, Japan bullied Korea into a trade agreement and, in 1894, invaded Korea, drove the Chinese from the peninsula, and captured the port of Weihai in China. That war ended in 1895 with China agreeing to pay Japan a huge indemnity and ceding Formosa, the Pescadores, and the Liaotung Peninsula to Japan.

France, Germany, and Russia banded together, in what would be referred to as the Tripartite Pact, to force Japan to return the Liaotung Peninsula to China. Japan was outraged over this reversal, which Emperor Meiji termed, "having to bear the unbearable," and the militarists never forgave the politicians for what they felt was a betrayal on the part of those who advised the emperor. Henceforth, the military would select the government ministers and control all advice given to the emperor.

Japan especially never forgave Russia, its chief rival for occupation of Manchuria. In February 1904, Japan, in a sneak attack, crippled the Russian-Asiatic fleet in Port Arthur and bottled up the czar's troops in the ports of the Liaotung Peninsula. In desperation, the czar sent his decrepit European fleet to the Strait of Tsushima between Korea and Japan where it was destroyed by the Japanese Navy under Admiral Heihachiro Togo. Togo became a popular war hero in Japan, but lost favor with the emperor in the early 1930s due to his support for the Strike-North faction. A young naval officer, Isoroku Yamamato, who would become the Combined Fleet commander and plan the attack on Pearl Harbor, lost his left middle and index fingers in the battle of Tsushima Strait.

President Theodore Roosevelt negotiated the end of the war in 1905, whereby Russia gave up her railroads in southern Manchuria, ceded the southern half of Sakhalin Island, and transferred her lease of the Liaotung Peninsula to Japan. Japan was now a great power but did not obtain all the reparations and territory it coveted. Japan lost some 200,000 soldiers in the war with Russia and depleted its treasury. One way to recover was to plunder the remaining possessions of Korea and Formosa, which Japan proceeded to do.

In 1931, Japan's military initiated a coup of sorts whereby, for the next fifteen years, the militarists controlled Japan's foreign policy. This spirit of militarism, with its extreme passion, brutality, and frenzy of determination, infected the Japanese Empire like a plague.

Two principles of Japanese conduct contributed to the militaristic expansionist policy of Japan in the 1930s, *hakko ichiu* and *kodo*. The first means making the world one big family. The second means that the first could only be obtained through loyalty to the emperor. Those who made military aggression the national policy of Japan made *hakko ichiu* the moral goal and *kodo* the way to achieve it.[2]

In actuality, the militarists were following the ideas published in a book by Dr. Shumei Okawa in 1924, wherein Okawa argued that "since Japan had been the first state in existence, it was Japan's divine mission to rule the world." Japanese civilians were repeatedly told that the Japanese were the master race and their mission was to "end the tyrannical rule and oppression of the westerners." Dr. Okawa was indicted as a major war criminal following the war, but was declared unfit for trial due to insanity. Following the trials, he promptly recovered his sanity and died of a stroke in 1957 at the age of 71.[3]

The next step in the expansionist policy was the suppression of freedom of speech and censorship of all written material. This measure was easy for the military to enforce since there had always been some limitations on the press in Japan.

As Japan's conquest of the Asian colonies began, it became immediately apparent that this was not to be one big family or the much-touted Asian Co-Prosperity Sphere. In each of the places captured by the Japanese, civilians and prisoners were murdered, bayoneted, tortured, beaten, and raped. The captured were robbed of their possessions and forced to work night and day in terrible conditions. They were kept in filth and squalor and either starved to death or reduced to "living" skeletons; all in the name of *hakko*

4

ichiu and *kodo*.

THE WASHINGTON CONFERENCE SYSTEM

Japan was a major power in the 1920s and enjoyed the reputation of being a respected member of the international community. In treaties signed in Washington, D.C. in 1921 and 1922, Japan, the U.S., and Great Britain were recognized as the three foremost naval powers in the world. Another treaty, which included Japan, France, Great Britain, and the U.S., required the nations to maintain an arms embargo and to consult with one another whenever there was a threat to stability in the Asia-Pacific region.

The most important document signed by Japan, the U.S., Great Britain, France, Italy, Belgium, the Netherlands, Portugal, and China was termed the Nine Power Treaty. This treaty established a period of international cooperation in China. The nine nations pledged to cooperate with China, uphold the independence and integrity of China, and provide a stable Chinese government. These treaties, known as the Washington Conference System, were meant to guard against radical change in China in order to enable China to take its place in the community of nations.

MANCHURIA

In 1928, Japan's Kwantung army secretly assassinated Marshall Chang Tso-lien, the warlord of the great, mineral-rich territory of Manchuria that bordered Korea. The action was made quite simple since Japan had annexed Korea in 1910 and could move freely across the border. To many Japanese, Manchuria was the promised land. It had vast coal and iron reserves, a source of abundant and cheap labor, and the potential to provide other resources that Japan needed as a foundation for its economic recovery.

The assassination was a major coup on the part of the army and a triumph for Col. Daisaku Komoto, senior staff officer who planned the explosion that killed Marshall Chang. Greatly disturbed by the army's unauthorized actions in China, Emperor Hirohito, for the first time, openly intervened in Japanese politics. He rebuked Prime Minister Giichi Tanaka for his handling of the incident, forcing the Tanaka cabinet to resign, and appointed Osachi Hamaguchi, president of the opposition party, as prime minister with instructions to form a new cabinet.

The "Marshal of Manchuria," Chang Tso-lin (in large winter hat), is saluted by the 15th Regiment, U.S. Army, then stationed in Tientsin, China 1927.
US Army/National Archives

CHINA EMERGES

From 1928 to 1931, China, under the leadership of Chiang Kai-shek, made significant strides towards its goal of a place in the community of nations. Chiang, with the title president of the Republic, established a central government in Nanking and extended political control far beyond that accomplished in recent history. China's infrastructure of transportation and communications networks, roads, bridges, telephone, and telegraph was established. A modern system of education was put in place, and foreign trade increased steadily. Gradually, the fiscal problems that hampered China for decades were being corrected.

The United States, which financed much of China's growth, as well as Great Britain, Japan, and others, recognized the Chiang government, signed new treaties, and began negotiations to elevate China to a first-class nation status. It was at this time that the Japanese military struck.

JAPAN REVOLTS

Japan revolted against the Washington Conference System because it saw only disaster in a system where its destiny appeared to depend increasingly on the goodwill of China and the Western powers. Later, Japan would argue that peace, order, and stability really meant a continuation of the status quo, whereby nations that had power retained such power and nations without power were denied the ability to gain it. Unless something was done immediately, the militarists argued, Japan would soon be at the mercy of outside forces and would lose control of its destiny. The solution the Japanese advocated was to remove the leadership currently devoted to internationalism and to defy the Washington Conference System.

The timing of Japan's revolt was good. In 1930, Japanese unemployment reached one million, farm prices plummeted, and many tenant farmers were forced to leave Japan and move to Korea or Manchuria in order to survive. Japan's export trade was especially hard hit. As a result, the Japanese public was receptive to the militarists' propaganda and agitation for radical reform.

A month after Japan ratified the London Disarmament Treaty, in November 1930, Prime Minister Hamaguchi was assasinated by a right-wing terrorist. The assassin was supported in the press and in mass rallies as a true patriot, one who was selflessly trying to purge the country of unpatriotic politicians. The incident kindled similar reactions resulting in the murders of a number of other leaders.

Chiang Kai-shek and his Wellesley-educated wife. Note the picture of Franklin D. Roosevelt on the mantle.

Associated Press

2

JAPANESE EXPANSION IN CHINA: 1931-1937

THE MUKDEN INCIDENT

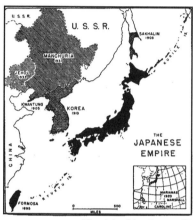
Honolulu Advertiser graphic

Japan's army in China, the Kwantung army, had its fair share of military zealots as did the military in Japan. Masterminding the incidents in China were Col. Seishiro Itagaki, Lt. Col. Kanji Ishiwara, and Maj. Kenji Doihara. Itagaki and Doihara were sentenced to death by the International Military Tribunal following the war, and Ishiwara died from cancer a few hours after testifying before the tribunal.

In November 1930, a right-wing terrorist assassinated Prime Minister Osachi Hamaguchi, and several other leaders identified with internationalism were also murdered. Various cabinet members who did not support the military's position were denounced verbally and threatened physically. Now that the leaders of Japan, including the emperor, understood their role, the army could make its move.

Late in the evening of September 18, 1931, two Kwantung Army officers led an attack on the south Manchurian Railway tracks five miles north of Mukden, China. The troops used explosives to destroy several feet of track and, under the guise of an incident being initiated by the Chinese Army, commenced a large-scale

9

attack on the Chinese forces stationed in Manchuria. Within a day, both Mukden and Changchun, the northern terminus of the railway, were under Japanese control.

The clash at Mukden developed into what would be a 10-year war between Japan and China. In retrospect, it now seems clear that this incident, staged by a few fanatical army officers, also marked the beginning of Japan's war against the ABCD powers, (America, Britain, China, and the Dutch.) The incident was also Japan's initial challenge to the Washington Conference System.

The Tokyo cabinet met shortly after the Mukden incident in the hope that a restoration of the previous status quo would be possible. The Army refused to consider such a position and stated that it would withdraw from cabinet participation if such a position should be adopted. The internationalists blinked, and, while they did so, the Japanese Army in Korea crossed the Yalu river and reinforced the Kwantung Army in Manchuria.

Propaganda concerning the Mukden incident was well-managed. Newspaper and radio accounts were screened, and the army controlled the release of all information. Releases and newsreels described in colorful fashion how the Japanese soldiers had reacted to Chinese aggression. Sensational headlines inflamed public opinion. In the process, some 30 million Chinese in Manchuria were working hard to raise the Japanese standard of living.

Chiang Kai-shek, as president and later generalissimo of China, was quick to call upon the League of Nations and the other members of the Nine-Power Treaty to condemn Japan for an assault on peace, civilization, and international morality. By doing so, China associated itself with international law and order and looked to the League of Nations and Washington Treaty members for support.

Japan refused to work in the international arena and dismissed its action in China as being only a police action in rebuttal for

Chinese intransigence. Chiang refused to deal bilaterally with Japan and was seen by the world as the champion of law and order. By refusing to cooperate, Japan was looked upon as the aggressor and violator of the several treaties concerning China. There would be many opportunities for Japan to reverse their expansionist policy, but the army would refuse to consider such a course.

JAPAN'S ISOLATION

The subsequent lack of action by the League gave additional courage to the militarists to encroach further into Manchuria and even Mongolia to establish control and expel Chinese forces. To initiate their plans, aircraft were launched from Mukden, on October 8, to bomb the city of Chinchow. The Chinchow bombing was followed by additional attacks throughout Manchuria, all aimed at severing the northeastern provinces from China.

Fifteen-hundred Chinese died when Japan bombed the Shanghai railroad station in 1937, but it was the cries of a battered baby that drew world attention to the "China Incident."   *Associated Press*

CHINA RESISTS: JANUARY 28, 1932

Japan proceeded to slowly and quietly enlarge its sphere of

influence in China until January 1932, when Chinese students and radicals in Shanghai organized to protest against Japanese aggression. These protests led to several armed skirmishes with Japanese forces in Shanghai. Once again, Japan argued that it was merely trying to restore law and order in the unorganized country of China. Chiang once again appealed to the international community, branded Japan as the violator, and pointed out that it was Japan that was so divided and unstable that its government was unable to control its army. Only the U.S. condemned Japan for its aggression. Great Britain, France, Italy, and Belgium were not ready to do so, their governments being occupied with more urgent issues at home.

ESTABLISHMENT OF MANCHUKUO

On March 1, 1932, Japan established the new government of Manchukuo. The act was solely the product of the Kwantung Army but was presented as the expressed right of self-determination by the local populace. Henry Pu Yi, the former "boy emperor" of the Manchu dynasty, was installed as the puppet emperor of the government. Japan refused to refer the question of Manchukuo's status to international arbitration, as called for by the Washington Treaty nations, and thus took another step away from the community of nations. The fact that the League condemned the action as unjustifiable scarcely mattered to Tokyo.

Back in Japan, Prime Minister Inukai was found not to be supportive enough to the military foreign policy and was assassinated. The cabinet collapsed on May 15, and, by fall, Japan withdrew from the League of Nations, the next step in Japan's isolation from world affairs.

Another obstacle now faced Chiang Kai-shek in China. The Chinese Communist Army had gained strongholds in Juichin, Kiangsi Province, and declared war on Japan. Its action posed a serious leadership problem for Chiang and the Nationalist government since Chiang's forces had been particularly aggressive against the Japanese. Chiang responded by mobilizing 500,000 troops and attempted to encircle and crush the communists. His efforts were not completely successful.

During 1933, Chiang's military commanders signed a quasi-truce with Japan. Chiang was forced to accept Japanese terms that acknowledged Japanese sovereignty of Manchukuo and agreed not to threaten Japan's presence in Inner Mongolia and the three northeastern provinces which now comprised Manchukuo. Although extremely humiliating to China, the agreement provided a cessation of hostilities which was sorely needed in view of the lack of outside assistance. Chiang reasoned that the truce was only a military agreement and not diplomatic recognition of the puppet regime of Manchukuo.

ABROGATION OF THE WASHINGTON TREATIES

Japan next suggested that, since it was the predominant power in the western Pacific, and America in the eastern, both countries should recognize this and not interfere with the other's area of predominance. Japan went on to insist on parity among the navies of the United States and Britain. When the United States refused to negotiate these issues, Japan abrogated the treaty in December 1934.

THE SOVIET UNION

The Soviet Union recognized the Nanking government in late 1932 and joined the League of Nations in 1934. During 1934, Moscow began strengthening its Manchurian-Siberian border defenses. Airfields were built, four-engine bombers deployed, trenches dug, defensive positions emplaced, and submarines added to their Pacific fleet. By 1935, Japan, or at least its war minister, Sadao Araki, was convinced that Japan's enemy was the Soviet Union. The Soviets were expected to move through Siberia and threaten Japan's territory of Manchukuo. Araki's position was opposed by Nagata Tetsuzan, bureau head of the war ministry, who agreed with Araki's call for military mobilization, but wanted

13

mobilization for a general war, not just for a specific war against the Soviet Union.

Tetsuzan was assassinated in August 1935 by an officer who favored Araki's policy. The differences between the two factions grew out of control by early 1936, when some 1,400 troops, loyal to Sadao, staged yet another coup, assassinated several cabinet ministers, and seized the war ministry, general staff, and several other government buildings. Surprisingly, the ringleaders were captured, the mob suppressed, and Tetsuzan's total-mobilization faction was in charge of the government.

When Chiang Kai-shek was forced to acknowledge Japan's sovereignty of Manchukuo in 1933, and after Japan signed a defense pact with Manchukuo, the Soviets signed a similar treaty with Outer Mongolia. When Japan began to develop the border areas of Manchukuo and to build railroads, the Soviets did the same in Outer Mongolia. When Japan mounted a massive attack near Nomonhan on the Manchukuo-Outer Mongolia border in May 1939, consisting of 70 tanks, 100 anti-tank weapons, 80 planes, 400 vehicles, and 15,000 men, the Soviets matched each border escalation and brought in General Georgi Zhukov to comand the Soviet-Mongolian force. By August 1939, Japan had suffered 8,440 killed, 8,700 wounded, and lost most of their weapons and equipment. The settlement of the Nomonhan incident was clearly a Soviet victory, so much so that two Japanese regimental commanders burnt their flags in dishonor, one disemboweled himself, and the other died charging into enemy fire.[1]

JAPAN'S FOREIGN POLICY GUIDELINE

Throughout 1935 and 1936, President Franklin D. Roosevelt showed little interest in either Tokyo's or Moscow's initiatives in China. Given a relatively free hand, Prime Minister Koki Hirota's cabinet drafted a foreign policy guideline that called for three basic objectives: one, maintenance of Japan's position in China; two, resistance to Soviet ambitions; and three, expansion into the South

Seas.

This was the first time that Japan had formulated a policy that, in effect, would pit Japan against the United States, the Soviet Union, and Britain as future enemies. The policy was a clear break from the Washington Conference System and established Japan as a renegade intent upon establishing itself as a power at the expense of other countries.

THE SIAN INCIDENT

In December 1936, Chiang Kai-shek was captured in the ancient Chinese capital of Sian by forces loyal to Chung Hsueh-liang, a former Manchurian warlord who now favored the Chinese communists. As a condition of his release, Chiang had to agree to end his anti-communist campaign and concentrate his resources against the Japanese. Chiang, with no recourse, accepted the condition. As 1937 dawned, the communists began incorporating their forces into the Nationalist army.

In Japan, the Hirota cabinet fell and was replaced by one headed by Senjuro Hayashi, former war minister. This cabinet proved to be unpopular with the army and was forced to resign in May. The new cabinet was headed by Prince Fumimaro Kanoye, who wholeheartedly favored military action in China as a means of obtaining the necessary rich resources for Japan. Konoye believed in Japan's manifest destiny and therefore its right to obtain the necessary resources to fulfill such a destiny. Kanoye appointed Hirota as his foreign minister, and the two, Kanoye and Hirota, would become the two civilians most responsible for Japan's further isolation from world affairs.

THE MARCO POLO BRIDGE INCIDENT

More incidents were staged by the Kwantung army, including one at the Marco Polo bridge in Peking on July 7, 1937. According to David Bergamini in his *Japan's Imperial Conspiracy,* a Japanese private was sent to relieve himself, and, while he was away, a roll call was held.[2] Finding one of his men missing, the Japanese commander ordered access to the Chinese fort to search for his missing soldier. Denied entry, the Japanese attacked and seized Peking, Tientsin, and large parts of North China and Inner Mongolia. Of course, the missing soldier had returned long before the action started and was able to participate in the search for himself. Bergamini says that, after the end of the second world war, plans were found in the emperor's library that detailed every specific of these incidents to include sending an enlisted man to relieve himself and holding a roll call in his absence.

President Roosevelt, still concerned that the American people would not support strong coercive measures against Japan, vetoed the economic sanctions of the Brussel's conference. Disappointed by the failure of the Western nations to act, Chiang turned to Germany for mediation in his war with Japan. As the German ambassador in Nanking, Oskar P. Troutman, prepared to act as an intermediary to work out the cease-fire agreements, the Japanese landed in force at Hangchow Bay, just south of Shanghai, and attacked the Chinese from the rear.

The Japanese strategy was excellent. The Chinese retreated pell-mell towards Nanking with the Japanese in hot pursuit. The Rape of Nanking in December 1937 and the attack on the U.S. Navy gunboat *Panay* on December 12 symbolized Japan's disregard of international treaties and individual rights. Japan was effectively isolating itself without League of Nations sanctions or other government actions. The Tokyo government quickly apologized and paid damages for the *Panay* attack but hardened their peace terms for China. It has been reported that Japan celebrated the Massacre of Nanking with lantern parades in the streets of Tokyo.

By now, the Chinese, led by Generalissimo Chiang Kai-shek, were fighting back. The stiffening resistance enraged the Japanese military who were determined to make the fall of Nanking the example that would force Chiang Kai-shek to capitulate.

3

THE RAPE OF NANKING: DECEMBER 1937

The coming of war

Japan

Nanking
•Shanghai
Yangtze

China

Honolulu Advertiser

Many Americans first learned of the Shrine of Remorse from David Bergamini's, *Japan's Imperial Conspiracy.* In his book, Bergamini described the shrine as being located on a green hillside some 50 miles south of Tokyo.[1] The centerpiece of the shrine was, and still is, a large statue of Koa Kannon, the Buddhist goddess of mercy.

The Kannon, which faces toward China, is made of clay, reportedly half of which came from Japan, and the rest dug from the banks of the great muddy Yangtze river. The shrine also houses a tea pavilion that features a wall portraying the skyline of Nanking, China. Nanking, in 1937, under Chiang Kai-shek, was the capital and model of unified China.

When Bergamini visited the shrine nearly 30 years ago, he found a priestess who chanted prayers and wept continuously. When asked why she wept, she responded that such was her duty, and that she has been weeping since 1938. In actuality, she wept because her kinsman, Gen. Iwani Matsui, on whose estate the shrine is erected, was hung by the neck until dead, in 1948, for his responsibility in the Rape of Nanking.

Few foreigners visit Koa Kannon, and most Japanese have never heard of it. The Kannon has, however, become a mecca for those elder Japanese who dutifully climb the unmarked steps on their annual pilgrimage to the shrine. During my recent visit to the Shrine of Remorse, there was no weeping priestess, but there were men dressed in the 1938 field uniforms of the Japanese Kwantung Army in China. The soldiers carried the classic long swords and waved the military rising sun flags. There were also members of the Koa Kannon Memorial Association who passed out literature that denounced the allied occupation of Japan and preached Japanese nationalism in the vein of Asian solidarity.

In December 1937, under the same guise of Asian solidarity, the Japanese Kwantung Army pushed the Chinese forces up the Yangtze Valley from the port of Shanghai, captured and closed off the city of Nanking on December 14, and then conducted six weeks of the most brutal and supervised terror imaginable. According to several historians, somewhere between 100,000 and 200,000 Chinese were executed of whom not fewer than 40,000 were innocent civilians.[2]

Nanking was normally home to 250,000 people, but the mass exodus from Shanghai had swollen the population to more than a million. The city had long been a cultural and intellectual hub of China, and was home to the University of Nanking and Ginling college for women. Both institutions were targeted for atrocities by the Japanese.

As the Japanese forces approached Nanking, Chiang Kai-shek made a decision not to defend the city. He supervised the evacuation of most of the government apparatus, and, on December 7, flew to Hankow, 350 miles inland, with his staff.

General Yasuhiko Asaka, prince and uncle of Emperor Hirohito, arrived at the front on December 8, and was informed that 300,000 Chinese troops were about to be surrounded in front of the Nanking walls. Preliminary discussions revealed that the Chinese would like to surrender.[3] Immediately, a set of orders was issued from Asaka's headquarters under his personal seal that said simply, "Kill all prisoners."[4] Knowing that defeat and death were inevitable, 30,000 of the Chinese troops laid down their arms and surrendered to the Japanese forces. Within 24 hours, the prisoners were lined up along the banks of the Yangtze river and machine-gunned to death.[5]

The remainder of the Chinese forces sought refuge inside the city walls and all but 75,000 of them were able to escape and join Chiang Kai-shek's army at Hankow.

Only 22 foreigners remained in Nanking when the Japanese entered the city on December 12. These foreigners, mostly Americans and Germans, with a few Danes and Englishmen, organized an international rescue committee and cordoned off a section of Nanking to serve as an international safety sector for refugees and non-combatants. The effort, though noble and dangerous to the foreigners, was of no avail in stemming the atrocities of the rampaging Japanese.

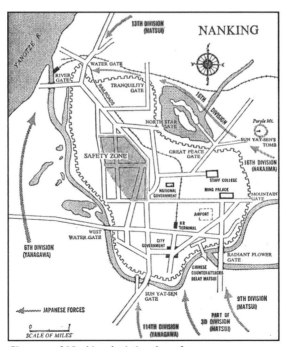

City map of Nanking depicting the safety zone.

Dyno Lowenstein

19

According to testimony given at the Tokyo War Crimes Trials, the Japanese troops did observe civilized rules of behavior when they entered the city. It was on December 14, when Col. Akira Muto, a member of the emperor's inner circle of advisors, and secret police chief Kesago Nakajima entered the city that the situation changed. Armed with Prince Asaka's directive to kill all prisoners, Muto and Nakajima ordered all Chinese to be shot on sight. Thousands of suspected Chinese military who had shed their uniforms and adopted civilian attire, were rounded up, tied singly, and in groups, marched to the edge of the Yangtze river and machine-gunned at close range. Their bodies were pushed into the river.

Women and girls were raped repeatedly by Japanese soldiers who then bayoneted them and mutilated their bodies. Rapes at the University of Nanking and Ginling college continued for 24 hours per day. The University was adjacent to the Japanese Embassy which had firsthand knowledge of the situation but was powerless to stop it.

Male Chinese were machine-gunned en masse, 20,000 in a single day. Others were used for bayonet and sword practice. Japanese officers made wagers on the number of Chinese they could kill, and their daily tallies were carried in Japanese newspapers. No women, from the aged to children, were safe from the ravages of drunken and howling Japanese soldiers. At least 15,000 were raped before they were slaughtered. Everything of value in the city was pillaged, and whole sections were burned to the ground. Soon the Yangtze river was a human logjam, thick with floating corpses.

An American Episcopal Minister, John G. Magee, testified at the Tokyo trials that he accompanied a Japanese Embassy official on a tour of the designated international safety sector of Nanking in hopes that the official would post a notice to the army to respect the zone. Magee and the official were unable to reach the zone due to layer after layer of charred bodies, men and women, which completely blocked the streets and alleys.

Drunken soldiers roamed the streets killing Chinese of both sexes, adults and children, without any provocation. Looting became routine after the first week. Everything of value was taken from homes and businesses and put on long supply columns that left the city. Torches were then put to the ransacked buildings causing the destruction of most of the city. When General Matsui triumphantly entered the ravaged city on December 17, riding a white horse, the gutters ran red with blood and bodies still covered the streets and alleys.

The rape of Nanking provoked worldwide moral indignation but not much action on the part of the West. In actuality, the sinking of the U.S.S. *Panay*, while Nanking was burning, caused far more uproar in the United States. The *Panay* and two of the three barges she was towing on the Yangtze were sunk by Japanese aircraft, and the survivors then strafed from a Japanese launch. Two American seamen and a foreign journalist were killed. Even this incident was considered closed by Christmas when the Japanese government delivered a check to the U.S. government for $2,214,007.36 as compensation.

It would be 1940 before President Roosevelt would respond to Japan's principle of *hakko ichiu*, bringing the eight corners of the world under one roof or making the world one big family. When he did act, Roosevelt froze Japanese assets in America, halted exports of finished steel and scrap iron to Japan, and cut off its oil imports.

Japan had two choices. The first was to withdraw its troops from China, lose face in the process, and condemn the militarists as a failure. The second was to continue the war in China and risk war with America, Great Britain, and, probably, the Netherlands. The war lords won. Prince Konoye, who was premier, resigned and was replaced by Gen. Hideki Tojo. The stage was set for the attack on Pearl Harbor.

Looking down on City of Atami from the lookout area at the Shrine of Remorse.

J. T. Hagen

This entranceway to the Shrine of Remorse. The Shrine is not well marked, and few Japanese know of its presence.

J. T. Hagen

22

The steps leading to the Shrine of Remorse. The Kannon is visible at the top of the steps.

J. T. Hagen

Kannon at Shrine of Remorse

J. T. Hagen

Facing the Kannon, one sees three stone monuments. The one on the right is in memory of the seven Japanese who were executed as class A war criminals. The center stone memorializes the 1,068 class B and C war criminals who were executed for their war crimes. The memorial on the left is for all people who died in the war. Note the horizontal slash across the stone monument on the right. The slash is the result of a terrorist bombing of the monument in 1971.

J. T. Hagen

The Yasukuni Shrine in Tokyo where Japanese war dead are venerated.

J. T. Hagen

4

THE ATTACK ON PEARL HARBOR:
THE *IAI*, DECEMBER 7, 1941

The *iai* is a surprise blow struck at the start of combat by a Japanese swordsman. The blow is struck in a single sweep as the sword leaves the scabbard, cutting up and through the opponent from the right hip to the left shoulder. Its purpose is to either destroy or incapacitate the enemy. The comparison to the Pearl Harbor attack is obvious.

On April 13, 1941, the Empire of Japan and the Union of the Soviet Socialist Republic, formerly Japan's hated adversary, solemnly agreed to respect the sovereign territory of each nation and signed a mutual nonaggression treaty.[1]

On June 22, 1941, Germany invaded Russia, the start of Germany's operation "Barbarosa." News of the war between Germany and Russia caused great agitation among Japan's political and military leaders. Foreign Minister Yosuke Matsuoka immediately called upon the Emperor and informed him, "Since war has broken out between Germany and the Soviet Union, Japan should cooperate with Germany and attack the Soviet Union."[2] So much for nonaggression treaties.

Cooler heads among the military advisors prevailed, and it was decided to wait and see how events progressed. The implications for Japan were critical. If the Soviets prevailed, Japan would abandon its "Strike North" strategy and instead strike south in southeast Asia. But if Germany should prevail, it would open the door for Japan's long cherished desire to advance, not only in China and Manchuria, but well into the southern Soviet Union. As events unfolded and the German advance stalled, Japan adopted the "Strike South" strategy. This strategy would have a major impact on the United States, because the architect of the plan, commander in chief of the Combined Fleet Adm. Isoroku Yamamoto, saw the destruction of the U.S. Pacific Fleet as a necessary first step in the plan.

Yamamoto had traveled extensively in the U.S. while he was the naval attache in Washington, D.C., and during his language course at Harvard. His knowledge of American industrial capacity convinced him that Japan did not have the national power for a military race with the United States. When Prince Konoye, the prime minister, made a confrontation with the U.S. inevitable, Yamamoto told Konoye face to face, "If we are ordered to do it, then I can guarantee to put up a tough fight for the first six months, but I have absolutely no confidence in what would happen if the war should go on for one or two years. . . . I hope at best you'll make every effort to avoid war with America."[3]

The attack on Pearl Harbor was not a sudden and unexpected event, at least not from the standpoint of the Japanese navy which had planned and trained for months to ensure its success. Vice Adm. Shigeru Fukodome, chief of staff to Admiral Yamamoto until April 1940, recalls that Yamamoto first spoke of such a plan in March or April 1940.

It was on the cold, windy day of January 7, 1941, that Yamamoto sat in his flagship *Nagato* in Hiroshima Bay, and wrote the strategy that was to decide the fate of the war with America on the first day, the attack on Pearl Harbor. Yamamoto's strategy, in hindsight, was extremely accurate, but there was much bitter opposition to the plan during its development. His staff officers argued against the terrible gamble of the surprise attack and the need for these precious naval resources to support the invasion of Malaysia, the East Indies, and the Philippines.

Yamamoto was, perhaps, the only naval officer who truly

understood that the entire Strike South strategy was dependent upon a crippling blow to the U.S. Pacific Fleet. Nevertheless, opposition and bickering to his plan went on throughout a critique of table maneuvers conducted on October 13, 1941. One by one, the admirals rose to speak against the attack on Pearl Harbor. After the final speaker took his seat, Yamamoto rose. He spoke slowly as he recognized "the points various officers have made here today." Then he eliminated any possible misunderstanding in a voice that cut like a knife. "So long as I am Commander in Chief of the Combined Fleet, Pearl Harbor will be attacked. I ask for your fullest support."[4] The issue was settled.

A few weeks later, Yamamoto believed the plan was ready to be briefed to the navy general staff in Tokyo. Accompanied by Adm. Matame Ugaki, the group flew from Hiroshima on November 3 and laid out Combined Fleet operation order no. 1. The navy general staff was astonished. The order went far beyond anything that the group had ever anticipated in the event that Japan should go to war. Here, in writing, was a plan that detailed Japan's simultaneous action in virtually every corner of the Pacific, including an attack against the most powerful navy in the world. Indeed, the first sentence of the Hawaii portion of the order stated that the task force will launch a surprise attack at the outset of war upon the U. S. Pacific Fleet supposed to be in Hawaiian waters and destroy it.

There were several objections to minor portions of the plan, but since none of the general staff expected the plan to ever be implemented in its entirety, Adm. Osami Nagano, navy chief of staff, approved it. Yamamoto's staff immediately began to produce 300 copies of the 151-page, top secret document.[5] When approved by the emperor, the plan would launch the war in the Pacific.

The Combined Fleet staff had been extremely busy while the plan was being prepared. For the past year, training exercises had been conducted simulating every aspect of the plan. Three major concerns remained. First, none of the large ships had any experience in refueling on the high seas. Second, their dive-bomber pilots had not demonstrated any great degree of accuracy in attacking ships at anchor. Finally, their current air-launched torpedoes were not suitable for the shallow waters of Pearl Harbor.

The problem of refueling the carriers and battleships at sea proved to be the easiest to resolve. Traditionally, when refueling smaller ships such as destroyers, the tanker took a position ahead of the destroyer, and, coupled by a towline connecting the two, dispensed the fuel. The smaller vessels could follow in the wake of the tanker with little difficulty. The large ships had too much power and momentum to maneuver behind the tankers, especially if it was necessary for the tanker to swerve or alter course. Snapped towlines and moments of sheer excitement made refueling of the large ships a spectator sport at best. The reversal of the tanker position, whereby the tanker followed the large ship, proved to be the solution. Although the solution was simple enough, someone had to think of it and test it. Thereafter, refueling practice during maneuvers gave the tankers and warships confidence that they could accomplish the voyage to Hawaii.

Through constant experimentation with dive angles, release speeds, and altitudes, the bomber pilots were able to raise their dive-bombing accuracy to over 70 percent. In addition, their high-explosive ordnance had been improved so that it would pierce the decks of U.S. carriers and battleships.

The air-delivered torpedo remained the most difficult problem to solve. Cmdr. Fumio Aiko, a navy expert on torpedoes, was given the order in the spring of 1940 to develop a torpedo that would be 100 percent effective in shallow water. Armed with Aiko's improvements, Commodore Minoru Genda, a resourceful tactical aviation expert on Adm. Chuichi Nagumo's staff, initiated a torpedo-improvement program in June 1940 that had the inhabitants of Kagoshima City ducking as the navy planes screamed across the city at tree-top level and launched their practice torpedoes at mock battleships in the bay.

Traditionally, air-delivered torpedoes were released at about 300 feet at high speed. Upon impact with the water, the torpedo would go to depths of 100 to 300 feet and then rise sharply, sometimes breaking the surface. At other times, the torpedo might remain deep and pass under the target. Genda's program had been able to reduce the water-penetration depth of the torpedo consistently to less than 60 feet, but that was not good enough for the waters of Pearl Harbor. It was starting to look like only the dive bombers would be used for the attack against the U.S. Fleet.

Through the use of a large aerial stabilizer fin, the torpedo sinkage was reduced to 20 meters (66 feet) on October 15. Continued trials managed successful runs in 12 meters of water. An unexpected bonus was that the fin so steadied the torpedo that it could be used in very narrow corridors.[6]

November 5 was a second dress rehearsal for the attack. Major concerns included: the ability of the torpedoes to level off and remain shallow on their way to the target; and the tendency of the bomber pilots to concentrate their attack on the outboard ships when two ships were moored together at a pier. Corrections were made to ensure the inboard ships would be bombed as well.

Following the rehearsal, Genda flew from the carrier *Akagi* to Kagoshima to consult with the torpedo pilots in one final attempt to solve the problems associated with the depth of sinkage. Genda introduced two new delivery methods. The first required that the pilots slow the aircraft to 100 knots and release the torpedo from an altitude of 20 meters in level flight. The second was similar but released the torpedo with a slight nose-down attitude. To everyone's amazement, both methods succeeded with 82 percent hits in very shallow water. The problem had been in the release speed. Now all that remained was to pressure the Mitsubishi plant, the manufacturer of the modified torpedoes, to deliver the necessary ordnance in the brief time remaining.

Just how well the Hawaii attack plan was executed can best be understood by visiting the Arizona Memorial at Pearl Harbor and watching any of the several videos on the subject. The carriers *Saratoga* (in San Diego) *Enterprise* (returning from Wake Island) and *Lexington* (returning from Midway) were not at Pearl Harbor. Otherwise, the results of the attack were everything that the planners hoped for. The final American death toll was 2,403, including 68 civilians. The wounded numbered 1,178. The attack cost the U.S. Pacific Fleet 18 operational warships and destroyed 84 navy and 78 army aircraft. Only 34 of the 400 sailors and marines trapped in the U.S.S. *Arizona* when it was sunk were rescued.

Those of us who condemn Japan for the surprise attack on Pearl Harbor would do well to reflect upon the words of Su-Tzu written 500 years before the birth of Christ. In the Chinese military classic *The Art of War*, Su-Tzu wrote, "If the enemy leaves a door open, you must rush in." He also wrote, "All warfare is based on deception."[7]

The afternoon of December 7, 1941, brought the news that Guam had been raided and Wake Island bombed and strafed. Singapore and Hong Kong had both been bombed. In Shanghai, the Japanese captured the U.S. gunboat *Wake* and the Philippines had suffered two bombing attacks. Later in the day, news was received that Japanese planes from Formosa had wiped out most of General Douglas MacArthur's air force in the Philippines. Though MacArthur and his staff were warned repeatedly by message and phone of the Japanese attack on Pearl Harbor, most of the 207 aircraft in the Philippines were destroyed on the ground.

Overall responsibility for the aviation catastrophe in the Philippines belongs to MacArthur. Individual responsibility long ago disappeared in a morass of divided authority, selective memories, conflicting stories, and missing records. Manuel Quezon, president of the Commonwealth of the Philippines, told General Dwight D. Eisenhower in 1942 that MacArthur refused to attack Japanese airfields on Formosa because MacArthur believed that, after the

Japanese attack on Pearl Harbor, the Philippines would be able to remain neutral. Lt. Col. Richard K. Sutherland, MacArthur's chief of staff, believed that MacArthur hesitated to launch his aviation assets due to the way the warning message from Washington was worded: ". . . if hostilities cannot, repeat, cannot, be avoided the United States desires that Japan commit the first overt act."

While MacArthur hesitated, Maj. Gen. Lewis H. Brerton, commander Aviation Forces, alerted his fliers for a possible strike against the Japanese airfields on Formosa. He was waiting to ask MacArthur for permission to launch the strike at 4:00 P.M. but was denied access to MacArthur by Lieutenant Colonel Sutherland who explained that General MacArthur was too busy.

Adm. Husband E. Kimmel in Honolulu radioed MacArthur's staff at 3:00 A.M., December 8 (Manila time) of the attack on Pearl Harbor. MacArthur was personally advised of the Pearl Harbor attack at 3:40 A.M. (Manila time) by the army war plans division in Washington, D.C. At 5:30 A.M., MacArthur was informed that a state of war existed between the United States and Japan. General Brerton continued to seek access to MacArthur until 8:50 A.M. (Manila time) when Sutherland informed him that there would be no strike against Formosa.

At 12:10 P.M. (Manila time), 108 Mitsubishi bombers escorted by 84 Zero fighters roared across the Boshi channel and struck the American P-40 fighters and B-17 bombers lined up neatly in rows at the several airfields. Only four American fighters were able to get airborne. After the strike, Clark field was unrecognizable. All the hangars had been destroyed, fuel tanks ignited, and nearly all of the aircraft destroyed.

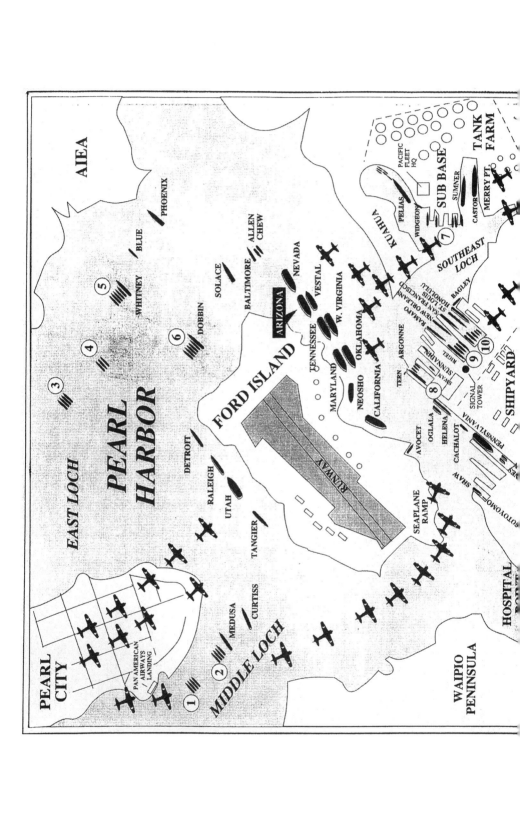

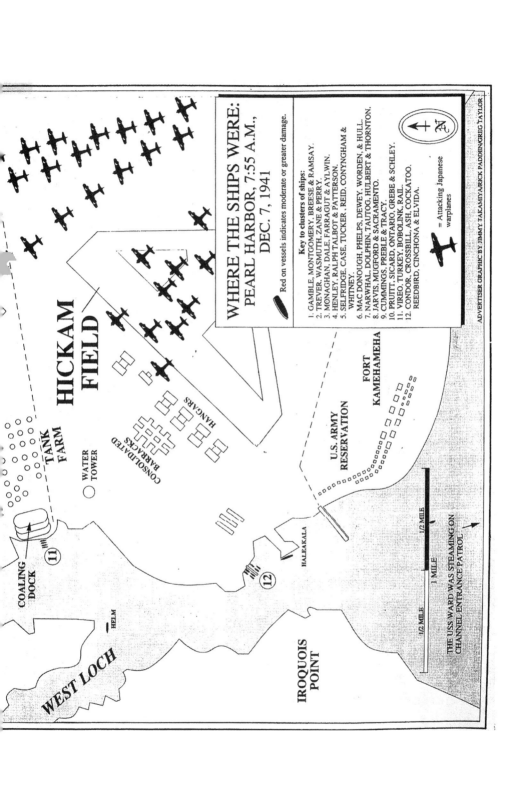

WHERE THE SHIPS WERE:
PEARL HARBOR, 7:55 A.M.,
DEC. 7, 1941

Red on vessels indicates moderate or greater damage.

Key to clusters of ships:

1. GAMBLE. MONTGOMERY. BREESE & RAMSAY.
2. TREVER. WASMUTH. ZANE & PERRY.
3. MONAGHAN. DALE. FARRAGUT & AYLWIN.
4. HENLEY. RALPH TALBOT & PATTERSON.
5. SELFRIDGE. CASE. TUCKER . REID. CONYNGHAM & WHITNEY.
6. MAC DONOUGH. PHELPS. DEWEY. WORDEN. & HULL.
7. NARWHAL. DOLPHIN. TAUTOG. HULBERT & THORNTON.
8. JARVIS. MUGFORD & SACRAMENTO.
9. CUMMINGS. PREBLE & TRACY.
10. PRUITT. SICARD. ONTARIO. GREBE & SCHLEY.
11. VIREO. TURKEY. BOBOLINK. RAIL.
12. CONDOR. CROSSBILL. ASH. COCKATOO. REEDBIRD. CINCHONA & ELVIDA.

= Attacking Japanese
warplanes

ADVERTISER GRAPHIC BY JIMMY TAKAMIYA/RICK PADDEN/GREG TAYLOR

HICKAM
FIELD

TANK
FARM

WATER
TOWER

CONSOLIDATED
BARRACKS

HANGARS

COALING
DOCK

U.S. ARMY
RESERVATION

FORT
KAMEHAMEHA

HALEAKALA

WEST LOCH

HELM

IROQUOIS
POINT

1/2 MILE   1 MILE

1/2 MILE

THE USS WARD WAS STEAMING ON
CHANNEL ENTRANCE PATROL

5

THE ATTACK ON HONG KONG

The Japanese attack on Hong Kong began at 2:00 P.M., December 7 (Hawaii time), with a raid of 35 bombers. One group attacked Kowloon, destroying the three British torpedo bombers and two Walrus amphibians located there. Another group attacked and damaged seven aircraft at the civil field.[1] Six Japanese infantry battalions, part of the 38th Division in China, attacked from the north. The small number of Canadian, Scottish, and Indian troops, along with 1,759 Hong Kong volunteers, were split by the Japanese advance, quickly pushed to the hills or to the southern end of the island, where they made a last-ditch defense of the colony.

For several days they held their defensive positions, but on the night of December 18, the Japanese launched a massive assault that broke the defense line. For the next seven days the defenders fought rearguard actions and yielded ground, yard by yard.

On Christmas day, the Japanese seized control of the power station and cut off all water supplies to the colony. Uncontrolled mobs of Japanese soldiers seized the hospital and began butchering the wounded and raping Chinese and British nurses. Maj. Gen. C. M. Maltby, the garrison commander, reluctantly advised Governor Mark Young that no further resistance was possible. That evening, in the Peninsula Hotel in Kowloon, Governor Young formally surrendered Hong Kong to Lt. Gen. Takashi Sakai, who was commanding Japan's 23rd Army. More than 1,200 defenders had died, about twice the number of Japanese dead.

This first occupation of a European colonial outpost was a major blow to Western prestige in the Orient and continued the pattern of savagery established by the rape of Nanking. The conquerors were especially cruel to the Chinese population throughout the Pacific, probably because the army was resentful of the long war against China on the mainland. In Singapore, a British colony, 70,000 Chinese were rounded up, 5,000 imprisoned, and many executed as live targets for bayonet practice.[2] The international observers in Hong Kong were horrified by the rape and murder of young girls and nuns as the victorious soldiers raped and pillaged the entire civilian population.

The Europeans fared little better. In Balikpapan, the Japanese murdered the entire European population as punishment for the destruction of the oil fields.[3] Dutch nationals suffered terribly on Java and Sumatra as did the British in Singapore and the Americans in the Philippines.

After the war, Japan's war criminals would explain such actions as being consistent with the code of *bushido*, the moral code of chivalry in Japan. *Bushido*, as a precept, held that the greatest honor for a warrior was to die for the emperor. Consequently, one had to fight to the death. Surrender was impossible, for the act of surrender would bring everlasting shame to the soldier and his family. In effect, by surrendering, the soldier would cease to exist. From such reasoning it follows that the prisoners and civilians captured during Japan's early successes had no rights. They were not prisoners but something less than animals, to be used as the Japanese saw fit until they died or were executed by their captors.

Lord Russell, in *Knights of Bushido*, explains that the code of *bushido* extended to anyone who was captured regardless of whether he fought well, was captured after being wounded, or taken while unconscious. Such captives ceased to exist as human beings.[4] It would be 1945 before allied carriers would raid Japanese air bases on Hong Kong. Chiang Kai-shek's Nationalist forces were never able to retake Hong Kong, nor create a supply port for the Chinese or a staging base for the final invasion of Japan.

6

WAKE ISLAND

Japanese air attacks on Wake (Wake Island, Peale Island, and Wilkes Island) began on Monday, December 8, (December 7, Hawaii time.) The first attack consisted of 34 land-based attack planes from Roi in the Marshalls. The low-level attack caught all of Marine Fighter Squadron (VMF) 211's Wildcat fighters on the ground and destroyed four of the eight aircraft. Fifty seven military and civilian personnel were killed, and both of the 25,000-gallon aviation fuel tanks were destroyed.[1] Japanese attack planes were back on Tuesday and Wednesday softening up the defenses of Wake prior to their invasion.

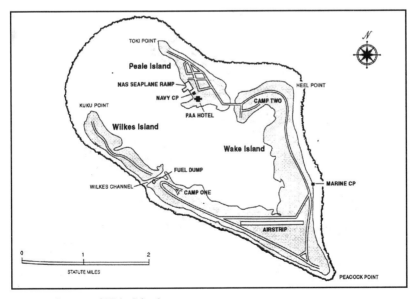

Japanese Capture of Wake Island

Honolulu Advertiser graphic

At dawn on the morning of December 11, Rear Adm. Sadamichi Kajioka, with a naval task force consisting of three light cruisers, six destroyers, two patrol boats, and two armed merchantmen arrived off the two-and-a-half square mile atoll. The cruisers and destroyers shelled Wake for forty minutes, and, having received no counter-fire, they moved closer to the beach to land the landing force.

Marine Maj. James Devereux, commanding officer of the Wake Detachment of the First Defense Battalion, purposely did not return the Japanese fire because the ships were out of range and needed to be decoyed into about 4,500 yards from shore before his five-inch guns would be effective. Now, he launched his four remaining Wildcat fighters and commenced firing with his shore batteries. The marines sank destroyer *Hayate,* killing all of her 167-man crew, and damaged destroyers *Oite and Mochizuki,* with their five-inch seacoast gun. VMF 211 sank destroyer *Kisargi,* damaged cruiser *Tenaryu,* caused an explosion aboard merchantman *Kongo Maru,* and shot down two Japanese bombers. Admiral Kajioka beat a hasty retreat to Kwajalein with his badly damaged task force.[2]

Japanese aircraft attacked Wake each day following Kajioka's failure. On Saturday, December 20, a PBY aircraft from Hawaii was able to land at Wake between air attacks and gave the defenders the news that a U. S. naval task force was on the way with reinforcements, ammunition, and replacement aircraft.[3] The task force would evacuate all the wounded and remove the 1,100 civilian contractors. Morale soared among the Wake defenders.

Instead of a U.S. Navy task force, Admiral Kajioka returned on December 23 with six heavy cruisers, two aircraft carriers, 54 planes, and 1,000 troops. Once again, the Wake Island marines gave the United States something to cheer about. For several hours they held off the invasion fleet, killing 800 Japanese in the process. The first Japanese landing was made on the tip of Peale Island at 1:45 A.M. on the 23rd. At 2:30 A.M., two landing craft and two destroyers beached on Wake Island. Marines and Japanese grappled in hand-to-hand combat in the murky darkness. Marines continued to slow the Japanese assault, but, by 3:00 A.M., Major Devereux and Cdr. Winfield Scott Cunningham, the senior commander on Wake Island, lost communications with most of their scattered forces. Communications wires had been cut and the radio net ceased to function. At 6:00 A.M., Cdr. Cunningham made the decision to surrender. Major Devereux began trying to get the surrender information to the marines who continued to fight until 1:30 P.M. The defenders suffered 49 marines, three sailors, and 70 civilians killed. Captured were 470 marines, sailors, and airmen, plus 1,146 civilian construction workers. A third of the captives would not survive captivity.[4] The Japanese lost two ships and 381 killed.[5]

By mid-afternoon, the prisoners were herded onto the runway, stripped, tied with rope, and laid out like trussed pigs awaiting appropriate means of execution. After the prisoners had lain in the sun for several hours without water, Rear Admiral Kajioka arrived for the formal surrender and gave orders that the prisoners were not to be executed. The POWs were untied but left naked on the coral runway to blister and burn in the tropical sun. In the evening, when the sun went down, the POWs began to shiver from the abrupt temperature change. At noon on Christmas day, some drums of water and moldy bread were provided to the prisoners who consumed their dinner still naked on the runway.[6]

On January 11, 1942, 1,200 of the prisoners were herded to the beach where they were embarked in the cargo hold of the *Nitta Maru* for transportation to Japan. Once embarked, the POWs were cursed, kicked, and beaten with heavy bamboo clubs. Down in the holds, air was foul, bodies were stacked on bodies, and the heat was unbearable. Water was not provided and men went mad for lack of it. On the second day, a routine was established whereby several buckets of a thin rice soup were lowered into the hold on ropes. Some days, a tiny rotting fish, head, scales and all, might be included in the slop pail. Dysentery became an epidemic, with many of the men so weak that they could not crawl to the slop buckets in the corner of the hold.

After several days of stifling heat, the temperature began to drop and the prisoners began to shiver and shake uncontrollably as they headed into the freezing midwinter of northern Japan. After a week of near-freezing temperatures, the *Nitta Maru* reached Yokohama. Five prisoners, two marines and three sailors were brought on deck, and, in front of hundreds of Japanese onlookers, were blindfolded. They were then forced to kneel, and a guard chopped off their heads with a long sword.[7] After the prisoners were decapitated, their bodies were mutilated by swords and bayonets until their captors were satisfied. Then, heads, body parts, and entrails were pushed over the edge of the dock.

Following the orgy at Yokohama, the *Nitta Maru* pulled anchor and left for Shanghai, arriving there on January 23. More prisoners were to be executed and mutilated at the Shanghai port in order to demonstrate Japanese superiority to the Chinese, but few people were at the dock. Instead, the POWs were marched five miles through freezing temperatures to the Shanghai War Prisoner Camp. Temperature at the camp was about 15 degrees below zero. There was no heat, hot water, or soap, and there were no indoor toilet facilities. Men slept as close to one another as they could, and covered themselves from the freezing wind with a single, thin Japanese blanket. Food was a scoop of rice three times per day with some occasional vegetable scraps.

The Wake Island POWs were later moved ten miles to Kiangwan, where they were used for heavy labor on construction projects with no tools or equipment. Many POWs were beaten with heavy objects, some were hung by their heels, their noses broken so they could not breathe through their nose, and then water was forced through their mouth until they suffocated.

It became common for prisoners to be put on display in front of their fellow POWs. Their noses and teeth would be smashed with heavy clubs. If the prisoner moved during this ordeal, he was smashed for moving. If he fell, he was bashed and pushed back onto his feet for more punishment. When he could no longer stand, the POW would be lashed to a pole. The guards would change shifts, but the POW beatings continued around the clock. Most of the Wake POWs that survived this first year were moved to Osaka, Japan, and then to various work camps in the Tokyo and Yokohama area.

During the first week of October 1943, when American planes bombarded Wake Island, all 96 American civilian contractors still alive on Wake were tied, blindfolded, and machine-gunned to death. Their bodies were pushed into shallow ditches near the island's shoreline. Rear Admiral Shigematsu Sakaibara, the atoll commander, was tried and found guilty for this atrocity and was sentenced to death by the War Crimes Tribunal following the war.

BATAAN TO CAMP O'DONNELL

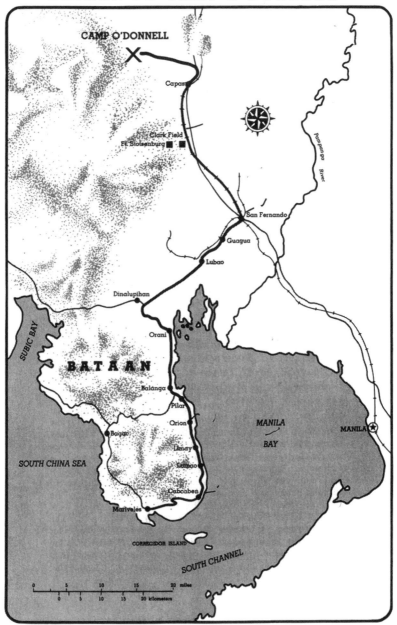

Honolulu Advertiser graphic

7

DEATH MARCH: BATAAN, APRIL 1942

When the emperor announced Japan's surrender in August 1945, some 4,000 Bataan survivors, about one-third of those captured, were still alive.[1] When the remaining survivors gathered for a reunion in 1984, none of them drove a Japanese-made car. The nightmares, scars, physical abuse, hard labor, malnutrition, and the outrage of what it took to survive had not dimmed. Nothing concerning the ordeal was forgotten even though very little was said.

The decision to surrender Bataan was made on April 9, 1942, by Maj. Gen. Edward P. King Jr., commander of the Luzon force. King made the decision based on the fact that one-third of his force was hospitalized and less than 50 percent of the remainder were fit for combat. Major General King had been expressly forbidden to surrender his forces by Lt. Gen. Jonathan M. Wainwright, commander of U.S. forces in the Philippines. Wainwright was then located on Corregidor where he had moved after succeeding General MacArthur on March 11, when MacArthur was evacuated to Australia. Prior to his departure, and by subsequent messages, MacArthur ordered Wainwright not to surrender but rather to attack the enemy when all food supplies were exhausted and to fight to the last man.

Maj. Gen. King unconditionally surrendered his forces to Col. Motoo Nakayama, senior operations officer of the Japanese 14th Army. In order to spare Wainwright from being implicated in his decision to surrender, King did not communicate with Wainwright on the subject.

Surrendered on Bataan were 78,000 troops, about 66,000 Filipino soldiers, and 12,000 Americans. For about three months prior to their captivity they had lived on a daily ration of 15 ounces of rice, canned meat, and milk, and an occasional monkey, snake, or lizard. Near the end, they were receiving less than a thousand calories per day instead of the 3,500 to 4,000 calories estimated as necessary to maintain a soldier on Bataan.[2] Dysentery, diarrhea, and beriberi were already in evidence as a result of malnutrition, vitamin deficiency, and poor sanitary conditions. Malaria would spread quickly after capture due to the lack of medicine and become the single greatest cause of death of the captives.

The Bataan Death March involved the movement of captured Filipino and American troops from Mariveles on the southern tip of the Bataan peninsula to a hastily established prisoner-of-war compound called Camp O'Donnell north of San Fernando, a distance of about 90 miles.

American soldiers Samuel Stenzler, Frank Spear, and James Gallagher, hands tied behind their backs, rest briefly during the Bataan Death March.

US Marine Corps

The poor physical condition and massive number of captives contributed, without doubt, to the death toll. The fact that the Japanese were far less concerned with the care and feeding of the captives than they were in capturing Corregidor, which continued to fight on and block the entrance to Manila Bay, was also a factor. A far greater factor was the inhumane treatment of the captives. Their story of terror began two days after the surrender when some 400 officers and men of the surrendered 91st Division were bound together near Balanga and executed en masse by sword and bayonet wielding Japanese officers and men.[3] Donald Knox interviewed many of the Death March survivors. Their story is well told in his book *Death March: The Survivors of Bataan.*

Pfc. Blair Robinette survived the Death March. He was about a half mile from Mariveles, when a Japanese soldier came across the road, stopped him, and took his canteen. The officer "took a drink, filled his canteen out of mine, poured the rest of the water on the ground, and threw the canteen at my feet." As Robinette bent over to pick up his canteen, the officer smashed him in the head with his rifle butt. "I fell face down . . . and crawled back up on my knees. . . . I left the canteen alone." The group moved a bit farther, suffering more beatings, and then a Japanese soldier grabbed one of the sick prisoners, guided him to the center of the road, and flipped him to the ground directly in front of an approaching tank. The tank rolled over him. "There must have been ten tanks in the column and everyone of them came up there right across the body." The body disappeared, but the uniform remained pressed into the cobblestones. "Now we knew, if there had been any doubts before, we were in for a bad time."[4]

Colonel Erwin wasn't so fortunate. Suffering from malaria and diarrhea, overheated and fatigued, he starting dropping back in the column. One of the guards struck him with a bayonet. Another guard pulled him to the side of the road, put his rifle muzzle in the colonel's back, and pulled the trigger. Maybe the colonel was lucky; the march was just starting.

Sgt. Ralph Levenberg remembered one of the tricks the Japanese enjoyed playing on the prisoners. When a truck passed, the Japanese soldiers in the back of the truck would snap their long black-snake whips and snag a prisoner around the neck or torso and drag him behind the moving truck. It was a game to see how far they could drag the helpless captive in this manner.[5]

Water, or rather the lack of it, was the greatest problem for most of the men. The sun blazed and the POWs had no protection against it. Capt. Mark Wohfeld recalled that there was a filthy buffalo wallow about 50 yards off the road. "It looked like green scum." Several dozen of the young enlisted men ran for the filthy water and almost drowned each other trying to get a drink. A short time later, a Japanese officer ordered the men pulled out of the water and moved to the rear. "When we marched out, after a short while we heard shooting behind us." The young troops were not seen again.[6]

Pfc. Cletis Overton remembers, "All along the road were artesian wells with water just flowing out of a pipe." Sometimes the column of prisoners would be stopped beside one of these gushing wells. "They'd make us sit there looking and listening to it for an hour or two. Then they'd move us along without any water . . . ."[7]

Capt. Loyd Mills recalled the corpses and filth all along the road. The stench and rot and maggots were indescribable. "I had dysentery pretty bad . . . but there was nothing you could do about it. You didn't stop on the 'March' because you were dead if you did." There was nothing to do but just let it go. "I was young so I had that advantage over some of the older men. I helped along the way. Course there was nothing you could do about the people who fell in the back."[8]

Private Leon Beck recalls, "The most abusive guards were the Koreans." They had been conscripted into the Japanese army but were not trusted. Consequently, they were used as laborers and service troops. "These guards hadn't seen any fighting and now they wanted to get a little blood on their bayonets. . . ."[9]

There was no water. The dust was so thick that sometimes the men couldn't see across the road, especially when the convoys of trucks were moving past. Everywhere there was confusion and despair. Here were men who had fought honorably for far longer than their condition warranted. Back home they would be heroes; here they were worse than slaves or animals. They had no rights, but, far worse, they had no leaders. This absence of leadership in an overwhelming and unexpected environment created the despair that caused many to just give up.

Pfc. Blair Robinette recalls his detail sitting in a field for three or four hours, sun beating down on the men's bare heads, and then being told to line up and march. Robinette collapsed. The next thing he recalled when he regained consciousness was a Japanese guard poking him with a bayonet. "Go ahead you sonovabitch, do it," he shouted. But before the Japanese could oblige, an air force sergeant pulled Robinette to his feet and into the line of march. "I couldn't manage to stand up and told them they should leave me." "Oh, no," the sergeant responded, "Couldn't do that. You need something inside you." The sergeant reached into his blouse and pulled out several sweet potatoes. After eating one or two, Robinette was able to continue.[10]

As the prisoners approached San Fernando, after 70 miles into their march, the word started to filter back that the remainder of the trip would be via railroad. Morale improved somewhat only to be dashed when they reached San Fernando. The overnight holding pen for the prisoners in the town of San Fernando was a cockfight pit or bullpen. The floor was bare dirt, and the prisoners were jammed in so tight that it was impossible to move.

Sidney Stewart, author of *Give Us This Day*, a narrative of the Bataan Death March, was in a group that spent the night in an open field outside San Fernando. If a prisoner tried to sit or slumped to his knees, the guards rushed in and jabbed the man with bayonets.

Soon the guards were walking by with American heads on their bayonets.[11]

Most Americans knew nothing of the fate of the 12,000 Americans captured on Bataan on April 9, 1942, for almost two years. In April 1943, a small group of Americans being held in the penal camp at Davao in the southern Philippines managed to escape. With the help of Filipino guerrillas, William E. Dyess, Melvin H. McCoy, and Steve H. Mellnik reached Australia and told the story of the beatings, starvation, denial of water, torture, and murder which characterized the Death March and became a daily routine for the remainder of their captivity.

Gen. Douglas MacArthur, in his book *Reminiscences*, states that he directed issuance of the story to the press, but officials in Washington, D.C. forbid the release of any POW atrocities until January 28, 1944.[12]

8

DEATH MARCH: CAMP O'DONNELL

Camp O'Donnell was nothing more than a partially completed American airfield about 10 miles west of the town of Capas. A high barbed-wire fence surrounded the camp, and there were several unfinished straw-roofed barracks. There were no medical facilities and only two partially functioning water pumps. By the end of April 1942, about 48,000 Filipinos and 9,300 Americans had arrived at the camp.

Following the march from Mariveles to San Fernando, the men were divided into groups of 100 and marched a few blocks to the railroad for the 30-mile trip to Capas, near Camp O'Donnell. When the boxcar doors were opened the heat hit us, recalled Cpl. Hubert Gater:

> We stalled for time. . . . but we knew by now to openly resist the guards would be fatal. We jammed in. . . . and the doors were closed. The three hours that followed are almost indescribable. Men fainting with no place to fall. Those with dysentery had no control of themselves. As the cars swayed, the urine, the sweat, and the vomit rolled three inches deep back and forth around and in our shoes.[1]

When the train reached Capas, the boxcar doors were again opened, and the men who could climb down did so and dumped the filth from their shoes. They were then lined up to march the final six miles to Camp O'Donnell.

The Reverend John J. Moret remembers that the route to O'Donnell led through the town of Capas. Filipino women crowded the sidewalk trying to pass fruit and water to the prisoners. The Japanese guards forced the women back, striking them with their rifle butts. Many of the women refused to leave, and Moret will never forget one brave woman who dashed towards him and thrust a square gin bottle filled with water into his hands. He was so grateful that he almost cried.[2]

At O'Donnell, the Americans learned that they would not be treated as prisoners of war because Japan had never ratified the international agreement on the treatment of such prisoners. 1st. Sgt. Houston Turner recalled, "A Japanese officer gave us a little talk. . . . told us that Americans were dogs . . . . and would be treated like dogs." Other POWs recalled that the officer was the camp commandant and told the men they "were slaves and that your comrades who died on Bataan are the lucky ones."[3]

According to Sgt. Charles Cook, to get water you had to get up early and head for the faucet. There would be hundreds waiting and you might have to stand in line all day. The Japanese would turn the water off with no warning or reason.[4]

The daily burial details became a consuming part of the routine. The prisoners tried to count the number of bodies being carried out each day, but there were so many sometimes they lost count. Often there were 20 to 50 bodies lying in the sun waiting for burial. At one point, 20 bodies of prisoners were buried per grave. An effort was made to keep track of who was buried by collecting dog tags or writing down names but, invariably, some were missed. The Filipinos died in great numbers. Their bodies were taken out in what seemed like an endless column that never ended, night or day. The Americans calculated that for every 40 Filipinos who died, 10 Americans died.

Capt. Loyd Mills recalls, "Death was all around. A thousand or more died because of dysentery and malaria. There was no medicine, no quinine. If you got something—that was it." The hospital was not a hospital, "it was a place to put guys who were going to die."[5]

Based upon Pfc. Eddy Loursen's testimony, "The flies were so thick. You'd get your kit of boiled rice and you had to fan your kit constantly to keep the flies off." The flies had just come from the slit trenches so if they got on your food, you were guaranteed dysentery or worse."[6]

At O'Donnell, the Japanese organized the work details into 10-man squads. If a prisoner escaped, the other nine were executed. If all 10 escaped, the Japanese would murder 100 prisoners. On the early morning of June 12, a Filipino guerrilla unit raided the camp exterior and killed three or four guards. About 2:00 P.M., the Japanese lined up all the Americans who could walk and held a roll call. They declared that one man was missing. A Japanese sergeant pulled 10 men out of formation, lined them up in front of the prisoners, and shot them.[7]

From Camp O'Donnell, the Americans were moved to Cabanatuan, a complex of three camps about 60 miles northwest of O'Donnell. About 5,850 Americans arrived at Cabunatuan. Of these, 764 died in June 1942, the month of the move, and about 2,061 more died by the end of 1942.[8] One of the first disappointments at Cabanatuan was the lack of water. Whereas the water faucet at O'Donnell trickled, the one at Cabanatuan dripped. It would take all night to fill a few five-gallon cans for the mess hall.

Corporal Gator lost all his close friends at Cabanatuan. The first week after working night and day, he was so exhausted that he fell into his bunk. The next morning, four men from his section were dead. Bataan, O'Donnell, Cabanatuan—death seemed to follow the Bataan death marchers.

Some of the prisoners at Cabanatuan were moved there directly from Corregidor. They had come by train and were in much better shape than the prisoners from Bataan. When the prisoners from Corregidor saw the emaciated, jaundiced, and sick survivors from Bataan arrive, at least three of the prisoners already at Cabanatuan decided to escape.[9] Phil Sanborn, Richard Truk, and

William Berry walked out of Cabanatuan shortly after they arrived. They ran for about 18 miles in the dark, through jungle, brush, vines, and swamp. They were able to survive for three months but were finally captured by Filipinos for the reward. When they were returned to Cabanatuan, the Japanese were not aware that they were escaped prisoners, but their senior officers, fearing for the lives of the other prisoners, forced them to confess to the Japanese that they were escapees.[10]

The men were tried twice by Japanese courts martial and sentenced to three years in prison as special prisoners under the control of the *Kempai Tai*, the dreaded Japanese military police. They were confined to special cells in Bilibid prison in Manila until the end of the war.[11]

From Cabanatuan many of the prisoners were moved to piers at Manila Bay, loaded into "Hell Ships," and shipped to Japan for use as laborers.

Filipino and American soldiers being disarmed and searched before the start of the Bataan Death March.

US Marine Corps

9

THE HELL SHIPS

By 1944, the Japanese military had utilized more and more of Japan's economy. The standard of living had decreased noticeably. The American submarine blockade prevented raw materials from entering the country, and American bombers were hitting the industrial centers.

Thousands of POWs had been brought to Japan as replacements for the labor force. The first Bataan prisoners were shipped to Japan as early as the summer of 1942. Shipments continued on a sporadic basis for the next two years and then increased as the Japanese sought to get the prisoners to Japan before they could be liberated in the Philippines.

The POWs shoveled coal, pushed dump cars, fed and cleaned blast furnaces, and unloaded and loaded ships and barges. They worked in mines, foundries, steel plants, dry docks, and piers. They worked in rain, snow, heat, and freezing temperatures without adequate clothing, food, or medical care.

Too many prisoners were put on too few ships for the move to Japan. The treatment aboard ship coupled with the prisoners' physical and mental condition caused large numbers of deaths and earned the antiquated freighters the name of "hell ships." These hell ships sailed in convoy with other Japanese shipping with no external markings. American submarines and aircraft attacked the convoys and struck several such freighters. The *Arisan Maru*, for example, when sunk by an American submarine, took hundreds of American prisoners to their death.

The last detail of prisoners from Cabanatuan left for Japan in early September 1944, aboard the *Orokyu Maru*. Capt. Marion Lawton, a survivor, would later state: "Inside the hold there was madness, claustrophobia, and total darkness. Then there was the heat, the desperate need for air. The temperature had to be near 120 degrees. Men became desperate. They went mad. Some drank urine."[1]

Pfc. Lee Davis, another survivor, recalls, "The men went literally mad. I saw Americans scrape sweat off the steel sides of the ship and try to drink it. Men would suck the blood from cuts on other men."[2]

As many of the men went mad and attacked one another, a Catholic priest, Father Bill Cummings, began to speak in a strong, clear voice. "Have faith," he said. "Believe in yourselves and in the goodness of one another." The men became quiet. "Know that in yourselves and in those that stand near you, you see the image of God. For mankind is in the image of God." Sanity slowly returned to many of the men.[3]

On the morning of December 14, U.S. planes found the convoy and the *Oryoku Maru* off the northern coast of Luzon. The ship was bombed and strafed and started to sink. Many of the POWs were injured or killed by the shrapnel and ricocheting bullets. Others were killed by the Japanese guards as they tried to escape from the flooding hold. The POWs who did survive swam to shore where more Japanese were waiting for them. The POWs were moved by truck to San Fernando which was well remembered from the earlier death march. Near the end of December, the POWs were moved to the port area again and were loaded aboard the *Enoura Maru* and the *Brazil Maru*. The *Enoura Maru* had unloaded a cargo of horses and the floor of the hold was covered in horse manure, urine, and flies. The POWs were not permitted to clean the hold prior to departure.

The convoy arrived in Formosa on New Year's eve. Shortly

thereafter, the ship was attacked by U.S. aircraft and mortally damaged. Half of the 600 men in one hold were killed during the attack. About January 12, the survivors were put aboard the *Brazil Maru* and the voyage continued. "Men died like flies. Their bodies were stacked against the bulkhead like cordwood. It was so cold the deck was covered with ice. We had no clothes, having just left the tropics," recalled Pfc. Lee Davis.[4]

On January 30, the *Brazil Maru* reached Moji, Japan, the same day that American troops recaptured Clark Field on Luzon. Only 497 prisoners survived the ill-fated trip to Japan. Seventy-six of these POWs would die in Moji, too ill to be moved. About 1,198 POWs died on the voyage. For many of the 421 survivors, there still remained yet another trip, a later move to Korea or to Manchuria in April 1945, if they survived their hard labor in Japan.

A rough count suggests that more than 5,000 Americans died when their hell ships were attacked enroute to Japan.

More than 175 camps were established in Japan to house POWs who would do hard labor so long as they remained alive. The work was hard, the hours long, the food inadequate, and the living conditions harsh. Typically, the men were forced to work 12 hours per day for 10 days before earning any kind of break. If work quotas were not met, there was no time off and the men were punished.

By 1945, the surviving prisoners entered their fourth year of captivity and chronic starvation. Perhaps more important than their physical deterioration, which reduced most of the prisoners to walking skeletons, was the erosion of the human spirit. Their cruel treatment had worked on their minds and spirits for so long that their source and sense of community had unraveled. Unable to prevail against the enemy, it was all anyone could do just to survive. Life had been brutal since they were captured but was becoming even more so as the Japanese themselves found life more and more difficult. The prisoners were kept alive for one day at a time so long as they continued to work. When the war ended, survivors of

Bataan were found in some 15 work camps in Japan, at Hoten, Manchuria, and Jinsen, Korea.

General Wainwright is being forced to broadcast his surrender instructions over station KZRH, on May, 7, 1942.

National Archives

54

10

THE BURMA AND LEDO ROADS

At the same time that Japan was running rampant in the Pacific, Generalissimo Chiang Kai-shek continued to oppose Japanese aggression in China. Following the closure of Chinese seaports, American lend lease to China was restricted to the Burma Road. In many ways, the Burma Road was the principal problem of all the American efforts in China, Burma, and India.

During October 1941, Brig. Gen. John Magruder, U.S. Army, and a support staff were sent from Washington, D.C. to China with orders to advise, assist, explore, establish, and maintain a supply link from the port of Rangoon in Burma to Chiang Kai-shek in Chungking, China. Following his defeat at Nanking, Chiang had been forced to relocate his capital to Chungking.

Following his initial meeting with Chiang Kai-shek in Chungking, General Magruder immediately began firsthand exploration of the various key points along the proposed supply route. These points included Kunming, China, where the convoys from Burma would first unload their materials in China. From there, the route went to Lashio, Burma, where the convoys would begin their 715-mile trip by road. From Lashio, the road travelled to Mandalay, a midpoint in the 650-mile railway portion of the route from Rangoon to Lashio. From Rangoon, General Magruder flew to Singapore which was seen as a major supply and communication link for American and British aid to China.

Magruder quickly discovered that the Burma Road was the worst logistical bottleneck in all of the Pacific. It was not an all-weather road and became nearly impassable during the monsoon seasons.

Communications along the China portion of the road were woefully inadequate. There were few, if any, sanitation facilities along its length, and the road passed through a significant malarial stretch of standing water.

The road was not restricted to the military, and since it was the only supply route remaining to China, it was a center of interest to speculators, traders, politicians, and bandits from all of the countries involved. It seemed impossible to control the traffic. There were so many checkpoints along the Road and so many inspectors, all of whom demanded payment in goods, that it was surprising anything at all got through.

There was no refueling capability for the truck convoys once they left Lashio. This meant that each truck had to carry its own fuel for the entire trip, thus significantly reducing the amounts of other materials carried. A military survey revealed that for 5,000 tons of materials to reach Kunming, China, 14,000 tons had to leave Lashio. Similar amounts of materials disappeared between Kunming and Chungking.

Magruder was able to determine that no fewer than 16 Chinese agencies operated inspection stations on the Road. They were all staffed with relatives of politicians or war lords. Few had any experience or education that prepared them for the task. There was no central authority to regulate traffic or control drivers. When one truck in a convoy of fifteen to twenty trucks stopped for maintenance, the entire convoy stopped. Trucks were overloaded and recklessly driven, and scheduled maintenance was never performed. Government drivers had no motivation to remain with the government since they could drive for a speculator, earn much more, and smuggle goods and passengers for profit besides.

The port of Rangoon itself was not a bottleneck, but the ludicrous numbers of custom inspectors and tax officials were. In July of 1941, for example, 79,000 tons of goods destined for China were tied up in Rangoon, meaning that it would take eight months to move the materials to Lashio. At Lashio, 30,000 tons of China goods were stored, another four-month backlog.

Another backlog on the Road proved to be the Gokteik gorge between Mandalay and Lashio. The gorge was on the Burma railroad line and posed a climb of 3,000 feet in 27 miles. Portions of the railbed required a climb of one foot every 25 feet. This was much too steep for the heavily loaded boxcars. The trains had to be disassembled and smaller sections moved to Lashio by rugged hill-climbing locomotives. The result was another backlog of materials. There was a road from Mandalay to Lashio, but it had a limited capacity due to dangerous stretches.

The end result, as Magruder quickly determined, was a massive congestion of materials destined for China and a failure of any central agency to deal with the problem. To add to Magruder's problems, Singapore became unavailable in December, due to the Japanese advance down the Malay Peninsula, and Chiang Kai-shek was warning that the Japanese were about to attack Yunan province and seize Kunming, the China terminus of the Burma road.

Such was the situation regarding the Burma Road when the Japanese attacked Pearl Harbor on December 7, 1941. The following day, the generalissimo convened a meeting of the representatives from the United States, General Magruder from Great Britain, Sir Archibald Kerr, Chiang's own minister of defense, General Ho Ying-chin, Madame Chiang Kai-shek, and several others. The meeting focused on the need for a combined alliance of Great Britain, the U.S., the Soviet Union, and China to meet the Japanese threat. Subsequent meetings would debate the pros and cons of ways to continue the flow of lend-lease materials to China should the Japanese invade Burma and cut the Burma Road.

On January 1, 1942, Chiang proposed to President Franklin Roosevelt that a road should be constructed from a point in northern India, across north Burma, to join the existing Burma Road north of Lashio. Chiang estimated the construction time as five months,

Washington conservatively estimated construction time as two-and-a-half years.[1]

Japan invaded Burma from Thailand on January 20. On January 24, the CBI (China-Burma-India) representatives selected Ledo as the start point for the Ledo Road. Also proposed was another road from Imphal to Kalewa, and associated port, road, and rail facilities in India to handle the supplies destined for China.

In early February, Britain and China concurred in the need for such facilities, and Washington agreed to fund the project. Simultaneously, Chiang proposed, as an immediate solution to the problem of resupply, that the 700 miles between Sadiya, India, and Kunming, China should be bridged by an air highway. One hundred DC-3s could fly 12,000 tons of supplies a month into China, Chiang assured Roosevelt.[2] President Roosevelt approved the plan and assigned responsibility for both routes to Gen. Joseph W. Stilwell, U.S. Army.

"Vinegar Joe" Stilwell was not a young man in 1942, having been born in 1883. Still, he was energetic, and big things were expected of him. He had served as a military attache in China, and had studied every Sino-Japanese battle of the 1937-38 time period. Stilwell had experience in training large troop units and in developing the kind of tactics needed for the defense of Burma and to organize the Chinese defense effort. Unfortunately, Stilwell was not a diplomat. His nickname "Vinegar Joe" was due to his acid tongue and gruff voice.[3] Despite all of Stilwell's positive qualities, his lack of diplomacy would sour his relationship with Chiang Kai-shek.

Stilwell arrived in Chungking on March 4, 1942, to be Chiang Kai-shek's chief of staff.[4] Within 10 days of his arrival, Rangoon fell to the Japanese. Stilwell was sent to Burma to command the Chinese expeditionary force and prevent the Japanese from advancing into North Burma. In April, the Japanese outflanked Stilwell's forces and captured Lashio, the terminus of the Burma Road on April 29. With the capture of Lashio, the Japanese gained

44,000 tons of allied ammunition.

WITHDRAWAL FROM BURMA. General Stilwell, followed by two aides, Lt. Col. Frank Dorn and 1st Lt. Richard Young, leads the way through the jungle.

US Army / National Archives

The scene in northern Burma was chaotic. The single-track railroad from Mandalay to Myitkyina was overwhelmed by troops from the various armies of the British, Chinese, Indian, and Burmese and hundreds of thousands of civilians all fleeing from the rapidly approaching Japanese. The railroad cars and engines were confiscated by the various military commanders, overloaded, and sent north until May 4, when a head-on collision put the railroad out of commission permanently. The Allied forces suffered 13,000 casualties in Burma and had over 9,000 troops missing when they arrived in India.

Since there was no highway to Myitkyina, the remaining evacuees had two choices: a long, difficult and dangerous walk to India; or to wait and become prisoners of the Japanese. Stilwell and large numbers of civilians chose to walk. Stilwell's party of 26 Americans, 13 British, and 16 Chinese military, plus a small number of nurses, cooks, and mechanics, started their march on May 6 and arrived in Imphal, India on May 20.[5] Many evacuees did not survive the jungle: rivers which had to be crossed with handmade rafts; steep mountains; diseases, especially malaria; animals such as elephants,

59

tigers, and snakes; hunger and heat exhaustion.

For the next 18 months, until winter 1944, Stilwell's struggle would be more political than military. The problem of supplying China and the training of 100,000 Chinese recruits who had been sent to India would absorb much of his time and energy. His relationship with Generalissimo Chiang Kai-shek would prove to be even more stressful.

The U.S. 45th Engineer Regiment relieved the British on the Ledo Road construction in December 1942. The distance from Ledo, in the northeast India province of Assam, to the juncture of the old Burma Road in the Hukawng Valley of Burma was about 103 miles through the Patka hills which rise to 4,500 feet and drop to 700 feet. The engineering report on the Ledo Road describes the area as:

> mountainous terrain, canyon sections, and narrow terraces along torrential streams. The area is unsettled and relatively unexplored. Existing maps were found to be highly inaccurate in their portrayal of ground conditions under the 150 feet of vegetation cover. . . . The total annual rainfall through this mountain section amounts to 150 inches but is concentrated in the monsoon season, May to September.[6]

By January 20, 1943, construction was on a 24-hour-per-day routine. The rate of advance was three-quarters of a mile of all-weather road per day. The road was a single lane and included turnouts for oncoming traffic. The Chinese army in India operated a day ahead of the construction crews to provide protection against any Japanese patrols. Work went well, and the Burmese border was crossed on February 28.

An airline route from northern India to China was seen as an immediate substitute for the Burma Road, but, in early 1942, the United States did not have the additional transports available for the long flights over the Himalaya mountains (the Hump) that such an airlift required. Instead of 100 DC-3's, only 57 were in place. Washington believed that these aircraft could ferry 5,000 tons per month to China. In actuality, the aircraft flew 80 tons in May, 106 tons in June, and 73 tons in July. In April, there were 45,000 tons of lend-lease material stockpiled in India with 7,000 more tons due in May and June.

In June, the generalissimo made his "three demands" which included the provision of 500 fighter aircraft in China and an airlift of 5,000 tons of lend-lease materials per month from India. Chiang strongly hinted through Stilwell that he would seek a separate peace with Japan if the United States did not meet his demands.

Roosevelt responded on August 1, promising the 500 fighters and 100 transport aircraft to meet the airlift goal of 5,000 tons per month by early 1943. In December, Stilwell shed his responsibility for the Hump airlift which became the Air Transport Command (ATC), a worldwide airlift command. Washington still figured 75 aircraft could meet the 5,000-ton goal. Stilwell argued that it would take 140 such aircraft.

In February 1943, 3,000 tons were delivered over the Hump; 3,200 tons in March and 2,500 tons in April. The problem seemed to be that the airfields near Chabua, in the Assam province of India, the termini of the air bridge to China, were not capable of supporting the new C-46 aircraft that were being assigned to the ATC.

A decision was made to divert the engineers and equipment from the Ledo Road to complete the seven airfields with 6,000-foot runways, associated parking, and loading and maintenance areas. Men, trucks, crushers, rollers, and other equipment were diverted and put to work on the Assam airfields. With the airfields completed and additional aircraft assigned, tonnage over the Hump gradually increased from 24,000 tons in October 1944, to 55,000 tons in June 1945.

Relieved of his airlift responsibilities, Stilwell was able to make an inspection trip of the Ledo road in August. He found the work at a virtual halt. From March until August 1943, the road had progressed 3.4 miles, from mile 47.3 out of Ledo to mile 50.7. The crossing of the Burma border had essentially marked the end of the forward progress. There were many reasons for this delay, chief among them the diversion of engineers and equipment to work on the airfields. Since May, when the monsoon roared in, all work had been halted.

Stilwell found other problems as well. Malaria, dysentery, scrub typhus, accidents, and the grim monotony of rain, heat, mud, mildew, insects, as well as boredom in a virtually unknown corner of the world were taking a toll on the work force. Equipment was constantly sliding off the roadbed into ravines and ditches with much time spent in recovering the vehicles. Resupply had become a major problem. Pack animals and Burmese porters could no longer handle the supply requirements. Airlift was tried but was unsuccessful due to jungle canopy and difficult terrain.

Work at night was done under illumination provided by buckets filled with sand and saturated with diesel fuel. There were generator-powered electric lights, but they could not be used during monsoon periods because the bulbs would break.

Bridges were built by hand by Chinese laborers. Fittings were carved with sledges and awls. On the Ledo Road portion of the highway alone, 10 major and 155 minor bridges were built in this manner. Many were carried away by the monsoon and had to be replaced.

Mr. Gerd Ramos, currently of Honolulu, worked on the Ledo Road and recalls the ground leeches as being especially bothersome. They were about one-and-a-half inches long and one-thirty-second of an inch wide. They came in many different colors depending on the color of the earth or vegetation where they existed. They would enter a man's boots through the eyelets and suck blood until filled.

In the process, they would expand to double or triple their size. When filled with blood, they would drop inside the wearer's boots where they would be stepped on and the blood squashed out. Hungry again, the leach would crawl back up and suck blood until it was once again filled. This cycle would be repeated many times throughout a 12-hour work period. Ramos says it was not uncommon to have a half pint of blood in your boots at the end of each workday.

There were 50 varieties of snakes, most poisonous and many very aggressive. They would wait in pathways until someone or something walked by and then dart forward to bite. They had no fangs and did not jump very high, but their bite could be fatal. Besides the leeches and snakes, there were over 1,500 varieties of flies, bugs, and mosquitoes, most carrying some type of disease.

Despite these obstacles, Stilwell was dissatisfied with the progress and brought in Col. Lewis A. Pick, U.S. Army, to take over the construction. His first night in Ledo, October 16, 1943, Pick called his supervisors to a staff meeting and announced: "I've heard the same story all the way from the states. It's always the same. . . . the Ledo Road can't be built. Too much mud, too much rain, too much malaria. From now on we're forgetting that defeatist attitude. The Ledo Road is going to be built, mud, rain and malaria be damned."[7]

Stilwell asked Pick if he could have a jeep path cut through to Shingbwiyang in Burma's Hukawng Valley by the first of January 1944. Sixty miles of the toughest mountain and jungle terrain in the world lay between the 50-mile point and Shingbwiyang. Pick replied that he wouldn't build a jeep trail but he would build a road to handle truck traffic in that amount of time. Pick's bulldozer broke the tape at Shingbwiyang on December 27, four days ahead of schedule. Pick rode the first truck in the first convoy to travel the entire route from Ledo to Kunming, arriving on February 4, 1945.

Following the defeat of the Japanese in Burma and the

occupation of Rangoon on May 3, 1945, the Ledo Road suffered from many of the same problems as the original Burma Road. A combined investigation by British intelligence and the U.S. Criminal Investigation Division in March and April 1945, called the Road a "Chinese army trade route," and found that there was no way to measure the tons or volume of non-military merchandise travelling the Road at any given time. Since convoys were guarded by Chinese soldiers who used force to keep the vehicles from being checked, the use of the Road was out of Allied control.[8]

The Ledo, or as it was sometimes called, the Stilwell Road, took four years to complete and played no part in the August 1945 surrender of Japan. The value of the Road, in hindsight, seems negligible. The decision to build the Road seems questionable. Only the dedication of the men who worked and died on the Road remains to be memorialized.

Graves are the milestones of the Ledo Road. This lifeline to China was paid for by the blood of Americans, British, Chinese, Indians, and Katchins, who lie in graves beside this dim trail in northern Burma and on the sheer mountainsides of China. Few people know of the price paid for this lifeline. Few people seem to care.

C-46 cargo plane flying the Hump. Photograph taken in 1944.

US Army / National Archives

The 21 curves of the Kunming-Kweilin Road.

US Army / National Archives

Chinese laborers level a roadbed for a portion of the Burma Road.

US Army / National Archives

11

THE FALL OF SINGAPORE: FEBRUARY 15, 1942

The Japanese earned their early victories in the Pacific. They planned, researched, and rehearsed every detail for months before they embarked on their campaign. So long as events unfolded as planned, the Japanese soldier appeared to be a superman. The invasions of Thailand, Malaya, and Singapore are classic examples of campaigns where everything went according to plan.

Planning for the invasion of Malaya began on New Years day, 1941, in Taihoku, Formosa, with the creation of Taiwan Army Unit No. 82, a research unit of some 30 officers, staff noncommisioned officers, and servants.[1] To date, most of Japan's planning had focused on the intensely cold region of Manchukuo. Unit No. 82 was given six months to collect all data on jungle warfare, not just Malaya and Singapore, but the Philippine Islands, Indonesia, Burma, and the Pacific islands as well. None of the research personnel had experience in the tropics. Assignment to Unit No. 82 was not considered choice duty. The funds allocated for the research were 20,000 yen or about $851.00.[2] Of this amount, 2,000 yen were set aside each month to be used to pay informants.

Two months of research revealed that: one, the back door of Singapore, facing Johore province, was essentially defenseless; two, the numbers of British fighter aircraft were greatly exaggerated in the media; three, the strength of the British forces was about 80,000 of which fewer than 40,000 were European troops; four, coastal defense and security around Mersing were strong.

Rehearsals for the invasion began in February. Troops were

embarked aboard ship in Formosa, and landings were made near Kagoshima on Honshu with Kurume as the objective. The rehearsals used the same equipment, weapons, and uniforms planned for the campaign and, most importantly, brought together the researchers, planners, and operational staffs that would conduct the invasion. Additional maneuvers were conducted in great secrecy in South China in June 1941.[3]

The movement by sea and landings of men, horses, bicycles, artillery, infantry, and engineer units in 120-degree temperatures were rehearsed in great detail. So was the subsequent movement of such units over 1,000 kilometers, the distance from the Thai border to Singapore.

In addition to research and planning, the 82nd Unit published a booklet that was issued to every man entitled, "Read this alone. . . . and the war can be won."[4] The booklet contained 18 chapters of simple, clear information about fighting in the tropics and was required reading for all troops.

Upgrading of airfields in French Indochina began in September. These earlier French-constructed airfields would be used to provide air cover for the landings at Singora, Patani, and Khoto Bharu. They would also provide the aircraft that would destroy the British battleships, *Prince of Wales* and *Repulse*.[5]

Disguised Japanese officers entered Thailand and Malaya and obtained detailed information on fortifications (or lack thereof), tides, landing beaches, airfields, and roads. Japanese officers flew reconnaissance missions from Saigon over areas of Malaya and Thailand. Maps were modified, plans adjusted, and operational commanders were required to memorize the topography from Thailand to Singapore.[6]

Gen. Tomoyuki Yamashita was appointed Army commander for the campaign on November 6 and decided to: land in strength at Singora, Patani, and Kota Bharu; move rapidly to the Perak river;

capture the bridges and Alor Star airfield; and press hard from Kota Bharu to Kuantan.

Troops were assembled from Japan, Shanghai, Canton, Formosa, and other areas, arriving at Hainan and Saigon for final embarkation on December 2. Space was minimal. Three men occupied one six-foot-by-three-foot mats aboard the troopships. The ships sortied two days later and commenced amphibious operations at Singora early in the morning of December 8.

Surprise was complete at Singora. The defenses were not even manned. The Thai police put up a strong fight inside Singora but were quickly overwhelmed, and the airfields were seized. Thai forces strongly resisted the landing at Patani. Japanese progress was slow, but a beachhead was established and penetration inland began.

Two Japanese ships were sunk at Kota Bharu, and the landing forces were attacked by groups of British fighter planes. Japanese forces soon prevailed, however, and moved quickly to seize the airfields at Kota Bharu, Tanah Merah, and Kuala Kulai. Many British field guns, machine guns, aircraft, cars, trucks, railway cars, and large quantities of petrol were also captured, prompting the first of Yamashita's colorful announcements that the Japanese could "depend on the Churchill ration for supplies."[7] The capture of vast quantities of such supplies would become a daily occurrence as the Japanese army pushed the defenders down the peninsula.

On December 10, *Repulse* and *Prince of Wales* were sunk. Churchill would later write, "In all the war, I never received a more direct shock."[8] The following day, Thai Premier Pibun Songgraml agreed to an alliance with Japan.[9]

Japanese forces reached the Perak River on December 9 and the British Jitra line on December 10. The Jitra line had taken the British six months to construct. It was defended by a whole division and was believed capable of stopping the Japanese advance for at least six months. The line of defense included multiple wire entanglements, deep trenches filled with gasoline which were wired to explode, mountains of artillery shells, provisions, and weapons.

In 15 hours, a detachment of 500 Japanese troops sent the British into full retreat. Japanese casualties were fewer than 100 men. And so it went. The Japanese would gather up the "Churchill rations" and push the British from one strong point to another. The Alor Star airfield was captured intact. Penang fell on December 15 without a single Japanese casualty. Ipoh, Kampar, and Kuantan were captured next.

The British had wired explosives on all five bridges that crossed the Slim River planning to stop the Japanese advance there. The Japanese outran the defenders, crossed all five bridges, and destroyed the arming wires. The British left 13 heavy guns, 15 anti-tank guns, 20 tractor-drawn guns, six anti-aircraft guns, 50 armored cars, 550 motor cars, and enough ammunition, food, medical stores, and supplies to enable two Japanese brigades to fight for a month.

Kuala Lumpur fell on January 11, 1942, without serious resistance, and the Japanese flag was raised over the Sultan's palace at Johore Baru on the last day of the month. The watchtower on the palace offered perfect observation of Singapore and the strait that separated Malaya from Singapore.

In 45 days, the Japanese had moved 1,100 kilometers, averaged two battles per day, and repaired four to five bridges daily, all in strict accordance with the timetable and plan they had so thoroughly developed and rehearsed six months earlier. More significantly, 35,000 Japanese troops had defeated 80,000 British forces in defensive positions while destroying five of their brigades (about 25,000 men). Japanese losses were 1,793 killed and 2,772 wounded.

General Yamashita and his senior commanders drank their ceremonial toast and launched the invasion of Singapore on February 8. By February 13, the Japanese had gained access to Alexandria Barracks Hospital in Singapore, where they bayoneted

323 of the hospital personnel including 230 patients.[10] On the morning of February 14, some survivors were sent back to British lines to explain what would happen to everyone in Singapore if they did not surrender.

Gen. Arthur Percival, the British commander, sought to delay the actual surrender for another day, but Yamashita would have none of it. "Do you consent to unconditional surrender?" he demanded. "Yes or No?" "Yes," answered the defeated General Percival.[11]

Following the fall of Singapore, Winston Churchill, Great Britain's prime minister and minister of defense, proclaimed the loss as the worst disaster and largest capitulation in British history. Contrary to Churchill's speech to the House of Commons on June 18, 1940, when he asked the British people to bear their duties so that men might say, "this was their finest hour," the surrender of Singapore was not Great Britain's finest hour.[12]

The day after the fall of Singapore, Emperor Hirohito rode his white horse across the moat that surrounds the Imperial palace and sat in the winter sunshine for an hour, basking in the gaze of his triumphant people.[13] The emperor took great pleasure in the destruction of Great Britain's bastion in East Asia. In Singapore, the Japanese army was busy arresting more than 70,000 Chinese who were suspected of having British sympathies. A large number of them were tied together, loaded on a boat, taken out to sea, and pushed overboard.

Emperor Hirohito astride his horse *Shirayuki* (Snow White) following the surrender of Singapore.

Private collection

12

THE RAID ON TOKYO: APRIL 18, 1942

The end of 1941 and start of the new year had been a bleak period for America and her allies. They had suffered one defeat after another: Pearl Harbor, Wake Island, Hong Kong, the Philippines; only Corregidor was still holding on.

The Japanese people had been told by their leaders that they were invulnerable and destined to lead the world. They were told that the homeland of Japan could never be touched by the enemy. Indeed, their defense line across the Pacific Ocean plus their occupation of much of China, Korea, Formosa, and Okinawa made such a statement seem most reasonable.

President Roosevelt needed a morale boost for the Americans and the allies. He also wanted to send his own message to the Japanese people, a message similar to the one the Japanese delivered at Pearl Harbor. He wanted to bomb Japan.[1]

Working in complete secrecy, Adm. Ernest J. King, chief of naval operations, had two of his operations officers, Capt. Francis Low and Capt. Donald Duncan, research a suggestion that U.S. army bombers could be used to fly from a carrier and strike Japan.[2] Army bombers were being considered because they had the necessary range to reach Japan from some 400 miles at sea where the attack would have to be launched.

Initial research revealed that the B-25 bomber could probably launch from a navy carrier at sea with a 1,000 lb. bomb-load, strike a target 400 miles distant, but could not be recovered back aboard the carrier. After completing their mission, the B-25s would have

73

to overfly Japan, land at friendly airbases in China, and then be used by either the American Volunteer Group in China or the Chinese Air Force.

Chiang Kai-shek did not want the bombers landing in China because he feared a violent Japanese reaction. The Generalissimo was notified at the last minute, and his objections were overruled by decision-makers in Washington.[3] Japanese reaction to the use of China as a haven for the B-25s was quick and efficient, the specifies of which are described at the end of this chapter.

Gen. Henry H. "Hap" Arnold, chief of staff of the Army Air Force, concurred with the initial research and designated Lt. Col. Jimmy Doolittle as the project officer on January 17, 1942.[4] Doolittle had a scant two-and-a-half months to obtain and train the pilots, modify the aircraft, select and plan the attacks on the targets and thoroughly coordinate all activities with the navy.

The B-25 was confirmed as the most suitable aircraft available, and the 17th Bombardment Group at Pendelton, Oregon, was selected as the project group and moved to Columbia Army Air Base in North Carolina. Auxiliary fuel tanks holding about 450 more gallons of fuel were installed on the aircraft, raising the total fuel load to 1141 gallons.[5] Training of aircrews began at Eglin Field, near Panama City, Florida, and the aircraft were then flown to California to load aboard the assigned carrier.

On April 13, 16 Army Air Force B-25s were lifted by crane from the pier at the Naval Air Station Alameda, California, to the deck of the new aircraft carrier *Hornet*. *Hornet*, with its escort of two cruisers and four destroyers, sailed to rendezvous with Adm. William F. Halsey's task force north of Midway. The task force with the flagship *Enterprise* and a total of 16 ships then headed west through heavy seas toward Japan.[6]

Admiral Yamamoto had anticipated that the allies might try a carrier raid against Japan and had created an early-warning system consisting of a picket line of small fishing craft equipped with radio communications over a thousand miles long, six-to-seven hundred miles off the eastern coast of Japan.[7]

Early in the morning of April 18, *Enterprise* picked up one of the picketboats on radar about 650 miles west of Japan. This was at least 150 miles further to sea than Halsey planned to launch his attack. The task force altered course but soon found another picketboat. Another course change and another picketboat. At 6:00 A.M., one of the scout planes dropped a message reporting that it had sighted one of the fishing vessels and, likewise, had been seen. A Japanese radio message was intercepted and a light was seen bobbing in the sea a few hundred yards away. At 7:30 A.M., *Hornet* sighted a vessel 12,000 yards away. It was obvious that the chance for surprise was in jeopardy. The decision was made to launch the B-25s at the distance of 650 miles, which would make it most difficult for the crews to reach safe airfields in China.

Jimmy Doolittle leads the raid on Tokyo in a B-25 from the carrier *Hornet.*

National Archives

At 8:00 A.M., *Hornet* turned into the wind and, with the flight deck rolling violently and green seas breaking over the bow, Lieutenant Colonel Doolittle led the rest of the squadron down the flight deck and then climbed laboriously into the sky.[8] It was the first carrier takeoff the Army fliers had made.

The 16 B-25s all flew individual routes to their targets. Crews saw numerous Japanese aircraft of all types and a number of barrage balloons but had no serious interference from them. The B-25s were at treetop level and nearly invisible to the Japanese aircraft. After dropping their bombs on Tokyo and other prescribed targets, the aircraft swung away on a course for China. A handful of Japanese fighters rose to intercept the bombers but did little damage.[9]

Fifteen of the 16 aircraft reached China and either crash-landed or the crews bailed out. Of the 80 airmen who carried out the Tokyo raid, 73 survived.[10] Eight of the crew were captured by the Japanese who executed three of them. Five crewmen were captured by the Soviets and were imprisoned for 14 months. One crew member died as a result of his bailout, two drowned at sea following the ditching of their aircraft, and one died of malnutrition (beri-beri) in a Japanese prison camp. The story of the release of the Doolittle flyers from the Japanese POW camp is told in the chapter "The Doolittle POWs" in this book.

It had been a 13-hour flight since the crews left the *Hornet*. Day had turned to night. When the fuel gauge on Doolittle's aircraft indicated zero, he ordered the crew to bail out and then followed. He landed in a rice paddy recently filled with nightsoil. Thoroughly disgusted with his situation and his smell, he spent the night trying to locate his crewmembers and to contact Chinese military forces. When he did find Chinese Nationalist forces the following morning, there was an extended period of tense negotiations and arguments before he was accepted as a U.S. pilot and allowed to keep his military pistol.

After a short stay in China, which included a decoration

ceremony by Chiang Kai-shek, Doolittle received orders to return to Washington, D.C. "by any means possible."[11] The only means possible was a China National Airways Corporation (CNAC), 21-passenger Douglas DC-3, piloted by Capt. Moon Chin. Chin was a native of Baltimore, Maryland, and had flown for 10 years with Pan American Airways which was under contract to fly CNAC routes.[12] Takeoff was on May 5, with the first scheduled stop at Myitkyina, Burma. En route to Burma, Chin received a radio message that Myitkyina was under attack by Japanese fighter planes. He landed at an isolated emergency field for an hour and then resumed his trip.

Myitkyina was in a state of chaos. Wreckage, fire, dead, and wounded were everywhere. Refugees flooded all transportation routes as the people fled from the approaching Japanese. Within minutes, the DC-3 was surrounded by refugees. As the aircraft was being refueled, Chin supervised the loading of passengers. Soon 30 people packed the 21-passenger cabin. Then 40 and then 50 people were brought aboard. Doolittle was understandably nervous. "I hope you know what you are doing," he said to Chin.

Moon Chin, not at all bothered by the American hero or the number of refugees, responded, "We're fighting a war over here. We do things you wouldn't do at home," and proceeded to load another 10 people.[13] Once the 60th passenger was loaded aboard, Chin shut the cabin door, climbed and crawled over the mass of humanity to get to the cockpit, and, despite the load, coaxed the DC-3 airborne well before the end of the runway. After a four-hour flight to Calcutta, the baggage compartment was opened and out tumbled eight more Chinese refugees. Doolittle believes that 68 passengers are still a record for a DC-3.

From Calcutta, Doolittle took a BOAC flying boat to Cairo, then, after 14 stops, he arrived in Washington, D.C. on May 18.

In retaliation for the B-25 raid, the Japanese sent 53 battalions slashing through Chekiang province where most of the B-25 crews had bailed out.[14] Some 20,000 square miles of countryside were searched in an effort to capture or prevent the escape of the U.S. airmen. In the process, 225,000 Chinese men, women, and children were brutally slaughtered.

The actual damage inflicted by the B-25s was small, but the psychological effect was huge. The army and navy had failed to protect the homeland and the emperor from attack. To Admiral Yamamoto, it was a mortifying personal defeat.[15] The navy general staff, in response to the attack, immediately moved up its timetable to attack New Guinea, the Solomon Islands, and Midway. The Japanese saw these land-based airfields as necessary to protect their bases at Rabaul and Truk and, eventually, the empire itself.

During the battle of the Coral Sea, *Lexington* explodes from gasoline vapors (above) after suffering Japanese torpedo hits. Men climb over the side of *Lexington* (below).

National Archives

13

THE CORAL SEA BATTLE: MAY 6, 1942

Historians and military strategists generally agree that no other single battle changed the balance of power and eventual outcome of the war in the Pacific as did the Battle of Midway. When it was over, the Japanese navy had suffered the most decisive defeat ever experienced, far less imagined. The defeat was so onerous that the Japanese navy put a lid of secrecy on the event. The wounded were transported to Japan and moved, after dark, through rear entrances into hospitals where they were placed in complete isolation. All information pertaining to the disaster was marked top secret, and even the Japanese army was not informed of the results. It would be 1951, when Mitsuo Fuchida and Masatake Okumiya published their book on the Battle of Midway, before the Japanese public would learn of the naval action.

The Midway invasion plan was conceived to extend Japan's perimeter and prevent the kind of carrier raids that the U.S. Navy had been conducting against The Marshall Islands, Rabaul, Wake, and Eastern New Guinea. In addition to occupying Midway, the Japanese Combined Fleet hoped to draw the US Pacific Fleet into a decisive surface battle and destroy it.

Adm. Isoroku Yamamoto approved the plan at the end of March, and it was briefed to the naval general staff on April 2. The plan to attack and occupy Midway, while simultaneously attacking and occupying the U.S. Western Aleutians, was not warmly received by the general staff. Objections centered on the complicated strategy and tactics, the tremendous number of ships and amount of equipment and material involved, the current shortfall of carrier aircraft, and even the questionable value of Midway as an outpost due to its proximity to Hawaii, which was only 1,137 miles away.

By the middle of April, the Midway plan was headed for a lengthy period on the shelf. Credit for revival and approval of the plan must go to Lt. Col. Jimmy Doolittle. Doolittle, on April 18, led a flight of 16 B-25 bombers from the flight deck of the carrier *Hornet* on a one-way mission against the Japanese homeland.

Although the Japanese had been alerted to the presence of the American carriers and launched interceptors against the anticipated raiders, all the B-25s were able to drop their bombs on the cities. Reports of Tokyo being bombed were followed quickly by reports of attacks on Kawasaki, Yokohama, and Yokosuka. Shortly thereafter, more reports of aircraft bombing Nagoya, Yokkaichi, Wakayama, and Kobe were received by the various military headquarters.

The result of the Doolittle raid was withdrawal of the general staff objections to the Midway plan. The army agreed to provide one reinforced infantry regiment to participate in the Midway assault, and May 25 was set as the date for assembly of the amphibious forces at Saipan. Although the army would withdraw its amphibious forces immediately after Midway was seized, its participation was a major compromise since it had long opposed the Midway plan due to its overextended area of occupation.

While Admiral Yamamoto's staff rehearsed the Midway and Aleutian invasion plans, Vice Adm. Takeo Takagi landed forces on Tulagi on May 3 and embarked forces from Rabaul on May 4 for the planned invasion of Port Moresby, New Guinea. To escort his 14 transports, Takagi had the heavy carriers *Zuikako* and *Shokaku*, the light carrier *Shoho*, seven heavy cruisers and 13 destroyers.

The invasion force entered the Coral Sea on May 6 and received reports of an enemy carrier force the next day. Admiral Takagi was aware of potential U.S. carrier forces because carrier aircraft had attacked the Tulagi beachhead during his amphibious operation three days earlier.

The first sighting of the American force included reports of one carrier about 160 miles south of Takagi's position. He launched all 78 planes from his heavy carriers, but they found only the destroyer *Sims* and the oiler *Neosho*. *Sims* was sunk and *Neosho* heavily damaged.[1]

While the Japanese were occupied with *Neosho* and *Sims*, about 100 bombers and torpedo planes from the carriers *Lexington* and *Yorktown* located *Shoho* and sunk it.[2] The naval forces of both sides moved apart during the evening, but Japanese float planes located the American carrier group early on May 8. All planes from *Zuikaku* and *Shokaku* were launched and reported sinking both American carriers, a battleship, and a cruiser.[3] At the same time, American carrier-based aircraft attacked the Japanese carriers, with *Shokaku* sustaining three bomb hits which forced her to withdraw. *Zuikaku* hid in a rain squall and was not attacked.

Lexington had been hit but not sunk; however, explosions below deck and uncontrolled fires forced the carrier to be abandoned and torpedoed by friendly forces the following day. *Yorktown* absorbed a single bomb hit, which caused extensive damage but did not put her out of action.

Both sides withdrew from the Coral Sea, and both sides proclaimed victory in this first naval sea battle in history in which the surface ships never saw one another or exchanged fire. Actual losses for Japan were the light carrier *Shoho* sunk, *Shokaku* damaged, 77 planes lost, and 1,074 men killed or wounded. The U.S. lost *Lexington*, *Neosho*, and *Sims*. *Yorktown* was heavily damaged, 66 planes were lost, and 543 sailors were killed or wounded.

Historians still argue over who lost the battle, but the long term effects all went against the Japanese. The damage to *Shokaku* would prevent her participation in the Midway battle, the aircraft and aircrews would prove to be impossible to replace, and the Port Moresby invasion was postponed indefinitely.

Japanese forces were ordered home to prepare for the Midway operation. According to author Fuchida, *Shokaku* arrived at the Kure shipyards with the distinction of being the most heavily damaged warship to enter the naval repair facility. Repair was estimated to take one month, too late for the Midway attack.[4] *Zuikaku* arrived a few days later, and although undamaged, it was learned that it would be impossible to replace the lost aircraft and train replacement aircrews in time for Midway. In effect, Yamamoto had lost three carriers, not one, for the Midway and Aleutian attacks.

Task Force 16, with carriers *Hornet* and *Enterprise*, arrived at Pearl Harbor on May 26, refueled, rearmed, and departed on May 28, the same day that Yamamoto's forces left Japan. The carrier task force, commanded by Rear Adm. Raymond D. Spruance, was escorted by six cruisers and nine destroyers.

Yorktown arrived at Pearl Harbor on May 27 and immediately went into drydock for repairs estimated to take three months. Repair crews worked around the clock for 48 hours and then pronounced the carrier "battle ready." She fueled, took on a replacement air group, and departed on May 29. This carrier task force was commanded by Rear Adm. Frank J. Fletcher and was escorted by two cruisers and six destroyers.[5]

14

THE BATTLE OF MIDWAY: JUNE 4, 1942

Midway was so important to U.S. strategy in the Pacific that Adm. Isoroku Yamamoto knew the Pacific Fleet would intervene. He was most confident that Adm. Chuichi Nagumo's heavy carriers and fast battleships could annihilate any force that Adm. Chester Nimitz, commander-in-chief, Pacific Fleet, could send to Midway. Certainly, the preponderance of power favored the Japanese. Their Combined Fleet included 25 flag officers commanding more than 200 ships and 600 aircraft. The Midway operation alone would include the carriers *Akagi*, *Kaga*, *Soryu*, and *Hiryu*, plus nine battleships, three of which were the strongest and fastest in the world.[1]

To offset the strength of the Combined Fleet, Admiral Nimitz had his Naval Intelligence Service. Through intercepts and decoding of messages, he knew the date and location of the planned attack and the planned diversionary attacks on Kiska, Attu, and Adak in the Aleutians.[2] He was determined not to fall for the Aleutian trap and made plans to set his own trap off Midway.

Midway, while not defenseless, could not have held out alone against the much stronger Japanese force. At best, it was a desolate post never mentioned by recruiters. Since 1940, it had been reinforced by construction and marine corps units who were improving defensive positions.

The island was shelled for 23 minutes on December 7, 1941, by two destroyers and proved to be a handy bombardment target for passing Japanese submarines on their way to and from the eastern Pacific. Most recently, Admiral Nimitz had reinforced the garrison with a marine corps dive-bombing squadron and army land-based bombers.[3]

A Catalina flying boat out of Midway first sighted the landing force of 11 troop transports some 700 miles west of Midway at 9:00 A.M., on June 3. Army B-17 bombers attacked the convoy in early afternoon, inflicting no hits or damage.[4] Marine torpedo planes attacked next, scoring one hit on a tanker which killed eleven men and wounded thirteen but did little damage to the ship.[5] During the Midway land-based air attack on the Japanese landing force, Admiral Fletcher positioned his carrier forces 200 miles north of Midway and waited. Their presence at Midway was still unknown to the Japanese.

The Japanese carrier force was located at first light on June 4, an hour after they had launched 108 aircraft to attack Midway. At 6:16 A.M., about 30 miles northwest of Midway, the old Brewster fighters of Marine Fighter Squadron-221 met the incoming attack force.

The first wave of the versatile Zero fighters shot down nine of the 21 Brewsters. The second wave of Zeros destroyed six more.[6] The Japanese lost four bombers and two zeros while causing heavy structural damage to the base at Midway, creating large fires, and inflicting many casualties. The runway was not put out of operation, however, which meant that Midway-based aircraft could continue to oppose the Japanese landing.

At 7:05 A.M., the first marine corps torpedo bombers from Midway, TBF "Avengers," attacked the carriers. Zero fighters destroyed three of the four Avengers, and the others withdrew. Next, Zeros destroyed three of the six army B-26 "Marauders" that attacked at low altitude. The others released their torpedoes without effect. Another B-26 was destroyed by anti-aircraft fire after the attack.[7]

At 8:00 A.M., 14 Army B-17s attacked the Japanese carriers

Hiryu and *Soryu* from an altitude of 20,000 feet. Each dropped four tons of bombs but scored no hits. Their altitude did save them from the Zeros however, and allowed them to survive. Next came 16 "SBD" marine corps dive bombers which made shallow glide-bombing attacks on *Hiryu*. Zeros destroyed eight of the SBDs, and six of the remaining eight aircraft that returned to Midway were damaged beyond repair. The SBDs scored no hits.

To this point, the Japanese were not impressed with the tactics or ability of the Americans. They had been subjected to about every kind of attack possible and had not suffered any damage while inflicting tremendous losses on the attackers. They apparently had little to fear from the uncoordinated and unescorted attacks of the Americans.[8]

As the Japanese were recovering their aircraft from the Midway strike and rearming for another strike against the runways, they received a report of one American carrier, five cruisers, and five destroyers 240 miles from Midway. Admiral Nagumo radioed Yamamoto that he would proceed there. Aircraft recovery was completed at 9:18 A.M., and the Japanese carrier force sped towards the reported U.S. position.

Adm. Raymond Spruance had waited until the Japanese carrier planes returned from their Midway raid and were on the carrier decks being refueled and rearmed. He then launched 131 of his own dive bombers and torpedo planes against the Japanese carriers. His first attack group of 15 torpedo bombers, VTB "Valiants," went after *Akagi* and were all shot down by Zeros before they could drop their torpedoes.

At 9:30 A.M., another attack on *Akagi* unfolded as two groups of torpedo bombers commenced an attack from both the port and starboard sides of the carrier. Seven of the torpedo bombers were destroyed before they could launch their torpedoes. The remaining aircraft scored no hits. So far, 41 navy carrier aircraft had attacked the Japanese carriers. All but six had been destroyed, and they had not inflicted any damage on the Japanese fleet. To compound matters, aircraft from *Hornet* never found the Japanese fleet and missed the battle.[9]

Yorktown (above) and the cruiser *Mikuma* (below) were both lost in the Battle of the Midway, but Admiral Spruance (top inset) clearly bested Admiral Nagumo (bottom inset).

National Archives

Despite the destruction of most of the Midway-based aircraft and the futility of the American carrier-based aircraft to that point in time, what happened in the next five minutes changed the course of the war forever. While the torpedo bombers were being blasted out of the sky by Zeros and anti-aircraft fire, 37 dive bombers from *Enterprise* and *Yorktown* attacked and put bombs in *Akagi* and *Kaga*. At the same time, 17 dive bombers from *Yorktown* attacked *Soryu* and scored direct hits. Within minutes, all three carriers were in shambles with blazing decks and exploding aircraft. All three carriers were doomed.[10]

In retaliation, the Japanese carrier *Hiryu* launched 40 aircraft which scored three bomb hits and severely damaged *Yorktown*. The damage was controlled until several hours later when *Hiryu* torpedo planes again hit *Yorktown*. The carrier was abandoned but remained floating for two days until sighted and sunk by a Japanese submarine. To avenge *Yorktown*, dive bombers from *Enterprise* located *Hiryu* at 5:00 P.M., and made a flaming wreck of the carrier in just a few minutes. She sank the following morning.

During the subsequent withdrawal ordered by Admiral Yamamoto, two of his heavy cruisers collided and were found by Midway-based aircraft the next morning. The old fabric-covered SB2U marine corps dive bombers attacked the well-armed cruisers. Capt. Richard Fleming, his aircraft on fire from the cruiser's guns, flew his aircraft into the cruiser *Mikuma* and destroyed it. His act earned Fleming the posthumous award of the Medal of Honor. The second cruiser, the *Mogami*, was crippled but eventually reached repair facilities in Japan.

The Aleutian diversionary force, which was intended to pull part of Admiral Nimitz's fleet away from Midway, occupied Attu and Kiska in the Aleutions for a short period of time, but such occupancy of American territory in no way made up for the loss of the four Japanese carriers.

The rigidity of Japanese planning and their tendency to abandon a project when events did not go according to plan would be widely communicated to Allied forces and would be repeated many times throughout the war.

The importance of the U.S. victory in the Battle of Midway cannot be over emphasized. In just five minutes, the entire position of the Japanese forces in the Pacific changed from dominant to doubtful. The expansion phase of Japanese aggression had ended. The road to victory for the Allies would remain long and hard, but the issue was no longer in doubt. In addition to the carriers *Akagi*, *Kaga*, *Hiryu*, and *Soryu*, Japan lost the battleship *Haruna*, the cruiser *Mikuma*, and 332 aircraft. The cruiser *Mogami* was heavily damaged. Lesser damage was suffered by three destroyers and an oiler. The U.S. Pacific Fleet lost the carrier *Yorktown*, the destroyer *Hamman*, and a total of 147 land and carrier-based aircraft.

General Douglas MacArthur, President Franklin D. Roosevelt and Admiral Chester W. Nimitz.

US Navy

15

THE LIGHT CRUISER *JUNEAU*

At 11:01 A.M., on November, 13, 1942, the light cruiser USS *Juneau* was seen to disintegrate in a mighty column of smoke and flames.

Capt. Gilbert C. Hoover, commander of the cruiser USS *Helena*, saw the torpedoes streak past *Helena's* bow and impact *Juneau*. He saw the plume of fire, smoke, and water that reached skyward for nearly a thousand feet. He clearly saw the disaster that killed his good friend, Captain Lars Swenson, commander of *Juneau*.

Hoover saw no debris or survivors in the water, and, fearing for the safety of his ship and crew, he ordered *Helena* to steam swiftly away from the site and directed that the destroyer *Fletcher*, which was racing to the scene to assist in a search for survivors, be signaled to turn back. Both ships then maintained radio silence and joined the remainder of the four-ship task force enroute to Espiritu Santo.

But Hoover was wrong. Dead wrong. Between 140 and 180 survivors of *Juneau* were in the water trying to survive. Some were without arms or legs, some had mortal wounds, and all were bloody and covered with oil. Those who were not hysterical had ample reason to become so as they watched the ships from their convoy race into the distance.[1]

Juneau was a new ship when the United States entered the war. Her keel was laid in 1940, and she was commissioned in October 1941. Juneau was 541 feet long, 53 feet wide, and displaced 6,000 tons. She had a crew complement of 26 officers and 587 men.

Following her sea trials and Caribbean patrols, *Juneau* joined Task Force 17 off the Hebrides Islands in September 1942. *Juneau,* the battleship *South Dakota,* and three destroyers were escorting the carrier *Wasp* to Guadacanal when *Wasp* was sunk by the Japanese submarine I-19. In October 1942, *Juneau* was part of an escort force for the carriers *Hornet* and *Enterprise* during the Battle of Santa Cruz. In the battle, the Japanese sank *Hornet,* three other warships, and shot down 74 carrier aircraft. The U.S. navy damaged four Japanese ships and shot down 66 planes.

Following the loss of *Hornet,* the navy advised all brothers and close relatives stationed aboard the same ship to request transfer to seperate ships to minimize family casualties. The Sullivan brothers on *Juneau* ignored the advice, but Joseph Rogers and his brother, James, transferred to a supply ship, leaving Patrick and Louis on *Juneau.*

Juneau assisted in the rescue of more than 1,900 of the *Wasp's* crew, including Charles Coombs, brother of Russell Coombs, a sailor on the *Juneau.* Ironically, Charles would later join his brother on the *Juneau* and become yet another family of brothers on the ship. Five Sullivans, two Rogers, and the two Coombs perished in the *Juneau* tragedy.

The day before *Juneau* was torpedoed, she was part of the protective screen for the Guadalcanal transport force that fought a major battle with a large Japanese naval force in "Ironbottom Sound." Only six of the 13 American warships had survived the battle. *Juneau* was badly damaged, and the cruiser *San Francisco* was in even worse shape. *Juneau* signalled *Helena* following the battle, "Torpedo flooded forward engine room and fire room x [stop] Plotting room out of commission x Down by the head four feet x Estimate eighteen knots speed x Flooding under control x All forward fire room personnel lost x. . . . x"[2] Swenson indicated he would follow the *Helena* to Espiritu Santo.

In spite of his damage, Captain Swenson realized how fortunate he was when he saw *San Francisco*. How was it possible for the ship to be afloat? The hull, superstructure, and turrets were no more than a mass of twisted and torn steel. The whole ship was a floating junkyard.

San Francisco's dispensary had been destroyed and then flooded during the battle. There was no warm water, the casualties were on the after deck, and other wounded and dying were in the hangar.[3] Burial sacks of the dead were being consigned to the sea the entire time *Juneau* could observe her. The crew of *Juneau* considered themselves lucky.

While the crew of *Juneau* stared at *San Francisco*, the Japanese submarine I-26, commanded by Comdr. Miroru Yokota, was tracking and figuring a firing solution to torpedo *San Francisco*, the largest ship in the slow-moving convoy. Chief petty officer Tsukuo Nakano fired two torpedoes at a range of 1,500 meters, with a deflection of 70 degrees.[4] The torpedoes passed astern of *Helena*, which was the third ship in line and just forward of *San Francisco*, the fourth ship. Nakano was aware that there was a ship on the far side of *San Francisco* but had not targeted it. After a long run, the torpedo impacted *Juneau*, the ship on the far side of the convoy, and exploded in the forward magazine. The explosion blew the ship apart.[5]

A B-17, piloted by 1Lt. Robert Gill, was flying a patrol mission about 40 miles south of the task force when he saw the huge column of smoke that marked the end of *Juneau*, and went to investigate. Debris littered the ocean for miles, and the oil-soaked heads of the sailors resembled coconuts more than people. His crew estimated that there were about 180 survivors in the water. Restricted by the same radio silence as the task force, Gill flew close to *Helena* and, using a blinker, signalled over and over that there were at least 150 survivors in the water.[6]

Helena responded with a "Roger" and continued on its way with the ships in the convoy. Later, on his way to Guadalcanal, Gill flew over the site again and circled the survivors. No one in the crew thought to drop rubber rafts or supplies. The men in the water located and tied three rafts together and attached parts of ten rope nets to the rafts for men to hold on to. Lt.(jg) J.T. Blodgett was the senior survivor. He tried to exercise leadership to save the men and was assisted by S1c. Lester Zook, who was able to compile a list of 125 survivors, but men were dying fast.

When Lieutenant Gill completed his search sector, he flew slightly out of his way to let the men know they had been sighted. He made three passes over the men and this time dropped some rafts and supplies. Upon landing at Espiritu Santo at 5:30 P.M., six and a half hours after the sinking, Gill rushed to the group headquarters to report the sinking and the survivors. He found that no one felt any sense of urgency over his report. It was treated as routine and filed in the daily operations report.[7]

About 12 hours after the sinking, Captain Hoover reported the sinking of *Juneau* to Adm. Richmond K. Turner but said nothing about the B-17 sighting of survivors. When the task force arrived at Espiritu Santo, Hoover notified Adm. "Bull" Halsey in Noumea that the task force had arrived, but did not mention the sinking of *Juneau*.[8]

The day following *Juneau's* sinking, a DC-3 sighted the survivors and dropped a rubber raft about a hundred yards from the sailors. Between the men and the raft were dozens of six-to-ten-foot sharks that had been aggressively tearing apart the bodies of men who had died or lost their hold on the nets.

S2c. Joseph Hartney, a good swimmer, eyed the raft all morning. He knew it should contain food and medicine desperately needed by the survivors. Finally, Hartney and his friend Victor Fitzgerald decided to swim for it. They had not gone 10 yards before the sharks closed in from three sides.[9] Hartney was scared. He and Victor thrashed the water as hard as they could and the sharks melted away, only to return in a few seconds. This scene was repeated several times with the swimmers gaining 10 to 15 yards each time. With 20 yards to go, the sharks were passing within inches of their bodies. A final thrashing and the men were at the raft. They pulled themselves aboard in time to receive several heavy jolts and scrapes from sharks passing under the raft. The men searched the raft and found nothing. No food, no medicine, and no water. Only a set of oars and a bailing bag.

By November 15, the third day in the water, conditions were becoming desperate. The bodies of the men hanging in the nets were starting to swell due to the saltwater, fuel oil, and reflection of the sun off the water. Most were hallucinating and all needed water. Their tongues were swollen, and they could not swallow or salivate. Their eyes were swollen shut. Some men drank saltwater, went mad, and jumped into the sea where the sharks consumed them. The sharks became braver each day and were coming out of the water to chew hands or arms that extended from the rafts.[10]

On November 15, Lieutenant Gill was flying his usual search mission and went slightly off course to the site of the sinking. Gill and his crew were speechless when they saw swimmers still bobbing in the water. The crew estimated the number of survivors as fewer than 100. "What kind of a navy would leave men in the water for days?"[11] Gill growled. Once again, radio silence precluded his transmission of the survivors. As soon as he landed, Gill again reported the sinking and survivors, and lamented the plight of the men in the water. The debriefing officer was not impressed.[12]

George Sullivan, the only remaining Sullivan brother after three days in the water, announced late in the afternoon that he was going to swim to a nearby imaginary island. The others tried to reason with George, but before he could be stopped, George went over the side and swam away. The sharks tore him to bits.

By November 17, the fifth day in the water, only about 40 men remained alive. By the morning of the sixth day, Blodgett was no longer in control. He was losing his mind and drifting in and out of delirium.

Again, on November 18, Lieutenant Gill diverted his aircraft to fly by the site of the sinking. "My God!" Gill thought, "The navy apparently doesn't give a damn about them! They are being left to die!"[13] Gill's crew estimated that 50 men remained alive. Once again, Gill did not break precious radio silence. When he returned to base, he reported the status of the survivors for the third time.

Shortly after Gill left the scene, the wind and waves loosened the ropes that were holding the rafts together and they detached. Now the men were separated into small groups of fewer than a dozen each. Sharks grabbed any part of a man that protruded out of a raft. A shark bit into a sailor who had been lying on the edge of a raft and ripped off a leg. Allen Heyn, the only other person in the raft, was able to hold on to the man and tried to pull him inside, but the shark struck again and tore off piece after piece of the remaining leg and finally pulled the victim into the water.[14]

As Arthur Friend stood up in another raft, a shark grabbed him by the buttocks and pulled him into the water. Friend still had some strength left and ripped out a large section of the sharks gills. The shark spit him out and Friend climbed back into the raft minus 15 pounds of buttocks just as another shark pulled a seaman named Brown from the edge of the raft and devoured him. Brown had previously tried to swim away from the raft and had been rescued by Friend, but not before Brown had lost both feet to a shark.[15]

At 5:30 A.M., on November 19, six days after the sinking, the navy alerted a PBY patrol plane to search for members of a ship sunk in the battle for Guadacanal. The *Juneau* was not mentioned by name, and there was nothing special in the mission assignment. Navy Lt. Lawrence B. Williamson assumed it would be another boring and uneventful search mission.

Williamson and his crew searched all day. About 5:00 P.M., he radioed a message to his headquarters that he was returning to base. As he made a turn to the south to head home, one of the crewman shouted, "There they are."[16] The PBY had spotted a raft with five to seven men on it, then a second raft with only one person in it, and after three circles of the area, a third raft with bodies in it but no movement. The crew did not see any other rafts or nets.

Williamson was told to remain on site until the Destroyer USS *Ballard* could arrive at about 11:30 P.M. Williamson estimated that he barely had enough fuel to remain on station for another six hours, and, besides, it would be difficult to maintain contact with the rafts after dark. He asked for permission to land and rescue the survivors and was told, "Use your own discretion."[17]

On the approach for the landing, the PBY did a full stall, lost lift, and headed down swiftly. It hit the water hard and bounced from wave to wave before Williamson brought it to a halt. Leaks were plugged with sharpened pencils and slowly the first raft was approached. The first sailor pulled aboard was Seaman Wyatt Butterfield. When asked, "What ship?," Butterfield responded, "The *Juneau* . . . we're the only ones left."[18] Then he passed out.

Williamson now had a difficult decision to make. The sea was much rougher than he estimated, and the plane was taking a pounding as he tried to taxi on the surface. It was almost dark and it would be impossible to find the other rafts after dark. With grave apprehension, Williamson decided to return to base, get the survivors he did have into the hospital, and return the next morning for the others.

The following morning, November 20, Arthur Friend lay alone in his raft, his buttock chewed off by a shark. He had no food and no water, with only the sharks that circled and bumped the raft to talk to. Friend was drifting into madness when he heard the roar of a plane. "I'm here, I'm here,"[19] he groaned feebly, but the plane kept going.

Several hours later, the mast of a ship appeared and kept coming until it was about 200 yards away. Then a motor launch was sent towards the raft. As the launch approached the raft, the sailors could see that Friend was preparing to jump. "Don't jump!" they shouted. Friend couldn't wait. With all his remaining strength, he jumped and landed face down in the launch. As he was gently carried to the destroyer *Ballard*, he passed out.

Ballard was then directed by the PBY to a raft containing Allen Heyn, who was too feeble to move. Heyn was carried to a bunk on the destroyer and was allowed to wet his lips with fresh water. The following day, November 21, another PBY would rescue three more survivors, bringing the total to 10. Lieutenant Blodgett who had worked so hard to maintain order and discipline among the survivors was not one of the 10. Blodgett, in a moment of madness, swam a few yards away from the raft and was devoured by sharks. He missed the rescue by four hours.[20]

On that same day, Adm."Bull" Halsey came aboard *Helena* and visited Captain Hoover in his cabin. Halsey left after about five minutes. When he was gone, Hoover turned to Cmdr. Charles Carpenter, his executive officer, and, without emotion, said, "I have been relieved of command." Hoover was the first to feel the wrath of Halsey. There would be more, but Lieutenant Gill, USAAF, would not be one of them. The subsequent investigation would exonerate him, and he was promoted to captain a few weeks later. The intelligence officer that took Gill's debriefings was not seen again.

Helena was subsequently torpedoed and sunk in July 1943 in the New Georgia area. Over a thousand members of *Helena* were rescued by destroyers that stayed on the scene.

16

THE DEATH OF ADMIRAL YAMAMOTO

Commander of the Japanese Combined Fleet, Adm. Isoroku Yamamoto, flew to Rabaul on April 3, 1943, to observe the major aerial operation that was to reduce the allied hold in the lower Solomons and the Papuan Peninsula. Neatly attired in his dress white uniform, he watched the first of 200 fighters and bombers take off from Rabaul to strike Guadalcanal. It was the largest Japanese air strike since the attack on Pearl Harbor.

The strike sank a destroyer, a tanker, and a corvette, but the excited pilots reported much more. Three more strikes over the next four days reported the sinking of a cruiser, 25 transports, and the downing of more than 200 planes. Even allowing for pilot exaggeration, Admiral Yamamoto believed his strategy was succeeding and decided to make a personal tour of the Japanese airfields to enhance the morale of the front-line troops.[1] It would prove to be a fatal mistake.

On the afternoon of April 14, Pearl Harbor radio intelligence intercepted the signal that announced Yamamoto's travel agenda and decrypted it.[2] Adm. Chester Nimitz, commander Pacific Fleet, determined that the first leg of the journey would bring the Japanese admiral within range of fighters from Henderson Field on Guadalcanal. Here was a chance to eliminate a man whose loss would be a tremendous blow to Japanese morale. On April 15, after the mission had been approved by Secretary of the Navy Frank Knox and President Roosevelt, Admiral Nimitz cabled approval for the interception.[3]

On Henderson Field, Maj. John Mitchell's P-38 squadron was

alerted, and 18 Lightnings were fitted with external fuel tanks to give them extra range. The pilots were briefed and sworn to secrecy. One P-38 blew a tire on takeoff, and another was unable to transfer fuel from the external tank, so only 16 planes would participate in the attack.[4] Promptly at 6:00 A.M., on April 18, Yamamoto's plane, a Mitsubishi "Betty" twin-engine bomber, departed Rabaul, followed by another carrying his chief of staff, Rear Adm. Matame Ugaki.

About 7:30 A.M., as the two bombers and their six escort Zeros were skirting Buin's coastal jungle at 6,000 feet, it became apparent to Yamamoto that something was wrong. Several of the escort fighters veered off to intercept planes that had been sighted 1,600 feet below. At the same time, Major Mitchell reported sighting the bombers ahead and high. The Lightnings jettisoned their drop-tanks and raced after the bombers who were now diving for the protection of the jungle canopy.

Four P-38s engaged the Japanese fighter escorts, while the remaining twelve planes went high to provide fighter cover in case the Japanese fighters from Kahili airfield on Buin were involved in the escort of Yamamoto. Mitchell had expected only one bomber and had no idea which one of the two was the target. Cannon fire tore into both of the bombers, sending one crashing into the jungle in flames, while the other, its wing torn off, pancaked into the sea.[5]

Rear Adm. Ugaki struggled ashore after his bomber sank, but Admiral Yamamoto lay dead in the wreckage under the trees. Next day, a party of Japanese soldiers hacked their way to the wreck and found the admiral strapped in his seat, his body unblemished except for holes that had been left by a bullet that passed through his jaw and came out his temple. Identification was positive, not only because of his diary and collection of poems by the Emperor Meiji, but by his gloved left hand that gripped his sword. The index and middle fingers were missing, casualties of the naval battle of Tsushima.

The elimination of Yamamoto was another victory made possible by American intelligence capability and was a heavy blow to Japan. His death was kept secret for more then a month and was only announced at the end of May, when his ashes were brought home by the battleship *Musashi* and paraded through Tokyo in a national day of mourning.[6]

Adm. Mineichi Koga was appointed to succeed Yamamoto, but Koga lacked Yamamoto's genius and implemented a very conservative policy.

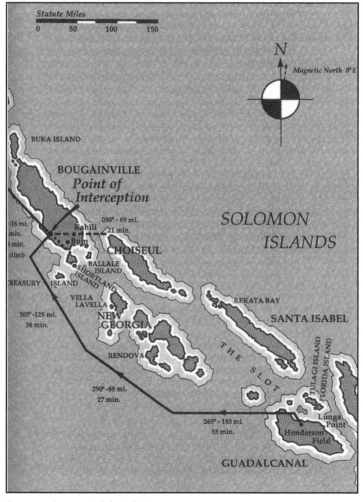

Route to intercept Admiral Yamamoto.

HPU Graphic

Admiral Isoroku Yamamoto, architect of the attack on Pearl Harbor, a gambler, drinker, and favorite of the geisha. The admiral attended Harvard University, and served on the staff of the Japanese embassy in Washington, D.C. He counseled against going to war with the United States, but when told to prepare for war, he developed the strategy to eliminate the U.S. Pacific Fleet on the first day of the war.

National Archives

17

THE DEATH RAILWAY

Russell Braddon in his introduction to Clifford Kinvig's *Death Railway*, describes the survivors of the ordeal in these terms: they have "the memory of monsoons and malaria; of bamboo and bashings; of cholera and corpses; of pain and putrescence; and of despair."[1] There are memories of cutting through solid rock with only sledgehammers and crowbars to create holes for the dynamite and of carrying thousands of tons of earth in straw baskets or blankets. There are memories of cruel and sadistic guards, "of burning corpses on unblessed pyres,"[2] and the doom reflected in the sunken eyes and emaciated bodies of fellow prisoners.

Braddon suggests that there is a great difference between the Japanese and Western cultures. He observes that we should have learned the difference on Saipan where Japanese soldiers, women, and children took their own lives rather than surrender; and, if not at Saipan, then at Cowra in New South Wales where hundreds of Japanese escaped into the wilds of the bush rather than face dishonor by being sent back to Japan. The rapes of Nanking and Manila should have convinced us. The Kamikazes should have instructed us, and the Death March should have taught us of the difference.[3]

The raids of Brigadier Orde Wingate's Chindits in North Burma did little to disrupt the Japanese in the spring of 1943, but the raids did cause the Imperial general staff in Tokyo to hasten the construction of the strategic rail link between Bangkok and Rangoon. The reaction brought additional misery and death to thousands of allied prisoners of war who had slaved from the previous autumn to build the single-track line through the most hostile terrain imaginable. The progress through the malarial swamps, jungle ravines, and swift-flowing streams was painfully slow.

The railway was begun in October 1942 by 3,000 Australian prisoners who had been working on Japanese airfields in Thailand since May of that year.[4] The prisoners began the herculean task, under the supervision of savage Japanese guards, of hacking out the railway trail through the dense rain forest with spades, pickaxes, hoes, and only an occasional elephant to drag away the monstrous teak trunks. Hundreds of thousands of tons of earth were scraped and carried by individual baskets to form the embankments that would carry the roadbed through the swamps. By the end of 1942, more than 10,000 prisoners were beaten, whipped, and bayoneted on a daily basis to increase the pace of construction. Inadequate food supplies and mosquitoes and parasitic diseases further drained the strength of the prisoners, 95 percent of whom had malaria, dysentery, or beriberi.[5]

Following Wingate's aborted thrusts into Burma and the inability of Japan's merchant marine force to supply her newly gained empire, the need for a land supply route to Rangoon became essential. Scattered in prisons and camps throughout Malaya, Singapore, Java, and Sumatra, were thousands of Allied prisoners of war who were a far greater problem for their captors than the Japanese military had planned for. Their use as slaves to build the railroad seemed perfectly logical to the Japanese.

By February 1943, the number of prisoners working on the railway was increased to 60,000 plus 300,000 native laborers.[6] Prisoners were forced to work 16-hour shifts extending throughout the night by the weak light of hand-powered generators.[7] The new prisoners were ill adapted to the rigors of the jungle; fever, disease, beatings, and endless miles of marching took a heavy toll. The rice ration was insufficient, there was no medicine, and the prisoners dropped like flies even before they reached the point where they would begin their work 180 miles into the interior.

The spring monsoon broke on May 22, 1943, and destroyed much of what the earlier prisoners had accomplished. Bridges were washed out, and sections of railbeds were turned into streams. Water lay everywhere in great stagnant pools. The rain made working conditions difficult and brought fresh outbreaks of disease. None of the difficulties could compare, however, to the cruel treatment of the guards who announced, "We will build this railway if necessary over the bones of the prisoners."[8] And they did. Beatings for no reason became routine. Guards would strike at the prisoners with whatever implements were on hand, usually bamboo staves, pick handles, or swords. Prisoners were knocked senseless, their bones broken, and their corpses left for the other prisoners to clean up after they had fulfilled their work quota for the day. Perhaps the coolie force of Asian peasants suffered even more. They had no leadership and extremely primitive standards of hygiene. They died at a rate of about nine native laborers for every Allied prisoner.

When the railway was opened in November 1943, more than 13,000 Allied prisoners and 90,000 native workers had died to complete the project. That works out to the lives of 412 men for every mile of the 250 miles of roadbed.[9]

Completion of the railroad was not the end of terror or death for many of the prisoners. At least 10,000 of the fittest POWs were shipped to mainland Japan for forced labor. A shipment of 2,300 such prisoners left Singapore on September, 6, 1944, aboard the transports *Kachidoki Maru* and the *Ryuku Maru* in a convoy of 15 vessels. On September 12, the convoy was attacked by U.S. submarines, resulting in the sinking of three vessels plus the *Ryuku Maru*. About 140 POWs were left clinging to the floating wreckage, some for as long as five days before they were rescued by U.S. submarines.[10] Nearly 1,500 POWs died in this attack. The prisoners who did reach Japan found conditions scarcely better then the jungle. Millet was being substituted for rice, winters were desperately cold, and the labor was long and hard.

Maintenance of the railroad took another heavy toll of

prisoners who remained in Thailand. In the fall of 1943, American bombers started bombing the tracks and sidings. As time went on, the bombings intensified. Prisoners forced to repair the damage suffered casualties as did those who were in the camps since the Japanese refused to relocate the camps away from the rail lines to make them less vulnerable to the air attacks. One Allied plane on September 6, 1944, killed 98 POWs and injured 330 more. The Japanese commander had no pity for the POWs and warned them, "This will happen many times again. You are soldiers, you must be prepared to die."[11]

Many prisoners reported that air attacks by their own forces were more terrifying than had been their previous captivity. Of course, the attacking aircraft had no knowledge of the prisoners plight, and, even if they had, they would likely have had to destroy the railroad anyway. Late in 1944, when the Allies became aware of the POW's situation, they started dropping pamphlets to the POWs encouraging them to "Take heart, we are coming." One prisoner allowed that it would have been more appropriate to say, "Take cover, we are here."[12]

By June of 1945, the POWs were becoming increasingly aware of the restlessness and tension of their captors, as well they should have. In the headquarters of Field Marshall Hisaichi Terauchi's Southern Army in Saigon, plans were completed for the massacre of all prisoners if the Allied invasion of South East Asia should occur.[13] Events were swiftly moving to a climax for the remaining Death Railway survivors.

18

THE KAMIKAZES

Vice Adm. Takajiro Onishi is generally credited with the plan to form aerial suicide units to attack the United States Fleet as it supported amphibious operations off the Philippines and Okinawa.[1] Onishi also played a major role in planning for the attack on Pearl Harbor and ordered the skillful attack on Clark Field that wiped out Gen. Douglas MacArthur's air forces in the Philippines.

In mid-October 1944, Onishi arrived on Luzon to command the Japanese First Air Fleet and discovered that he had fewer than 100 planes to oppose the American landing.[2] Onishi's suggestion was to crash dive Zero fighters into the decks of the American carriers. Each Zero would be armed with a 250-kilogram bomb set to explode on impact. Onishi's staff, which worshipped the flamboyant admiral, eagerly supported the concept and immediately started to implement the strategy.[3]

The word "kamikaze," used to describe the volunteer pilots and their tactics, came from an earlier attempt by an enemy to invade Japan. In 1281, Khubilai Khan mobilized hundreds of ships and over 100,000 warriors under the joint command of Korean Adm. Hong Tagu, the Chinese Fan Wen-hu, and a Mongol Hsin-tu.[4] Khubilai was the grandson of Genghis Khan (1162-1227) who led the Mongols across Asia, through China, India, and Russia, into Europe. The armada landed on Kyushu and encountered stiff resistance from the Japanese. The two armies fought to a standstill until August.

On August 15 and 16, intervention came in the form of an east wind which grew to typhoon force, swamping the Chinese fleet and drowning many of the invaders. The soldiers already ashore on Kyushu were slaughtered, captured, or drowned in their attempt to escape.[5] The typhoon was a typical occurrence for this time of year, but the Japanese choose to regard it not as an accident, but as a divine wind (kamikaze) sent by the gods to save Japan.

The modern kamikazes were young men who had scarcely finished flight training. The more experienced pilots were saved for other operational missions. The kamikaze pilots were assigned to aircraft that were no longer fit for conventional missions. The aircraft were stripped of all radios and instruments; not even a compass remained. The gas tanks were fueled with just enough gasoline for the plane to reach the enemy fleet and to dive upon a ship. The kamikazes were guided and escorted to their targets by more experienced pilots in fighters and bombers.

Before leaving on his first and last mission, the kamikaze pilot often participated in his own funeral service and drank several cups of ceremonial sake. More than once the young pilots climbed into cockpits on legs made wobbly by too much sake.

The last surface battle of World War II, the battle of Leyte Gulf, preceded the first organized kamikaze attacks of the war. The surface battle ended on October 25, 1944, when Vice Adm. Takeo Kurita withdrew his much stronger force from the battle. The kamikaze attack began an hour later, and the timing for the attack was perfect. The escort carrier *St. Lo* and the remnants of Task Group Taffy 3 had just come off general quarters and were tending to their dead and wounded.[6]

The kamikazes had been forced to wait for five days to strike the enemy and were highly motivated when the carriers were sighted. Suicide groups took off from fields on Mindanao and Mabalacat. The Mindanao group of six suicide planes escorted by four Zeros crashed into the escort carriers *Santee* and *Suwanee* of the Taffy 1 Escort Carrier Group.[7] The damage to both jeep carriers was light, and repairs were made on the spot. The suicide unit from Mabalacat headed for the escort carriers of Taffy 3. Five of the planes were suicide craft; the remaining four were escorts to assist the kamikazes in reaching their targets.

At 10:53 A.M., the first Zero entered into a steep dive and crashed into the *Kitkun Bay*. Two more attacked *Fanshaw Bay* but were destroyed just short of the jeep carrier. The final two kamikazes were hit by antiaircraft fire from *White Plains*, but one continued on just above the water, pulled up, and then dove into the deck of *St. Lo*.[8] The resulting explosion spread fire to the gasoline stored below decks and resulted in a huge internal explosion. *St. Lo* sank at 11:30 A.M.[9]

The tally for the first suicide attack was five Japanese planes and pilots lost, one U.S. escort carrier destroyed, and three other escort carriers badly damaged. Onishi was elated and formed new units immediately. Over the next three months, more American warships were sunk and damaged off the Philippines than in all other Pacific War battles combined. Author Hoyt cites the numbers as 16 ships sunk and 87 damaged.[10]

The carrier task groups moved to within 70 miles of Iwo Jima on February 21, and the kamikazes were waiting. At 5:00 P.M., six Zeke aircraft, a variant of the Zero, attempted to crash the carrier *Saratoga*. The first two Zekes were shot down, but the next two managed to smash into *Saratoga's* hull at the waterline with both bombs exploding inside the carrier. Zeke number five crashed into the port catapult and exploded while kamikaze number six crashed into the starboard side. All action occurred within three minutes. *Saratoga* had the fires under control by 6:30 P.M. and was jettisoning the burning aircraft overboard when five more kamikazes arrived. Four of the attackers were shot down clear of the carrier, but the fifth dove very steeply, released his bomb which exploded on the flight deck, and then crashed his plane into the deck. *Saratoga* survived and by 8:15 P.M. was recovering her own aircraft. The ship was subsequently out of action for three months for repairs and suffered 123 sailors killed, 192 wounded, and 42 planes destroyed.[11]

On the same evening off Iwo Jima, kamikazes crashed the escort carriers *Bismark Sea* and *Lunga Point*. *Bismark Sea* exploded and, after burning for over three hours, finally sank. The toll was 119 dead and 99 wounded. *Lunga Point* survived a suicide crash on the flight deck with little damage and no casualties.[12] The net cargo ship *Keokuk* and the *LST-477* were also crashed by kamikazes. *Keokuk* had 17 killed and 44 wounded; *LST-477* had minor damage.[13]

Following the seizure of Iwo, Vice Adm. Marc Mitscher's task force ranged from Hokkaido, the northernmost island of Japan, to southern Kyushu, destroying Japanese aircraft on the ground and in the air. Once again, the kamikazes exacted their toll.

The first suicide attack off Japan occurred on March 18, when Rear Adm. Masafumi Arima dove his Zero fighter into the flight deck of the heavy carrier *Franklin*.[14] Arima was commander of the Twenty-sixth Air Flotilla. His pilots were poorly trained and no match for the veteran American carrier pilots. Arima set an example that many of his pilots would emulate. At the same time, a Betty bomber tried to crash the aircraft carrier *Intrepid*. The Betty missed but was shot down so close to *Intrepid* that the debris killed two men and wounded 43 others. *Franklin* suffered 724 dead and 265 wounded, and repairs would keep the ship out of action for the remainder of the war.

The following day, a kamikaze missed the new carrier *Wasp* by a few feet. The explosion killed 101 and wounded 269. The next day, a kamikaze narrowly missed the carrier *Hancock* and crashed into the destroyer *Halsey Powell*.[15] The kamikaze's bombs went through the destroyer's hull without exploding, but 12 men died and 29 were wounded. *Halligan* was sunk on March 26, with 153 dead and 39 wounded.

March 21 saw the first use of the "baka bomb." This was a 4,700-pound bomb with short wings, five booster rockets for propulsion, and a suicide pilot at the controls. The bomb was delivered by a Betty bomber, released, and then glided to its target under control of the suicide pilot. The U.S. sailors called them "baka" or crazy.[16] Fifteen "baka" bombers and 55 escort fighters were launched against the Carrier Group and were intercepted by 150 U.S. carrier aircraft 60 miles from the carriers. Later in the day, five of the Japanese escort aircraft returned to their base at Kanoya. They were all that remained of the "ultimate weapon," the "baka" bomb group.[17]

Kamikazes figured prominently in the Japanese strategy for the defense of Okinawa. The plan was for Gen. Mitsuru Ushijima, commander of the Imperial Japanese Army on Okinawa, to delay the allied advance once the forces were ashore. The kamikazes would then destroy the fleet which would have to remain in Okinawa waters to support the landing force.

The operational code name for the massive air attack was "Ten-Go." The kamikazes of operation Ten-Go bore the less-than-descriptive title of *kikusui* or "floating chrysanthemums." In all, 10 separate attacks involving several thousand aircraft were planned.

The landing force went ashore on Easter Sunday, April 1. The next day, the *kikusui* arrived. These first kamikazes were locally based and came in pairs or small groups. Because they were so close to their targets, they did not need more experienced pilots to lead them, and they tended to attack the first ships they saw. These were usually the landing ships and attack transports that were bringing troops and equipment to the beaches.

At least 15 aircraft went after the attack transports *Dickerson*, *Chilton*, *Goodhue*, *Telfour*, and *Henrico* on April 2. *Dickerson* was sunk. *Henrico* survived, but her repairs would take longer than the war. The ships suffered more than 265 casualties with more than 100 dead.[18] The violence associated with the *kikusui* attacks also took a heavy toll on the survivors. Often, while the ships were fighting off conventional torpedo and dive-bombing attacks, the kamikazes would come in low and fast and be in their fatal dive position before guns could be trained on them. Even if they were shot down, they often crashed on or near their target. On the ships, the men's concern for the kamikazes added greatly to their fatigue.

The suicide craft returned on April 3, 1945, with about a dozen planes crashing *LST-599* and attacking picket destroyer *Prichett*, a new 2,200-ton destroyer, the *Mannert L. Abele*, and the escort carrier *Wake Island*. *Wake Island* was forced to depart for repairs with an 18-by-45-foot hole below the waterline.[19] *Prichett* accomplished her repairs quickly. *Abele* was not damaged on that day, but her time was to come. *LST-599* had 21 men wounded, and the marine corps fighter squadron equipment aboard was destroyed.

Rain and a heavy overcast provided some respite to the sailors on April 4 and 5. April 6 was also overcast in the morning with sunset due at 6:49 P.M. The mainland-based kamikazes began to arrive in mid-afternoon and converged on the isolated picket ships that formed the exterior watching and listening posts for the fleet.[20]

A dozen kamikazes concentrated on the picket destroyer *Newcomb*, and three were able to crash the ship with near-fatal results. The destroyer *Leutze* raced to assist the blazing *Newcomb* and, while helping to put out fires, was crashed by a kamikaze. The fire spread to the ammunition room and opened 17 compartments to the sea.[21] *Leutze* began to settle, and, as she pulled away from the burning *Newcomb*, destroyer *Beale* moved in to help. Shortly thereafter, *Leutze* was able to control her flooding and was taken under tow by the minesweeper *Defense*, which had been damaged by two kamikazes only minutes before. *Newcomb* got her fires under control and was towed to the anchorage at Kerma Retto by the fleet tug *Tekesta*. The two destroyers had 47 dead and 58 wounded.[22]

The destroyers *Bush*, *Cassin Young*, and *Colhoun*, on picket duty about 50 miles to the north of Okinawa, were the first to meet the kamikazes from the mainland. Earlier in the day, *Colhoun* had fought off 11 bombing attacks. About 50 kamikazes circled over *Bush* and a dozen more went after *Cassin Young*. Both crews were exhausted by the strain of the constant, nerve-wracking vigil at general quarters. *Bush* shot down the first two planes, but number three came from dead ahead, just off the water, straight at *Bush*. *Bush's* gunners fired every weapon they had, and the commander turned the ship desperately to avoid a collision. At 3:15 P.M., the aircraft crashed into *Bush* between the two stacks with the bomb exploding in the forward engine room.[23] *Bush* was afire, but it seemed possible to save her.

Colhoun hurried to assist *Bush* and came under simultaneous attack from seven kamikazes. Several of the aircraft were destroyed, and one exploded so close that the water from the explosion put out the fires that were raging on the ship.[24] For over an hour, despite continuous air attack, the crew of *Bush* worked to repair the damage, treat their wounded and remove the dead. For the next hour, *Bush*, *Colhoun*, and the support craft, *LST-64*, fought dozens of suicide planes despite being crashed repeatedly.

At 4:35 P.M., the friendly air cover over the destroyers disappeared, and a dozen more enemy fighters approached from the north.[25] The aircraft circled and then, one after another, peeled off and dove at the ship. One Zero smashed into the port side, almost severing the ship. All that remained of *Bush* was floating wreckage and the dying encircling the ship. Yet the remaining crew members worked on. Just before twilight, when the crew was hoping that their ordeal was over, a single plane flew over the wreckage at mast height, turned back, and flew a low-level course into the ship.[26]

The aircraft ripped into the center section of what remained of the destroyer, and the ship began to settle into the water. Her crew abandoned ship as the battered destroyer slid below the surface. In the darkness, the struggle of the day-long battle took its toll. Many of the exhausted officers and men sank beneath the waves. According to author William Craig, 87 men from the USS *Bush* died on April 6. Kamikazes sank or damaged a total of 24 ships on that day.[27]

More than 380 Japanese aircraft attacked the fleet on March 9, of which 185 were kamikaze aircraft. Following the kamikazes came Betty bombers with baka bombs. The first baka bomb hit was recorded on the destroyer *Mannert L. Abele*.[28] *Abele* had been crashed moments before by a kamikaze and sank immediately. Shortly thereafter, a baka exploded on the destroyer *Stanly*.

Unfortunately, April 6 and 9 were only preludes for the suicide attacks against the fleet off Okinawa: 930 kamikaze pilots hurled themselves to death while sinking 10 destroyers, an escort carrier, and 6 lesser ships. They heavily damaged 198 other vessels, including 12 carriers, 10 battleships, five cruisers, and 63 destroyers. In the process, according to author Werstein, they killed 4,907 sailors, and wounded 4,824 more.[29]

The final kamikaze mission against naval forces off Okinawa was flown by 11 torpedo bombers from their base at Oita, late in the day of August 15, after the emperor's announcement of surrender. After drinking the ritual toast, Adm. Matome Ugaki tucked a short samurai sword into his belt and climbed into the rear cockpit of the lead aircraft. Several hours later, a message was received at Oita from Admiral Ugaki stating that he was going to ram an American ship.[30]

No American ships were attacked by kamikazes that day, so one is left with the conclusion that the planes ran out of fuel, dove into the ocean, or were shot down by allied night-fighters, or, possibly, a combination of all three.

USS *Bunker Hill* on fire after being hit by two kamikazes off Okinawa in 1945.

U.S. Naval Academy

The flight deck of *Bunker Hill* after kamikaze strike. Note the buckled aft elevator.

U.S. Navy

This Japanese kamikaze missed his target off Okinawa but the suicide planes took a heavy toll of U.S. Navy ships.

National Archives

Bomb hole in the flight deck USS *Bunker Hill*. The bomb exited through the side of the carrier and exploded 100 feet away.

US Navy

19

LORD JAMES BLEARS: MARCH 1944

Each of us can remember the day that someone special came into our lives. That's what happened on Saturday, August 19, 1995, when Lord James "Tally Ho" Blears spoke to my history class. Blears is best known by his nickname, "Tally Ho," but I will not be using his nickname here. Somehow, it just does not connote the respect due to this man of such unusual courage, compassion, humility, and humor. Without elaboration, this is his amazing story.[1]

Blears was a British citizen, serving as a radio officer aboard the Dutch freighter *Tjisalak*, en route from Australia to Ceylon with a cargo of flour, food, supplies, and 27 passengers. Most of the crew were Dutch and Indian.

Just before 6:00 A.M., on March 26, 1944, Blears was jolted out of his sleep by the sound of a torpedo explosion below decks. As the ship began to sink, Blears worked his way to the radio room where he found the first officer already sending out a distress signal. He then reported to his alternate emergency position, a four-inch gun on the aft deck, and, after loading some supplies and a radio transmitter into a lifeboat, he began to pass shells to the aft gun.

Due to the rapid sinking of the ship, it soon became impossible to elevate the gun sufficiently to engage the periscope of the submarine which was surfacing nearby. The ship sank within six minutes with 21 members of the crew.

The remaining 103 survivors were in four lifeboats, with the ship's captain, a Dutch officer named Hens, and most of the officers being in the only lifeboat with a motor. Verna Gordon Britain, an

American nurse, was the sole woman passenger on the ship and was also in this lifeboat. Mrs. Britain was going to India to join her husband who was in the British army, stationed in Calcutta .

Shortly after the survivors had settled into the lifeboats, the Japanese submarine *I-8* surfaced and the crew called to the survivors to come to the submarine or they would destroy the boats with the submarine's deck guns.[2] Captain Hens' boat reached the submarine first, and the officers and woman were taken inside the submarine. This was an enormous submarine and carried a patrol aircraft on deck to search for possible targets. [3]

Blears' lifeboat was the last to reach the *I-8*. As the survivors were pulled aboard, they were manhandled, stripped, slapped, and had their hands tied behind their backs. They were then prodded with swords to the foredeck, where they were forced into a kneeling position and told that they would be shot if they looked back towards the conning tower. As soon as all the survivors were aboard the *I-8*, the submarine engaged engines and left the scene of the sinking.

Blears remembers that crewmembers of the *I-8* laughed and enjoyed the situation immensely. The officers of the *Tjisalak*, who were taken below, were tortured for information, killed, and their bodies dumped over the side. Mrs. Britain was asked if she wanted a blindfold, refused, and was shot in the head.

Then, one at a time, the remaining survivors were pulled to their feet, led aft past the conning tower, and their heads chopped off with a long sword. Blears tensed himself to jump over the side in an attempt to escape the massacre when suddenly a Hindu sailor beat him to it. The Hindu was wearing a life jacket and consequently was unable to get below the surface of the ocean. The Japanese riddled him with rifle and machine-gun fire as soon as he hit the water. Blears decided that jumping from his present position might not be such a good idea.

Several of the prisoners were then hit with swords until they stood up and were tied together. Blears was tied to his best friend, Peter Bronger, the ship's fifth officer. As Blears and Bronger were pushed forward towards the conning tower, Blears could see the bloody deck and the grinning sailors awaiting them. Two Japanese officers were poised on the other side of the tower; one had a large sledgehammer and the other a sword. As the officers moved towards the two prisoners, Blears kicked at the one with the hammer and dove from the submarine, pulling Bronger with him.

Blears dove as deep as he could and succeeded in loosening one of his hands. The submarine, which had been moving, passed over them with the twin screws of the sub thrashing just over their heads. When he had to come up for air, Blears raised his head above the surface just enough to get a gulp of air and immediately heard bullets hitting the water all around him. He dove again and this time stayed under until he could bear it no longer. When he surfaced, the submarine was quite a distance away, but the officers on the stern were firing rifles at any bodies they could see, so Blears dove again. Finally the firing ceased, and Blears turned his attention to Bronger.

Bronger had been sliced by the officer with the sword, and his back was laid open to the spine. He was covered with blood and did not respond during the five or 10 minutes that Blears spent untying their ropes. Blears had to assume that he was dead.

Blears then picked out some clouds on the horizon at a spot in the general area of where he thought the ship had gone down. About 8:30 in the morning, he began what would be a seven-hour swim to where he hoped some floating wreckage might be. Before dusk, a huge wave lifted him up high enough in the water and he spotted a heavy oak card table which the men had used to play cards. He grabbed the table and hung on until he felt some of his strength start to return.

When he was feeling a bit better, he noticed that there was a lot of garbage floating on the water and many sharks tearing the mess apart. Shortly thereafter, Blears noticed a raft with an arm waving from it and heard a voice calling. He let go of his table and swam to the raft. On the raft was Chief Officer Frits de Jong.

Officer de Jong owed his life to the fact that he was six-feet, six-inches tall. When the shorter Japanese pulled the trigger to blow de Jong's head from his body, the angle caused by the difference in height was so steep that the bullet only opened up the back of his head. De Jong was in the first group of prisoners who were killed so did not have to swim as far as Blears.

As Blears treated de Jong's nasty head wound, they heard a voice that turned out to be Third Engineer Spuybrock. The engineer, like Blears, had dived off the side of the sub and was in good shape. Shortly thereafter, the men spotted the lifeboat that Blears had loaded with the emergency supplies and transmitter, and were able to paddle to it and get everyone aboard. The boat was nearly full of water but had not sunk because of air tanks under the seats. After several hours of bailing, the men rowed to another life boat, obtained the waterproof containers of food and medicine, and decided to rest for the day.

It was completely dark when the men heard another voice and discovered Second Officer Jan Decker and a Hindu sailor named Dhange clinging to a hatch cover. Dhange had been the last one to escape and therefore had to swim further than anyone to reach the area of debris. Once the men were brought aboard, they heard the story of how the Japanese had tied the last 25 prisoners together with one long rope, tied the rope to the end of the submarine, and dived. Dhange had been the last man on the rope, and the few extra seconds allowed him to loosen his knots and swim to the surface.

Before Blears finally collapsed from exhaustion, he rigged the mast for the lifeboat, took a compass reading, and concurred with the crew's decision to head away from Java where the prevailing winds seemed to be taking them.

The five survivors huddled in the life raft would later learn that they were the only survivors from the 102 men and one woman who had been taken aboard the *I-8*. All of the rest of the crew and passengers of the *Tjisalak* had been murdered.

For three days the crew tacked and rowed in an effort not to be blown to Java which was then occupied by Japan. Chief Officer de Jong's condition worsened considerably, and the men decided to risk a short emergency transmission that evening although they all lived in fear that the message might be intercepted by the *I-8* which would come back to finish them off.

About 4:00 P.M., on March 30, after putting the antenna as far up the mast as possible, the crew broke open a tin of peaches, drank the juice, and each ate a large peach. The food had such a positive impact on morale that Blears continues to observe the anniversary date each year with a can of peaches. While the men waited for darkness before sending their SOS, the silence was broken by a loud explosion and the sight and sound of a shell that landed just in front of the boat.

Another explosion and another impact a bit farther away occurred and then another a bit closer to the lifeboat. Was this the end? Had the *I-8* spotted them? As the men tried to decide what to do, the structure of the vessel that was shooting at them came into sight. It was not a submarine, but was it a Japanese supply ship? As the ship came closer, still firing, Blears recognized it as an American liberty ship, one of some 5,000 built during the war.

Finally, the ship, the SS *James A. Wilder*, stopped firing, came alongside the lifeboat, and threw down a cargo net. After explaining that the Dutchmen were not Germans, and getting the injured de Jong to sick bay, Blears was taken to the shower where he was helped to scrub off the accumulation of oil and salt. Then, while he was fed a beer, the ship's cook came right into the shower and told Blears, "I run this ship. What do you want to eat, Limey?"

The real captain was also there grinning at the scene. Blears recalls that he has never been so happy as he was at that moment. "The reception was so fantastic: Americans are the greatest people in the world."

Lt. Cdr. Ariizumi Tatsunosuke, the captain of the *I-8* had a well-deserved reputation as a butcher. Under Tatsunosuke's command, the *I-8* repeated the slaughter of ships like the *Tjisalak* several more times. Certain to be indicted for his war crimes, he committed suicide on August 31, 1945. Two of the lower-ranking officers of the *I-8* were convicted in 1948 and spent five years in prison.

Lord James Blears married an American, became a United States citizen, and lives on Oahu. He remains vigorous, full of life, and an inspiration to us all.

20

FIREBOMBING: MARCH 1945

In the Marianas, at twilight, on March 8, 1945, 334 B-29s started their engines and prepared to taxi to the ends of three separate runways.[1] The aircraft were unarmed but carried more than 2,000 tons of incendiary bombs. Eight hours later, more than 100,000 Japanese would be dead as the result of the most ferocious holocaust ever visited on a civilized community.

High-altitude bombing of Japan with high-explosive bombs had not been effective. In Europe, where industrial targets were clearly discernible, where winds were light and predictable, and where distances to targets were much shorter, U.S. strategic bombing had been quite effective.

The weather between the Marianas, home base for the B-29 fleet, and Japan was atrocious. Jet streams at 30,000 feet often exceeded 200 miles-per-hour. In six weeks of high-altitude bombing, only one opportunity arose for visual bombing of the target on mainland Japan due to the targets being obscured by cloud cover. All other missions were completed using the new radar bombing systems.[2]

Another factor mitigating against the more conventional bombing tactics was the dispersal of much of Japan's war production to highly populated urban areas. Such targets were difficult to locate visually and nearly impossible to pinpoint on radar. Also, the long distance from Saipan to Tokyo against heavy winds with huge payloads caused many mechanical breakdowns in the B-29 fleet. Often, less than half of the giant bombers were operational, and many would have to abort after takeoff and return to home base due to mechanical problems.

Gen. Curtis LeMay had proven to be a brilliant and resourceful bomber division commander in England, where he flew against the Luftwaffe. He was recalled and told to tackle the problems that the B-29s were having in the Pacific. On paper, the B-29 should have substantially altered the balance of the war against Japan. So far, the planes' lack of effectiveness had been most frustrating.

Built by Boeing, the four-engine monster was 99 feet long and 27 feet, nine inches high, and had a wing span of 141 feet. It carried twelve 50-calibre machine guns and a 20-millimeter cannon in the tail. It could operate at 38,000 feet, cruise over 350 miles-per- hour, and fly 3,500 miles with four tons of bombs.[3] But it had not been able to destroy the industrial targets of Japan.

Lemay studied the problem and decided to gamble on a low-altitude fire-bomb attack, centered on the northeast urban section of Tokyo which contained a large percentage of Tokyo-based war production capability. Bombing runs would commence just after midnight. All guns would be removed from the B-29s to permit the carriage of more ordnance. Finally, bombs would be released between 5,000 and 9,000 feet, hopefully in visual conditions.

This unconventional bombing procedure was a tremendous gamble. So much so that LeMay decided not to notify Gen. Hap Arnold, U.S. Army Air Corps chief of staff, in advance.[4] The flight crews objected strenuously. Not only would the low altitude of their attack make them sitting ducks for the estimated 600 antiaircraft guns and 415 fighters and interceptors estimated to be in the Tokyo environs, but the loss of all their guns made them completely defenseless.

In Tokyo, a chill, 28 mile-an-hour wind tossed paper through the narrow streets.[5] The first 12 B-29s dropped a preplanned series of E-46 bombs, each of which exploded at 2,500 feet and scattered

38 more pipe-like canisters into the wind. The two-foot long projectiles fell into the clusters of wooden homes which began to burn furiously, thus marking the target area for the remaining onrushing B-29s. The huge bombers arrived singly and in small groups, each dropping their incendiaries with visual precision.

In 30 minutes, the blaze was completely out of control. There was no way to stop it. More B-29s arrived with more magnesium, more phosphorous, and more napalm. The target area became larger and larger. Violent updrafts from the firestorm tore at the arriving B-29s. Turbulence tossed the huge aircraft several thousand feet in seconds. Aircraft went straight up or down at dizzying rates.

On the ground, there was a frenzy as the heat rose. Breath was pulled from people's lungs. Many died standing upright in close-packed, airless shelters. In the Meiji-za theater, bodies were stacked eight feet high.[6] Many ran for the ditches and streams to escape the fire but sank beneath the surface as the fire sucked away the oxygen. Hundreds of people died in rivers, packed so tightly that they were still standing days later when rescue workers began their gruesome task. Miwa Koshiba and her three children survived by spending the night in a sewer drain pipe that emptied into the Sumida River.[7]

By 3:00 A.M. on March 10, the last B-29 had dropped its seven tons of bombs. Of the 325 B-29s that took off, 279 dropped their bomb loads on the target. According to William Craig, 14 B-29s and 140 airmen were lost.[8]

At 6:00 A.M., four miles to the north of the target area, a student standing on the roof of her home called her family to come see the beautiful sunrise. It was not a sunrise she was watching but the funeral pyre for 100,000 Japanese citizens.[9] Almost 16 square miles of Tokyo were totally destroyed and lay scorched and smoldering; 250,000 buildings had crumbled under the flames that reached an intensity of 2,000 degrees fahrenheit.

Rescue workers were overwhelmed. Despite their gauze masks, they vomited and wretched helplessly as they tried to lift and separate the remains of their countrymen. Many victims were badly charred; almost all had suffocated. In short order, the people of Tokyo knew that the B-29, which from previous experience they had learned to ignore, now ruled their lives.

A week later, after elaborate security precautions, Emperor Hirohito walked informally through the acres of devastation. He was seen to shake his head and gaze sadly at the heaps of ash and charred bodies still in evidence. His loyal subjects would stop their work to bow reverently and, perhaps for a moment, dry their tears. But the war continued.

LeMay immediately ordered additional low-level fire-bombing missions, and, in the next few days, Nagoya, Osaka, Kobe, and other industrial cities were struck. There was a brief respite during the last week of March while the B-29s were used to drop some 12,000 mines in the inland sea, but then it was back to fire-bombing cities.[10]

More than 50 percent of Tokyo was completely burned by the middle of July 1945. Eight million people were homeless. Hunger was a constant torture. Clothing materials were unavailable. Family units eroded. The use of public baths was sharply curtailed. There was no lumber for coffins to transport the dead to the crematoriums. The B-29s and carrier planes dominated the people's every movement. The Japanese people were on the edge of desperation.

21

THE BATTLESHIP *YAMATO*: APRIL 6 1945

The largest ship in the world, the colossal Japanese battleship *Yamato*, accompanied by the cruiser *Yahagi* and eight destroyers, departed Hiroshima on April 6, 1945, enroute to Okinawa for what was generally understood to be a one-way or suicide mission. Short on fuel and lacking air cover, the *Yamato's* captain, Kosaku Ariga, and his 3,000-man crew hoped only for a surface confrontation with the allied fleet.

In actuality, this "decisive surface battle," for which the Japanese had wished since the start of the war, had already occurred. It took place at the battle of the Philippine Sea on June 19-20 when the U.S. sank three of Japan's five heavy carriers and shot down 400 of her 473 carrier planes. In that battle, the U.S. lost 100 of its 956 airplanes and no ships. The big guns of Japan's super battleships were never a factor.

The Japanese decision to build the *Yamato* was due, in large part, to their calculation that the U.S. would have to move ships from the Atlantic to the Pacific through the Panama Canal. According to these calculations, the biggest battleship that could go through the canal locks would displace 63,000 tons with a maximum speed capability of 23 knots and armament of ten 16-inch guns. The largest U.S. warship at the time displaced 34,000 tons. The Yamato-class battleship would be larger than any ship the U.S. could build if it had to pass through the canal. Therefore, reasoned the Japanese, the Pacific Fleet would be outgunned and outclassed.[1]

The first design was for a ship of more than 75,000 tons with

200,000 horsepower turbines and a speed of 31 knots. Final plans were for a ship of 71,659 tons with 18.1-inch guns that would fire a one-and-a-half-ton projectile 22-1/2 miles. Maximum speed would be 27 knots.[2]

Construction of *Yamato* began in 1937 at Kure, and the keel for her sister ship, *Musashi,* was laid in 1938 at Nagasaki. The keel for the final *Yamato* class battleship *Shinano* was laid down at Yokosuka, also in 1938.

It was ironic that before *Yamato* was commissioned, the Japanese carrier attack on Pearl Harbor rendered all battleships obsolete. In recognition of such a fact, the half-completed *Shinano* was converted into an aircraft carrier. *Shinano* left the building dock at Yokosuka on November 29, 1944, en route to Kure for further work. She was detected by the U.S. submarine *Archerfish* and sunk with six torpedoes. It was not known until after the war that *Shinano* had a cargo of 50 "ohka" kamikaze flying bombs aboard, each of which could have destroyed a U.S. warship.[3] *Musashi* was sunk during the battle of the Philippine Sea in October 1944. She went down with 13 torpedo hits on the portside and seven more to starboard.

Yamato had been at Midway as the flagship for Admiral Yamamoto but saw no action in the carrier war there. For the first three years of the war she had not fired her guns in anger. Mostly, *Yamato* spent her time moored at Mitajiri anchorage where the U.S. submarine *Skate* put a torpedo into her waistline on Christmas day, 1943. The torpedo penetrated the supposedly impenetrable hull and caused considerable damage, but the damage was repaired and *Yamato* was seaworthy.

During the Philippine Sea battle, *Yamato* took two bomb hits and, with two older battleships, eight cruisers and 14 destroyers, went through the unguarded San Bernardino strait at night and attacked the escort carriers and destroyers protecting the U.S. landing force.

The sea battle for which the Japanese had prayed was at hand. The American fleet was extremely vulnerable. At the precise moment that total victory should have been achieved, Adm. Takeo Kurita, the Japanese force commander, feared for his fleet and retreated. *Yamato's* great 18-inch guns had not scored a hit. She returned to Mitajiri as the flagship of a paper fleet.

Yamato was headed for Okinawa to do battle with the American fleet but not in the manner anyone wanted. Hers was a one-way mission with no air cover and only enough fuel to reach the enemy, where she was to attack the landing ships, run the ship aground when ammunition ran low, and then have the ship's company abandon ship and join the ground forces in the defense of Okinawa.

Agreement to the mission went down hard. For one of the few times in Japanese naval history, a vote was actually taken among the commanders to determine if they would obey the orders of the navy commander-in-chief, Adm. Soemu Toyoda. Perhaps the sortie would not have taken place at all had not Vice Adm. Ryunosuke Kusaka, Toyoda's chief of staff, reminded the commanders, "I think it is necessary to understand that *Yamato's* reputation is open to criticism. This ship's only action was a failure. People are wondering whether it has become a comfortable hotel for unemployed admirals."[4]

Shortly after 5:00 P.M. on April 6, *Yamato* and the task force were sighted by the submarines *Treadfin* and *Hackleback* as they made their way through the Bungo strait. Information on the direction and speed of *Yamato* was quickly sent to the U. S. Fleet.[5] At 8:22 the next morning, April 7, a plane from the carrier *Essex* sighted the monster heading for Okinawa at 24 knots. For the next four hours, Catalina flying boats kept the Japanese convoy under surveillance.

Shortly after noon, massed carrier air attacks commenced. "Thad" Coleman, one of the Essex air group commanders, commented: "The Japanese gunnery officers were handicapped because they didn't have the faintest idea from where the next attack would develop. Nor did we for that matter."⁶ More than 250 U.S. aircraft circled the zigzagging Japanese task force in a slow counterclockwise circle, flying in and out of the clouds and rain showers.

Almost every type of U.S. carrier plane was there. Marines flew the gull-wing F4U Corsair they made famous on Guadalcanal. The SB2C1 Curtis Helldivers, which had replaced the Dauntless dive-bombers made famous at Midway, were there. There were a few Grumman F4F Wildcats, lots of F6F Hellcats, and squadrons of the big TBM-1 Avengers, replacements for the earlier outclassed Devastators.

Bennington's Helldivers led the first wave of attackers. For 22 minutes, *Yamato*, *Yahagi*, and the destroyer escorts absorbed bomb and torpedo hits. The destroyer *Asashimoto* was the first to fall, disintegrated from torpedo and strafing attacks in less than three minutes. She sank at 12:30 P.M. *Hamakaze*, another escort, sunk in seconds after being hit simultaneously by bombs and torpedoes. It was 12:43 P.M.

Yamato had taken two 1,000-pound bomb hits aft and two torpedoes on the port side forward but weathered the first wave of attackers. Captain Ariga had the Z flag hoisted. This was the historic signal Admiral Togo flew at the battle of Tsushima. In effect it meant, "On this one battle rests the fate of our nation. Let every man do his utmost."⁷ The time was 12:59 P.M.

As the aircraft from *Bennington, Hornet,* and *San Jacinto* departed, attackers from *Essex, Bunker Hill,* and *Cabot* moved into position. For 13 minutes the convoy was pounded. *Yamato* took three more 1,000-pound bomb hits and three torpedo hits on the port side. Minutes later she was rocked with four more torpedoes on the port side and one to starboard. Four armor-piercing bombs penetrated the deck. Ariga corrected the starboard list by flooding and chuckled as he welcomed the torpedo hit on the starboard side which helped to correct the imbalance of flooding. He quickly checked their position on the charts and found that, for the past two hours, they had only advanced 10 miles towards Okinawa. "Don't worry," he said to himself, "*Yamato* will never sink."[8]

Now it was time for the third wave, the aircraft from *Yorktown*, *Langley*, and *Intrepid*, to attack. A torrent of bombs and torpedoes quickly sank the cruiser *Yahagi* at 2:05 P.M. *Yamato* had taken three bomb hits at 2:02 P.M., and three more five minutes later. Two torpedoes struck the port side at about the same time. Near misses heeled Yamato to 15 and then 20 degrees of list. Ariga ordered the starboard outer engine room flooded to correct the list. The flooding corrected the list, dropped speed to eight knots, and drowned 300 engineers in the engine room. At 2:10 P.M., a torpedo from a *Langley* Avenger hit the stern and jammed the rudder hard left. *Yamato* spun helplessly counterclockwise with no electrical power.

Yamato was clearly sinking and pilots from *Yorktown* were determined to finish her. Lt. Tom Stetson and three other torpedo bombers adjusted their depth settings to 18-20 feet, made two approach runs, and then, when satisfied that the preparations were perfect, released their torpedoes at 800 feet of altitude at a range of 1,000 feet from *Yamato*. The fish hit the exposed underbelly of the battleship below the waterline. The time was 2:20, P.M.[9]

Ariga ordered the crew to abandon ship and had himself lashed to a support with a heavy cord. *Yamato* continued her tilt toward the sea until its tall bridge tower was nearly horizontal to the sea. The list continued, gun platforms tore loose from their mounts, all loose objects hurtled across the deck, bulkheads inside the hull were ripped away, and the aircraft catapults crashed overboard. Underwater explosions came next, killing the few survivors who had managed to escape being sucked into the undertow.

At 2:23 P.M., *Yamato* rolled, exploded, and disappeared. Ariga and a loyal seaman who refused to leave his side went down with the ship. The smoke from the explosion was visible on Kyushu, 90 miles away.

The destroyers *Isokaze* and *Kasumi* were still afloat but battered beyond recognition. Both were sunk on the spot by the remaining four Japanese destroyers as they rescued survivors. The convoy lost 4,250 men, 3,063 from Yamato alone. The U.S. lost 10 planes and 12 men.

A favorite poem of kamikaze pilots, and, in this case, kamikaze sailors, has to do with giving up their life for the emperor while they are still in the prime of their life. Captain Ariga's crew aboard *Yamato* certainly epitomized the poem:

> If only we might fall
> Like cherry blossoms in the spring - -
> So pure and radiant.

The cherry blossoms were still blooming at Sasebo on April 8, when the four surviving destroyers reached port. Of the four, *Hatsushima* was sunk by a mine in the Japan sea, and *Yukikaze* was given to Nationalist China after the war. *Fuyutsuki* and *Suzutsuki* were sunk to become harbor breakwaters. According to author Russell Spurr, each year the decreasing number of *Yamato* survivors commune with their dead comrades' souls at the Yasukuni shrine in Tokyo.[10]

Yamato was the largest battleship ever built. Picture was taken at sea in April, 1945.

Japan Self Defense Force Archives

22

THE USS *INDIANAPOLIS*

This is a story that needs to be retold. It is the story of a proud ship with noble service yet an ignominious end. It is a story of kamikaze attacks, a record-setting 5,000-mile race of atomic bombs, torpedoes, shock, death, and dying. It is a story of men abandoned at sea and of the court martial of those believed responsible.[1]

Just after midnight on the morning of July 30, 1945, Capt. Machitsura Hashimoto, commanding the large Japanese submarine *I-58*, locked the USS *Indianapolis* in the crosshairs of his periscope and directed his crew to launch six torpedoes at the prize target. The heavy cruiser capsized and sank in 12 minutes after absorbing two torpedoes on her starboard side. The survivors who did not perish with the ship rightfully expected to be rescued at first light the following morning, but such was not to be.

The only indication of the sinking was an intercepted message at Naval Fleet Headquarters in Hawaii late on July 30. The message indicated that the Japanese had sunk something big in what was later determined to be the approximate predicted position of the *Indianapolis*. Since the Battle of Midway, the Japanese had constantly sent erroneous reports of sinking U.S. combatant ships. This intercepted message seemed to be just one more such exaggeration, and so it was ignored. As a result, it would be noon on August 2, before the pitiful survivors would be spotted by a routine patrol plane 250 miles north of Peleliu, midway between Guam in the Marianas and Leyte in the central Philippines.

Why was the *Indianapolis* travelling alone in hostile waters? Why didn't the navy respond to routine departure and expected arrival times which should have triggered near automatic search operations? Why wasn't a distress signal sent? Therein lies this story.

The heavy cruiser *Indianapolis* was commissioned at the Philadelphia Naval Yard on November 15, 1932. She was a sleek 610 feet long and displaced 9,800 tons. She was 66 feet wide at her beam and was capable of racing through the ocean at a speed of 32 knots. She mounted eight-inch guns and carried a normal ship's complement of 1,269 officers and men.

Indianapolis was not a behemoth in the sense of a battleship. Comparatively, the Japanese battleship *Yamato*, was 863 feet long and displaced 71,659 tons. *Yamato* mounted two monstrous forward casements with triple 18.1-inch guns which fired a 1-1/2 ton projectile 22-1/2 miles. *Yamato* had a top speed of 27 knots.

Following her shakedown cruise, *Indianapolis* hosted President Roosevelt, the secretary of the navy, and various official groups during visits, tours, and inspections. The cruiser was subsequently transferred to the Pacific Fleet and was spared the fate of the battleships on December 7, 1941, since she was on maneuvers near Johnston Atoll. Following the attack, she joined Task Force 11 for combat operations.

Indianapolis participated in action south of Rabaul in February and near New Guinea in March 1942. She then returned to the Mare Island Navy Yard in San Francisco for overhaul and alterations. Following her overhaul, she escorted convoys to Australia and participated in the recapture of Kiska and Attu in the Aleutians. On February 16, 1943, *Indianapolis* was credited with sinking the Japanese cargo ship *Akagane Maru*, which was trying to resupply Japanese forces on Attu.

Indianapolis sortied from Pearl Harbor on November 10, 1943, as the flagship of Vice Adm. Raymond Spruance, commander of the Fifth Fleet. The long-awaited U.S. offensive in the Pacific, code named "Galvanic," began shortly thereafter with the landing of 18,000 marines on Tarawa in the Gilbert Islands. The flagship was credited with destroying her first enemy plane on November 19 while providing supporting gunfire off Tarawa.

On board Indianapolis, Capt. Charles Moore, Spruance's chief of staff, watched the pre-landing bombardment of Tarawa and predicted that the assault would be a walkover: "No living thing could be on the island. Everything had been destroyed by the naval and air bombardment." The Officer of the Deck on the USS Ashland agreed with Captain Moore, further predicting, "There aren't 50 Japanese alive on that island." The comments proved tragically inaccurate as the marines suffered 3,000 casualties from the 5,000 Japanese survivors.

The invasion of Makin Island was next. More than 200 ships and 20,000 sailors supported this assault. The conquest of the Marshall Islands followed the U.S. victory in the Gilberts, and Indianapolis led the way. On February 1, 1944, she silenced shore batteries and destroyed blockhouses and other shore installations on Kwajalein atoll.

From the Marshalls, the fleet moved to the Western Carolines. In late March, carrier planes of the fleet sank three enemy destroyers, 17 freighters, and five oilers, and damaged 17 other ships off Palau. Indianapolis was credited with her second enemy plane, a torpedo bomber.

During June, the Fifth Fleet assaulted the Marianas and bombarded Saipan. On the 19th, the two fleets met in the Battle of the Philippine Sea. The U.S. Navy destroyed 402 enemy planes while losing 17. Indianapolis was credited with the destruction of her third enemy plane. With enemy naval aviation virtually eliminated, U.S. carrier aircraft pursued the enemy and sank two carriers, two destroyers, and a tanker. Indianapolis resumed fire support on Saipan for six more days and then moved to Tinian to smash enemy shore installations.

For the remainder of 1944, Indianapolis participated in the bombardment of the Japanese home islands, destroying planes, ships, trains, and ground installations on southern Honshu and the harbors of Kure and Kobe.

The pre-invasion bombardment of Okinawa began on March 24, 1945. For seven days, Indianapolis fired eight-inch projectiles into the beach defenses. Enemy aircraft, including kamikazes, repeatedly attacked the fleet. Indianapolis was credited with shooting down six more enemy aircraft and assisted in the destruction of two others.

On March 31, the day before the Easter Sunday invasion, a single-engine Japanese fighter plane emerged from the morning twilight and hurtled itself towards the bridge of Indianapolis in a vertical dive. The gunners were alert and directed all anti-aircraft guns at the kamikaze. Tracer shells impacted the plane, it swerved, but was too close to miss the cruiser. There was no time for the ship to maneuver to avoid the collision. At a height of 25 feet, the pilot released the armor piercing bomb and then crashed into the port side of the rear main deck.

The plane itself skidded off the deck and toppled into the sea, causing little damage. Not so the bomb. It plummeted through the deck armor, the crews' mess hall, the enlisted berthing compartment, and the fuel tanks before crashing through the bottom of the ship and exploding in the water.

The explosion blew holes in the ship's bottom and flooded compartments, killing nine crewmen. The flagship settled slightly and listed to port, but this was a battle-tested crew. Prompt emergency-repair procedures contained the flooding, and she proceeded under her own power to a salvage ship for emergency repairs. Subsequent inspection revealed that her propeller shafts were damaged, fuel tanks ruptured, and her water-distilling equipment ruined. She was ordered to return alone to the Mare Island shipyard in California for repair.

Following overhaul and repair on July 14, Indianapolis was scheduled for a normal post-repair and crew-training cruise. The training was especially important since many of the ship's officers and more than 250 of the crew were new replacements, most right out of recruit training or officer training schools. However, the training would not be conducted. A mission of greater importance was delivered to Capt. Charles B. McVay III in sealed orders which directed the *Indianapolis* "to deliver secret cargo to Tinian." The cargo was to be guarded night and day, and the trip was to be made as rapidly as possible. The orders also stated, "Everyday that you can save on your voyage will cut the length of the war by just as much."

Indianapolis departed San Francisco on July 16, unescorted and at high speed. She covered the 2,091 miles between San Francisco and Honolulu in 74 and one-half hours, setting a new world's record for that distance. There was no liberty for the crew at Pearl Harbor. After unloading passengers and refueling, the ship continued to race for Tinian, arriving there in the elapsed time of 10 days and replacing the previous record for the 5,000-mile trip by a full day. After unloading the special cargo, the lead-encased Uranium 235 and other components for the "Little Boy" atomic bomb, *Indianapolis* departed Tinian with orders to Leyte in the Philippines and a stop at Guam for additional instructions. McVay anticipated accomplishment of the long-delayed crew training at Guam.

Upon arrival at Guam, Captain McVay and his navigator visited the office of the port director for the required briefing concerning the next portion of their trip. The route selected to Leyte was a routine track for combatant ships, essentially a straight line between Guam and Leyte, a distance of 1,171 miles. The route was considered well within the "acceptable risk" category.

The briefing included information on possible enemy submarines, the expected weather, and alternate routes. The decision to zigzag along his course was left to the discretion of Captain McVay, although tactical orders then in force required ships to zigzag during conditions of good visibility, in waters where enemy submarines were expected to be present. The weather forecast was for good visibility.

135

At the time, it was impossible for a submarine to attack a ship travelling at a speed of 24 knots or more. However, in order to conserve fuel, regulations limited transiting ships to a speed of 16 knots. McVay established a 15.7-knot speed of advance which would put him off the entrance to Leyte Gulf at first light on July 31. The port director at Guam sent the routine dispatch to all appropriate parties including the port director at Tacloban, Leyte, which gave the route, date of departure, and estimated date of arrival at Leyte. Due to a shortage of escort ships, *Indianapolis* would travel alone.

Indianapolis departed Guam on July 28. At 12:15 A.M., on July 30, she was staggered by two huge explosions on her starboard side forward. The ship lifted slightly out of the water, seemed to pause, then settled back to her normal position. A huge plume of water soared high into the dark sky. Flame, steam, and smoke erupted from the forward stack, and a wave of flame swept the entire forward half of the ship.

There was no panic. Men reacted automatically and began to perform their assigned tasks. Flood control was lost immediately, and the damage-control teams were unable to function due to heavy casualties, rapid flooding, and intense fires in the forward section of the ship. All mechanical and electrical communications, power, and lights were lost, making it impossible to contact the engine room to stop engines or the radio room to ensure that a distress message was sent. McVay repeatedly sent messengers below and to the radio room, but none returned.

Within minutes of being torpedoed, men began to emerge from the heavy smoke and flames below to report that the forward compartments were rapidly flooding. It was suggested to McVay that he should give the order to abandon ship, but since the list was still slight, the captain wanted more time to try to save her.

Again McVay sent messengers below to report back on conditions and, again, none returned. Eight minutes after the ship was hit, McVay gave the order to abandon ship. The order was passed verbally as much as possible in the low visibility and short time remaining. Most of the crew were standing by their stations waiting for orders. Nothing had been done to prepare for evacuation. As a result, much of the life-saving equipment, such as rafts, boats, and radios, went down with the ship. Most of the men had only their life jackets, and many did not even have these.

McVay started for the radio room to check on the distress signal, but, as he turned to leave the bridge, the ship rolled 60 degrees, paused momentarily, and then continued to a full 90 degrees of roll. The ship's decks became vertical to the ocean, and everyone was forced into the sea.

As the ship sank, the front end went down first. The last 100 feet of the ship reached the full vertical position and seemed suspended above the ocean. The number 3 turbine was still generating power, and the huge screw seemed, to the men in the water, to be a giant meatgrinder about to fall on them. Instead, the ship slipped straight down, disappearing quickly and silently. *Indianapolis* capsized and sank at 12:27 A.M., just 12 minutes after she was hit.

Captain Hashimoto and the crew of the *I-58* danced with joy as they observed the effect of their torpedo hits on the ship. Then the submarine dived and spent over an hour reloading the torpedo tubes. When the *I-58* surfaced, there was nothing to see. According to Hashimoto, there was no ship, no debris, and no survivors. After searching for more than an hour, the *I-58* departed on the surface to the northeast. At 3:00 A.M., the submarine sent the message to Kure that was intercepted by Naval Fleet Headquarters in Hawaii.

No one knows how many sailors survived the sinking. From subsequent interviews, it seems certain that at least twice the number of eventual survivors were alive and left floating on the tranquil surface of the ocean with nothing more than their kapok life jackets to support them. All of the initial survivors suffered from some form of injury. Hundreds were badly burned, most were in shock, and all were coated by the oil slick that formed and encircled the various groups.

The stronger of the survivors encouraged the weaker to just hang on until morning. They were confident that rescue aircraft and ships were already on the way and that they would be spotted and rescued at first light. The very weak and badly injured did not make it through the first night. Most simply gave up and sank quietly beneath the surface.

Morning mercifully came but rescue did not. The scattered band of survivors had no way of knowing that a distress message from *Indianapolis* was never sent and, consequently, never received by any plane, ship, or station. With daylight came the first opportunity to recognize other survivors and improve one's position. Some life jackets were found floating among the debris as well as a desk, a toilet seat, lard cans, and even a sack of potatoes which McVay climbed aboard to use as a raft. A few rafts were also found, and these became the nucleus of various sized groups of survivors for the remainder of the tragedy. Each group believed they were the only survivors. Men whose eyes were nearly closed by salt water and oil did not see very far when floating only a few inches above the water in a sea with 12-foot swells.

During the first day, Monday, most of the survivors persevered. Only those who gave up hope or whose injuries sapped their strength drowned. During the afternoon, the telltale fins of the sharks encircled some of the groups. At first, the sharks seemed satisfied to tear apart and devour the still-floating corpses, but then became braver and would attack any swimmer who strayed away from the group. At night there would be terrible screams as men suddenly disappeared. Only a pool of blood would remain to stain the ever- present carpet of oil.

The second night was a nightmare. Many of the survivors were so exhausted by the ordeal that they fell asleep and drowned.

The moon reflecting off the oil created a luminescence which some mistook for lights, and men began to swim to some imagined beach. These hallucinating men would expend their energy in the attempt to reach shore and drown with a desperate thrashing that signified a will to live but a lack of strength to remain afloat. The following days and nights followed the same pattern with the number of survivors decreasing each day.

After the second day, many of the survivors could not see. Their eyes had closed from the effects of the sun, oil, and sea water. Some lost their sight permanently. All had blisters and ulcers on body parts that were above water. Their skin dried, cracked, and bled. Only the strongest, physically and mentally, would survive.

By the third day, Wednesday, thirst became obsessive. The men were in a state of extreme dehydration due to the effects of the sun and sea and also from vomiting up their fluids when they would try to rid themselves of the fuel oil they swallowed. Some men would take a small drink of sea water. Nothing seemed to happen so they would take a larger drink and then another. Delirium soon followed. The men would thrash violently so that it was impossible to help them. They would babble in a demented stage and then die. Stronger men would remove the life jackets of the dead and give them to someone without support. The corpse would sink or drift a short distance away before the sharks came for it. Many of the men hallucinated, seeing green islands, hotels, and even the *Indianapolis* lying just below the surface with the ice cream machine and fresh water spigots flowing freely. The power of suggestion was strong enough to cause dozens of the men to start swimming and diving for the imagined delights.

By Wednesday, the kapok life jackets had exceeded the 48-hour saturation time, allowing the survivors to sink so low in the water that their lips were only inches above the sea. Morale deteriorated badly, and leadership of the small groups disintegrated. Men were approaching the final stupor stage that precedes death.

By the fourth day, Thursday, there was no talk or movement among the men in the water. Black oil-coated heads lay flat on the sea. Those who were still alive had no strength to raise their heads. Then, miraculously, one of the numerous patrol planes that often passed over the survivors turned, dropped altitude, and came back.

At 11:25 A.M., August 2, Lt.(jg) Wilbur Gwinn, flying a routine sector patrol, spotted an oil slick about 250 miles north of Peleliu. He lost altitude to investigate and, after several passes, identified some 30 of the small black oily lumps in the water as people. Gwinn dropped a life raft and radio transmitter to the group and alerted all sea and air rescue units in the area. After nearly four days, help was on the way.

Additional aircraft arrived within two hours and dropped more rafts and radios. At 5:05 P.M., a Catalina flying boat arrived and took aboard 58 of the survivors who were not in life rafts. The plane was so badly damaged in landing, however, that it was only able to serve as a floating aid station until surface ships arrived during the night to rescue everyone.

Before the search was abandoned on August 8, an area within a 100-mile radius of the first group of survivors was thoroughly searched. A total of 316 men out of a crew of 1,199 survived the disaster.

Following a debrief of the survivors, Admiral Nimitz ordered a board of inquiry to determine what did happen and why the men were abandoned at sea. There were many issues of mitigation. The report that was sent by the port director at Guam was garbled and not understood by several of the addressees. The port director and his operations officer at Tacloban were relatively new to the job. The operations officer erroneously believed that the departure/arrival of combat ships was not to be reported.

There had been a huge expansion of naval facilities and personnel in the Western Pacific as the U.S. offensive moved towards Japan. The difficulties associated with such expansion were acknowledged in the inquiry. The failure to correctly evaluate the intercepted message of the *I-58* was mitigated because of the large number of exaggerated and false claims made by enemy reports. Acknowledgement was also made of the outstanding contribution of the Fleet Combat Intelligence Center in Hawaii whose work had strategic significance for the entire course of the war. The communicators on the *Indianapolis* had tried several times to send distress signals, but the complete lack of electrical power precluded the transmission.

Following the board's report, which did not charge McVay with wrongdoing, the blame appeared to lie with the lack of action when the *Indianapolis* failed to arrive at Leyte in a timely manner. Admiral Nimitz recommended that letters of admonition be given to the port directors, their operations officers, and to Captain McVay. Such letters were quite common in wartime and had little effect upon the recipient's career. It had been a long, hard war, and the operational side of the navy was not in a mood to punish people who had otherwise performed well through extremely difficult times.

The Pacific Navy's mood of forgiveness is probably most obvious in the release of the inquiry findings that state that, even under the best of circumstances with all procedures operating correctly, it would likely have been some time in the morning on August 1 before the survivors would have been spotted. The report also acknowledges that the sighting of the survivors was largely accidental since the plane that sighted them was on anti-submarine patrol and flying too high to see the survivors. Had it not been for the oil slick, it seems likely that there would have been no survivors.

The mood in Washington was quite different, however, as the press and parents bombarded the secretary of the navy and the chief of naval operations demanding to know who was responsible. The navy was accused of a coverup to shield senior officers who should be held accountable. Thus, the United States Navy, after losing more than 700 ships during the war, decided that Capt. Charles B. McVay III would be the first commanding officer to be tried by naval court martial for losing his ship in combat. The charges against him were: one, failure to give timely orders to abandon ship; and two, negligence for failure to follow a zigzag course during periods of good visibility.

The court martial began on December 3 and ended December 19, after 57 witnesses had testified, including Captain Hashimoto. In an unprecedented move, the prosecution called the enemy commander to testify against McVay on the issues of visibility and whether the vessel was following a zigzag course, issues which McVay had never disputed.

McVay was acquitted of the first charge but found guilty of the second, failing to follow a zigzag course. The port director at Tacloban, Leyte, and his operations officer were issued letters of admonition by the commander-in-chief, Pacific Fleet. The immediate superior of the port director and his operations officer were issued letters of reprimand by the secretary of the navy.

Later, the letters of admonition and reprimand were officially removed from the other four officers' records, and McVay's sentence, which was a loss of numbers on the seniority list, was remitted. The navy announced, however, that it was the sentence that was being remitted, not the conviction. The finding of guilty stood.

McVay was a beaten man. He tried hard to put his life back in order, but the navy was the only life the McVay family had known for generations. Hounded by the navy's finding and the abusive letters from parents who could not put the disaster behind them, McVay committed suicide on November 16, 1968. During July 2001, Congress directed the Secretary of the Navy to attach an official exoneration of guilt to Captain McVay's service record, clearing him of any wrongdoing in the sinking of USS *Indianapolis*. McVay's son, Kimo, tried for 55 years to have his father's name cleared, but did not live to witness the event. Kimo died on June 20, 2001.

Traditionally, the flagship of the powerful Fifth Fleet, *Indianapolis* served with honor from her commissioning through the last major offensive of the war and earned 10 battle stars.

USS *Indianapolis*.

US Navy

Lieutenant Adrian Marks, fourth from the right, and the crew of his PBY rescued 56 men of the *Indianapolis* from shark-infested waters.

US Navy

Captain and Mrs. McVay enter the courtroom on
the first day of the trial.

US Navy

Cmdr. Mochitsura Hashimoto uses a model of the
Indianapolis to describe where his torpedoes struck
the cruiser.

US Navy

23

THE BATTLE FOR OKINAWA

For many Americans, the battle for Okinawa was lost somewhere among Joe Rosenthal's picture of the flag raising on Mount Suribachi in April 1945,[1] Germany's surrender in May, the massive fire bombings in June and July, and the use of the atomic bombs in August. Except for several historians and those who were there, few seem to recall the viciousness of the fighting and the tragic number of casualties that characterized the battle of Okinawa.

The amphibious phase of the battle began on April 1, 1945, and the battle was declared officially over on July 2.[2] The battle still stands as the largest amphibious operation ever undertaken, involving some 1,400 ships and 500,000 men. It was also the only Pacific battle in which both adversary commanding generals lost their lives.

The battle for Okinawa had different meanings for different people. For the troops on the ground, it was the bloodiest, muddiest, most brutal combat ever experienced or imagined. For the sailors at sea, it was hell itself as thousands of kamikaze pilots hurled themselves at whatever naval combatant vessels they could find. For the *Yamato* task force, which sortied to Okinawa without air cover on April 7, it was suicide, pure and simple. For the peaceful and friendly Okinawans, it was all of the above.

The American Tenth Army included 102,000 army personnel and 88,500 marines. The army had four divisions under the XXIV Corps, the marines two divisions under the III Amphibious Corps.[3]

The Japanese 32nd Army, under Lt. Gen. Mitsuru Ushijima,

numbered about 77,000. Ushijima had decided not to contest the beachhead, but rather to construct strong, interlocking defensive positions and let the enemy come to him. These positions were cut into coral and rock caves above and below ground and linked by elaborate underground tunnels in the southern one-third of the island. The Americans would pay dearly for every inch of Japanese soil.

Lt. Gen. Mitsuru Ushijima, Japanese commanding general on Okinawa.

Public Information Office, Japan Defense Agency

Lt. Gen. Isamu Cho, chief of staff to Lieutenant General Ushijima.

Public Information Office, Japan Defense Agency

Following the unopposed landing, the marines turned north and secured the northern two-thirds of the island with minimal casualties. The army divisions turned south and soon encountered strong resistance which slowed and then stopped their advance. The marines were brought south to assist. Lt. Gen. Simon Bolivar Buckner Jr., commanding general Tenth Army, made the decision to envelop the Japanese defensive position of Shuri Castle. His goal was the total destruction of the Japanese force defending Shuri and the elimination of the remaining forces of Ushijima's command.[4]

The battle for Shuri lasted two weeks and highlighted the ferocity of the fighting. Obstacles in the approach to the castle faced each of the attacking divisions. For the 96th Army Division it was Conical Hill; the 77th Army Division faced Shuri itself; for the 1st Marine Division it was Wana Ridge and Wana Draw; and for the 6th Marine Division, which relieved the Army 27th Division, it was Sugar Loaf Hill.

The torrential spring rains arrived at the front lines a day after the marines. For the next three weeks, the rain, water, and mud would become nearly as formidable obstacles as the Japanese.

1st Division marines resort to hand-carrying of supplies and wounded as roads are washed out by torrential rains.

US Army / National Archives

The advance of the frontline divisions followed the procedures learned on Iwo Jima.[5] First came naval gunfire and close air support against the defensive positions. Next was massed artillery fire by all divisions and supporting artillery. Tanks, some with flamethrowing capability, mortar fire, and crew-served weapons, would then pound the positions. Finally, it would be the individual Japanese and American infantrymen who would use rifles, grenades, dynamite, knives, entrenching tools, teeth, and fingernails to crawl, dig, fight, and kill their foe.

Naval gunfire, close air support, and artillery fire did little damage to the coral and rock fortifications. The Japanese would retreat into the caves until the barrage was over and then pour steady streams of automatic weapons and mortar fire on the advancing enemy. The advance stalled and stopped.

Sgt. William Manchester, one of those who would have to take Sugar Loaf Hill, remembers the battlefield as being similar to the trench warfare of World War I: two huge armies slugging it out from static positions. He also recalls that the front lines were one vast cesspool.[6] Mud was knee deep everywhere, and men had to fight, sleep, walk, bleed, relieve themselves, and die in the same mass of mud.

Cpl. James Day was one of thousands of marines wounded on Sugar Loaf Hill. Forty years later, he returned to Okinawa as a major general to command the Third Marine Amphibious Force. During his 43-year career, he saw combat in four separate conflicts, earned three Silver Stars for bravery, and was wounded seven times. General Day remembers that Sugar Loaf Hill on Okinawa was the toughest battle he ever fought. The battle lasted 10 days, and more men were killed per square foot on Sugar Loaf than in any other battle area of the war: 2,662 battle casualties and another 1,289 lost to combat exhaustion and disease.[7]

Day recalls that when his platoon leader was killed, his replacement fell almost immediately. So did the battalion commander and executive officer. A new regimental commander came forward to replace the colonel who was seriously wounded and was, in turn, killed. So were most of the troops. Day lost his best friend on Sugar Loaf.

Day's battalion started with 1,145 men on April 1. When the fighting ended, more than 3,000 men had come and gone in the battalion. Each man had been numerically replaced twice. More than 2,000 casualties had occurred in just one battalion.[8] James Day earned the Bronze Star for heroism on Sugar Loaf. After the Battle for Okinawa, he was sent to Guam to prepare for the invasion of Japan. He retired in 1986 and was awarded the Medal of Honor by President Clinton in 1998.

E.B. "Sledgehammer" Sledge was with the 1st Marine Division on Peleliu and Okinawa. Later, he earned a doctorate and became professor of biology at Montevallo University in Alabama. Sledge authored the highly acclaimed book, *With the old Breed: at Peleliu and Okinawa*, a graphic account of the battle for Okinawa. He calls the fight for Dakeshi Ridge and Wana Draw an appalling chaos, with a near-continuous thundering, deadly storm of steel impacting upon the men who were trying desperately to do their job and stay alive in the process.[9]

Sledge thought the fighting at Peleliu was about as tough as it could get, but it now paled in contrast to the brutality on Okinawa. The terrain was completely devoid of trees or bushes as artillery and naval gunfire had eliminated all vegetation. The rain was heavy and continuous. Everyone and everything was bogged down in mud nearly up to their knees. The troops were always soaked; utility uniforms hung from the body dripping water and caked with mud and perspiration. The landscape was such a sea of mud that even the tanks had problems operating.

The stench of death became overpowering. There were rotting corpses and rusting weapons and equipment everywhere. The corpses would be partially covered by mud and water, but there would always be a cloud of flies and a mass of moving maggots on the bodies. As the troops tried to dig defensive positions in the mud, they would uncover corpses, rotting and covered with maggots. When one fell, slipped, or was sucked into a muddy depression, often his hand would come in contact with a hidden corpse. The troops tried to cover the bodies with mud but it proved impossible. The rain would wash the dirt away, and a man could not expose himself long enough to throw more than a shovelful of mud or he would be spotted and become a casualty himself.

Sledge recalls that there were even marine dead who had not been recovered for evacuation, a most uncommon sight since marines have a strong tradition of removing their dead. The elements and the enemy made such a task impossible for extended periods of time. It was nearly as difficult to evacuate the wounded and then bring up fresh water and ammunition on the return trip.[10] Typically, when a marine was hit, four volunteers would slog forward with a stretcher to recover him. Two of the bearers would themselves become casualties, and another marine would move forward to help. He, too, would buckle and fall backward into the mud with steel in both legs. Recovery would have to wait until dark.

Like Day, Sledge remembers that no one envied the lieutenants. Their replacements were constant. They were killed or wounded with such regularity that they were seldom known by the troops they were supposed to lead. Sledge suggests that the position of a second lieutenant in a rifle company was made obsolete by the fight for Wana Draw and Dakeshi Ridge.[11]

Bob Boardman was an enlisted marine serving with a tank company in support of the 7th Marine Regiment. Forced from his burning tank, Boardman and three buddies were behind Japanese lines and trying to make their way to a marine position on Wana Ridge when a sniper cut all three of them down with a single well-aimed shot. Boardman was shot through the throat and finger and was losing blood. He began to hobble and crawl toward the forward-most marine position, and just as he was about to lose consciousness, one of the tanks from his company came in sight. The driver stopped the badly damaged tank, and the crew put Boardman on a stretcher on the back of the tank. When the tank came under sniper fire, Bud Brenkert, a marine buddy of Boardman, climbed out of the tank and placed his body over Boardman's. If Bob was going to be hit again by enemy fire, the steel would have to go through Brenkert first. The damaged tank broke down in the battle area, but a tank from another company reached the survivors and successfully evacuated them.

When Boardman initially vacated his burning tank, one of those expendable second lieutenants, Jerry Atkinson, suffered a large shrapnel wound in the thigh and had to be helped from the tank. When the Japanese sniper shot the three survivors with one round, the bullet went through Atkinson's neck, and Boardman left him for dead. Later, he learned that Jerry was still alive and that the sniper had proceeded to shoot him again and again. Five more bullets tore into the lieutenant's body.

A short time later, the last operational tank in A Company found

A truckload of marines clad in ponchos against the monsoon downpour moves to the front lines through several feet of sticky mud.

US Marine Corps

Atkinson, but mistook him for the enemy and opened fire on him. Atkinson put up his only usable arm to protect himself and received another bullet in the hand. Out of arms, he put up his last usable limb which just happened to show a red sock over the top of his boot. Red socks are not issue equipment for marines and they sure weren't worn by the Japanese. The tank driver, 2Lt. Charlie Nelson, recognized Jerry's red socks, and Atkinson, nicknamed "the sieve," was saved.

Bob Boardman earned two Purple Hearts and the Silver Star for bravery in three Pacific campaigns. Boardman was so impressed by the show of devotion on the part of Brenkert and his fellow marines that, following the war, he devoted his life to missionary work among his former enemies.[12]

Dakeshi Ridge was finally gained, and after two days of vicious counterattacks, the marines held the position. The army captured the western and northern slopes of Conical Hill on May 13, while Sugar Loaf changed hands 14 times.[13]

The 4th Marine Regiment came out of corps reserve on May 18 and immediately received its introduction to Sugar Loaf. By May 21, Sugar Loaf, Horseshoe, Half Moon Hill, and Wana Draw were captured. Following another week of heavy fighting, Capt. Julian D. Dusenberry, a native of South Carolina, and a bit of a rebel, and a small marine patrol climbed the wall and raised the confederate battle flag, not the stars and stripes, over Shuri castle.[14] The flag created some adverse comments between units and services. It was soon replaced, and the issue died.

More brutal and punishing fighting remained as Ushijima withdrew his forces to the south. From the middle of June, nearly 1,000 Japanese were killed every day as the battle became a series of fierce contests for caves.[15] The American procedure was to use a flamethrower to keep the Japanese from the mouth of the cave and then to blast the entrance closed. The Okinawan civilians suffered terribly from the fighting. Gradually, the remnants of the Japanese army and the civilians were driven to the southern end of the island to a defensive perimeter near the villages of Makabe and Mabuni near the seaside cliffs. Naval gunfire pounded the remnants from the ocean side, and U.S. soldiers and marines came down the land side with flamethrowers, tanks, and dynamite. They reduced or sealed everything in their path. Allied aircraft blasted everything in between. With defeat near, the Japanese soldiers turned on the civilians, as if to blame them for everything that had gone wrong.[16]

On June 18, General Buckner suffered fatal shrapnel wounds while observing the progress of the battle in the 1st Marine Division area. Although a corpsman and plasma were immediately available and a doctor arrived within 10 minutes, the chest wound was fatal. Roy S. Geiger, the Marine Amphibious Corps commander, was promoted to lieutenant general and assumed command of the Tenth Army the following day.

Lieutenant General Buckner (right) is pictured observing an attack by the 8th Marine Regiment on June 18. Moments later, an enemy shell splintered the rock to Buckner's left and drove a sharp fragment into his chest. He died within minutes.
US Marine Corps

153

On June 21, General Geiger announced that the island had been secured by American forces. Late on the afternoon of June 22, when the Japanese command had been driven to its final cave, Lt. Gen. Ushijima and his chief of staff, Lt. Gen. Isamu Cho, committed ritual suicide.[17] Gen. Joseph W. Stilwell, U.S. Army, relieved Geiger on June 23 and, after two more weeks of mopping up, declared the battle officially over on July 2, 1945.

The toll of U.S. casualties was the highest experienced in any Pacific campaign against the Japanese. Total casualty figures for the Okinawa campaign vary somewhat and have risen substantially in recent years due, primarily, to increases in the estimated numbers of Okinawan civilian and home guard casualties. The U.S. 10th Army reported 75,362 total U. S. casualties, including 9,731 navy dead and wounded.

The cost to the Japanese and Okinawans was even higher. Approximately 107,539 dead Japanese military personnel were counted on Okinawa. An estimated 20,000 more were sealed in caves or buried; 7,400 surrendered. Initially 42,000 Okinawan civilian casualties were announced. On June 23, 1945, a Peace Wall Memorial with the names of 234,000 casualties was unveiled at Itoman, Okinawa. Some 147,110 Okinawan names are inscribed on the memorial along with the names of 11,000 Americans. The actual number of those killed is estimated to be substantially higher.[18]

The U.S. lost 34 ships, and suffered 368 damaged. More than 763 carrier-based aircraft were lost. Japan lost 7,800 aircraft; 16 ships were sunk and four more damaged.

As the allied planners began to prepare for the forthcoming campaign on the main islands of Japan, the Okinawa casualty figures were used to estimate the losses of life which could be expected on the island of Honshu. Estimates were 20,000,000 Japanese military and civilian casualties, and 200,000 to 500,000 U.S. casualties. Such estimates would play a large role in President Harry Truman's decision to use the atomic bomb against Japan.[19]

Lt. Glen Slaughter is accepting the surrender of four Japanese navy men on the Oroku Peninsula of Okinawa. Moments after this picture was taken, a marine corps sergeant knocked Slaughter aside and threw away the live hand grenade that the Japanese was preparing to hand to Slaughter. Note the Okinawan youngster coming forward to surrender with his hands raised.

US Marine Corps

U.S. Army 77th Division infantrymen on Okinawa trudge toward the front lines past mud-clogged tanks.

US Army

Native Okinawans receiving food allotment provided by the American Military Goverment.

US Marine Corps

In a gesture of friendship, a Marine shares his rations with a frail old woman. Each American division brought along special supplies of fish and rice to distribute among the civilians.

US Marine Corps

156

24

HIROSHIMA: THE FIRST ATOMIC BOMB, AUGUST 6, 1945

The morning of August 6, 1945, was clear in Hiroshima, Japan, with visibility of 10 to 15 miles. A few clouds were visible at high altitude, and the wind was from the south at four-and-one-half miles per hour. An air raid was sounded at 7:31 A.M., when the aircraft that circled the city had departed. At 8:15 A.M., three aircraft were reported 15 miles east of Hiroshima, but the alert was not sounded. At 8:16 A.M., the three aircraft were over Hiroshima at an altitude of 28,000 feet. At that moment, the lead B-29 dropped the first atomic bomb ever used against human beings.

Hiroshima had been struck by aircraft only two times previous to August 6. On March 19, 1945, four U.S. navy aircraft combined to drop a 250-pound bomb in the Ota river, three miles north of the city and one 250-pound bomb in a residential section. The second bomb caused two deaths and destroyed two houses. The Navy Grumman aircraft also strafed the railroad tracks but caused no damage. On April 30, a lone B-29 dropped ten 500-pound bombs resulting in damage to the Nomura life insurance building, a buddhist temple, a warehouse, 20 residential homes, and a building on the Hiroshima University grounds. Casualties from the 10 bombs were 12 killed and 28 wounded. Inasmuch as the residents of Hiroshima had become used to seeing enemy aircraft bypass the city but seldom attack it, the three B-29s were not considered cause for alarm.

At 8:17 A.M., the "bomb" detonated in the air, 2,000 feet above a post office slightly northwest of the city. As estimated by scientists, the nuclear-fission bomb changed into a fireball hotter than the center of the sun (70,000,000 degrees centigrade) during the detonation that was over in a millionth of a second. Pressures developed in the bomb were of the order of a thousand billion times atmospheric pressure.

Survivors of the atomic bomb blast stated that the detonation seemed like a vast combustion of magnesium filling the entire sky. The city was darkened by a dense pall of smoke and dust; visibility was reduced to a few feet.

From a distance, a mushroom-shaped cloud was seen expanding and covering the entire city. The cloud rose to a height of 23,000 feet within four minutes after the explosion. Few people in the center of the city heard any noise associated with the explosion; they were killed instantly by the blinding flash and violent blast of overpressure. Directly after the explosion, survivors reported a substance which emitted a weak, bluish-white fluorescent light. The substance burned through to the flesh, producing extremely painful blisters.

The immediate casualties of this single bomb totaled 70,000 killed and a like number injured. Another 100,000 people become casualties or developed radiation sickness as long as 20 years after the "bomb."[1]

'Little Boy'

"Little Boy" was a four-ton, torpedo-shaped bomb with the power of 12,700 tons of high explosive.

National Archives

25

THE LIE OF MARCUS McDILDA

On the evening of August 8, 1945, in Osaka, Japan, several *kempei tai* (Japanese secret police) were questioning an American flyer who had been shot down earlier in the day. The flyer, Lt. Marcus McDilda, had been recovered from the ocean, bound, blindfolded, and forced to walk the gauntlet of angry civilians through the city streets. When the beatings at the hands of the civilians ended, McDilda was taken to a typical *kempei tai* interrogation room where Japanese officers began to question him.

McDilda was questioned for hours. The same questions would be asked again and again, and each time he was beaten if his responses were not to the liking of his questioners. The questioning intensified as did the beatings. What did he know of the atomic bomb dropped on Hiroshima two days earlier? Absolutely nothing, McDilda responded.[1]

Believing that they were on to something, the *kempei tai* brought in a general officer just before midnight to break McDilda. The general demanded that McDilda tell him about the atomic bomb. When McDilda said nothing, the general drew his sword and held it before McDilda's face. Then he jabbed forward, cutting through McDilda's lip. Blood streamed down the pilot's chin and flight suit. The general screamed, "If you don't tell me about the bomb, I'll personally cut off your head."[2] Then he stalked from the room.

McDilda had been beaten up enough. His body ached from the beatings received during the march, his lip throbbed from the sword cut, and now a fresh crew of questioners approached. According to author William Craig, McDilda embarked upon a lie worthy of the best storyteller.[3] McDilda began:

> "As you know . . ., when atoms are split, there are a lot
> of pluses and minuses released. Well, we've taken these
> and put them in a huge container and separated them from
> each other with a lead shield. When the box is dropped out
> of a plane, we melt the lead shield and the pluses and
> minuses come together. When that happens, it causes a
> tremendous bolt of lightning and all the atmosphere over
> a city is pushed back! Then when the atmosphere rolls
> back, it brings about a tremendous thunderclap, which
> knocks down everything beneath it."[4]

When pushed to further describe the bomb, McDilda added
that it was about 36 feet long and 24 feet wide.[5] The interrogators
were delighted but needed to know one thing more. Where was the
next target for the new weapon? McDilda chose the two Japanese
cities he could think of and responded, "Kyoto and Tokyo. Tokyo
is supposed to be bombed in the next few days."[6] The *kempei tai*
continued to ask questions, but McDilda had reached a point where
he could only go back and repeat his lies. One of the interrogators
left the room and put through a call to the headquarters of the
secret police in Tokyo.

The next morning, McDilda was flown from Osaka to Tokyo
where he became a "very important person" to the Japanese secret
police. McDilda's questioner in Tokyo was a civilian who wore a
pinstripe suit. "I am a graduate of CCNY College," he told McDilda,
"and most interested in your story about the atomic bomb."[7]
McDilda repeated his story again. After several minutes, the official
knew that McDilda was a fake who knew nothing about nuclear
fission. When asked why he was telling such a lie, McDilda responded
that he had tried, without success, to tell his interrogators that he
knew nothing about the bomb but had to invent the lie to stay alive.
The Japanese official laughed. McDilda was taken to a cell, given
some food, and waited for the unknown.

McDilda, at the time, had no idea that his lie had saved his life. Shortly after the emperor had broadcast the news of defeat, more than 50 American prisoners at the Osaka secret police headquarters were beheaded by vengeful Japanese soldiers.[8]

Nineteen days later, on August 30, the Fourth Marine Regiment landed near the Omori POW camp on the Tokyo waterfront. Cmdr. Harold Stassen, USN, later senator from Minnesota, walked to the gates of Omori where he was challenged by the Japanese commandant, who said that he had no authority to turn the prisoners over to him. Stassen kicked him squarely in the backside, looked coldly at the officer, and said, "You have no authority period."[9] Among the prisoners released were McDilda and Pappy Boyington, the marine corps ace of the South Pacific.

Fat Man was five feet in diameter, weighed five tons, but needed only a few kilograms of plutonium to devastate Nagasaki.

Associated Press

Atomic mushroom cloud over Nagasaki. Photo taken at 11:00 A.M., August 9, 1945.

US Naval Academy

26

THE SECOND ATOMIC BOMB

On the evening of August 8, 1945, B-29 number 77, *Bock's Car* by name, waited under heavy security and the glare of flood lights near the runway on Tinian. In its bomb bay, the "Fat Man," the first plutonium bomb, also waited. Fat Man measured ten-feet and eight-inches long by 55-inches in diameter. Inside the bomb, precisely machined plutonium components were arranged. When these components came together, another Japanese city would die. The city selected for this mission was Kokura.[1]

Bock's Car, with pilot Chuck Sweeny in command, lifted off the runway at 1:56 A.M., August 9, Japanese time. At 7:45 A.M., the cloud cover broke as forecast and the island of Yakoshima was sighted. The weather planes at Kokura and at Nagasaki, the alternate target, reported clear skies over both cities. At 8:09 A.M., *Bock's Car* rendezvoused with a specially modified instrument plane, but after circling an additional 40 minutes trying to locate the camera plane, Sweeny headed for Kokura.[2]

The radar in *Bock's Car* locked onto Kokura before the city could be identified visually. The bomb bay doors were opened, the signal that the bomb was ready was received, and the crew prepared for the bomb release. Kermit Beahan, the bombardier, picked up the city in his bomb sight, and waited for the enormous arsenal factory to pass across the sight. He saw streets and buildings but no arsenal. "No drop," Beahan announced to the crew.[3] Sweeny told the crew to relax and that they would try it again.

Bock's Car made a complete turn and approached the target on a second run. Once again everything was in order. Once again the

163

city went past, the river next to the arsenal emerged clearly, but no arsenal. Once again the bomb was not dropped. Beahan was following his orders to drop only on visual sighting, not by radar.

As Sweeny turned the B-29 to line up for a third run, the stadium close to the arsenal appeared, but it was not the arsenal itself. Now Sweeny faced a low fuel situation. He could not return to Tinian or Iwo Jima. In Kokura, more and more people paused in the streets to gaze at the two B-29s whose actions were so strange. Civilians began to crowd into the several air raid shelters.

Suddenly, the fighter direction circuits on the console of the B-29 began to light up, indicating that enemy interceptors were on the way, and flak from anti-aircraft batteries began to follow the B-29. "Major, the damned flak is right on the tail and coming closer all the time," the tail gunner reported. "Forget it Pappy," Sweeny answered, "we're on a bomb run."[4]

One more time Beahan saw the streets and river go by but never saw the arsenal. Once again the bomb was not dropped. "Fighters below and climbing," Sgt. John Kuharak, the engineer, told Sweeny, "Fuel getting very low."[5] Sweeny had already made up his mind to attack the alternate target of Nagasaki, but his fuel supply was so low that he would not be able to bypass the fighter fields on Kyushu. He would have to fly directly over them to reach Nagasaki with enough fuel for a bomb run and then an emergency landing on Okinawa. Sweeny rolled the aircraft on a direct course for the alternate target, and Kokura was saved.

Danger seemed remote to Nagasaki, a city of 200,000 people who were busy at work. Ninety percent of the labor force worked in the Urakami Valley on the northwest side of town. Here was the Mitsubishi complex of war plants that manufactured torpedoes and small arms. On this day, the factories were functioning at full capacity. At 10:55 A.M., a man north of the Urakami railroad station gazed through a pair of binoculars and spotted a B-29 heading towards Nagasaki. Air raid sirens began to sound.

Bock's Car was in trouble. The plane had barely enough fuel to make one pass over the target, and then fly to Okinawa. Any further delay would result in a crash landing in Japan and the possible dumping of "Fat Man" in the ocean. The crew was becoming tense. They had been in the air for nine hours with a very dangerous weapon and had started mission briefings long before that. Nothing seemed to be going right. As they approached Nagasaki, the clear visibility reported hours before became nine-tenths cloud cover as a frontal system moved in and covered nearly the entire city.

Sweeny called navy commander Fred Ashworth, a weapons expert assigned to the flight, to the cockpit, and came right to the point. "We have enough gas for one pass over Nagasaki . . . or we won't make it to Okinawa. How about dropping it by radar?" Ashworth had been dreading this scenario. He had strict orders not to do a radar drop. He hesitated, but then gave a firm "No."[6] Sweeny continued to try to convince Ashworth that the drop would come within a thousand feet of the target and that would be better than dropping it in the ocean. "I'm sure the radar will work," Sweeny said. Hearing the conversation, Jim Van Pelt, the navigator, shuddered. Should they drop by radar, the responsibility for the detonation would be his, and he did not share Sweeny's confidence. Ashworth asked for a moment to think about it and then said, "Go ahead and drop it by radar if you can't do it visually."[7] Kokura had survived because of smoke. Nagasaki had nearly survived because of clouds—but the odds had changed.

"Fat Man" was supposed to be dropped in the heart of downtown Nagasaki, where its power would spread through the relatively flat land around the bay. At 30 seconds before bomb release, Beahan found a huge hole in the cloud cover, spotted a stadium one-and-one-half mile up the valley from intended ground zero, and accepted the responsibility for dropping the bomb visually. By so doing, he relieved Van Pelt and Ashworth of the necessity for a radar drop. He asked for a correction to the right, got it, and put his cross hairs on the stadium. *Bock's Car* lurched as the bomb fell away, and Sweeny turned the aircraft left towards Okinawa.

In China, just a few hours before the thunderclap of the second nuclear detonation over the Japanese homeland, the emperor's soldiers had been subjected to a massive artillery bombardment, which signalled the charge of hundreds of Soviet tanks and aircraft that rolled over the Japanese positions like a tidal wave. Yet, as unexpected and powerful as the Russian offensive was, it did nothing to change the views of the war party in Tokyo.

Urakami Cathedral. The Catholic church, which had 14,000 parishioners, was destroyed beyond recognition. Father Saburo Nishida and a dozen parishioners were killed by the crumbling dome and other debris.

US Navy

27

NAGASAKI: AUGUST 9, 1945

Nagasaki's prefectural governor, Mr. Wakamatsu Nagano, had just met with city officials to discuss the startling news from Hiroshima. Takejiro Nishioka, publisher of a local paper, had been in Hiroshima and suffered burns and radiation exposure. His story concerned Nagano who was already starting to coordinate a major indoctrination program for the inhabitants of Nagasaki.[1]

The city of Nagasaki is surrounded by mountains on three sides and is open to the sea on the other, thus forming the Urakami Valley. On the east side of Urakami Valley, hundreds of people were worshipping in the Catholic church on the bluff. Nagasaki remained the center of Christianity in Japan and contained numerous Christian churches and schools.[2] At the Nagasaki Medical Center, Dr. Susumu Tsunoo was still contemplating the horror of the destruction at Hiroshima, which he had personally witnessed. He had somehow escaped serious injury and hurried back to his school to consider just what was happening. At the Urakami railroad station, a young woman, 20-year-old Aiko Tagawa, struggled with baggage, while children chased dragonflies in the nearby park.

At an altitude of 1,540 feet, the arming and firing switches closed on the "Fat Man," and Nagasaki became a graveyard. The bomb detonated several hundred yards northeast of the stadium in the Urakami Valley. Twenty-four hundred feet to the northeast, the roof and masonry of the Catholic cathedral fell on the worshipers, killing them all. At the Nagasaki branch prison, just north of the explosion, 118 guards and convicts saw the brilliant light of the explosion but nothing else. They died immediately.[3]

The baggage master at the Urakami railroad station did not live to meet an incoming train. His assistant, Aiko Tagawa, survived the collapse of the station and, torn by flying glass, rushed to the street where people were jumping headlong into the river to find relief from burns.[4]

Most of the people in the train that had stopped to discharge passengers died instantly as the white light flooded over them. Windows were blown in, bodies were severed and burns appeared instantaneously. Out in the harbor, two-and-one-half miles from the blast, craft burst into flames and burned to the waterline. Crew members screamed from burns on exposed portions of flesh.

The fireball of the bomb widened in seconds to fill the entire valley. The blast wave leaped the crests and raced through the seaport. People by the hundreds lay on the streets among the wreckage and cried for water. Creatures who barely resembled human beings walked aimlessly, not knowing where or why they were moving.

At the Nagasaki Medical Center, Dr. Raisuke Shirabe was left in total darkness as his room collapsed. Later he stumbled to the corridor and joined other survivors struggling to reach higher ground behind the hospital. At their backs were the terror-filled cries of patients trapped in their beds and now facing the fires which began to ignite everywhere.[5]

Nagasaki was in flames. Lines of refugees, including allied prisoners, limped and crawled from the inferno. Many would collapse and expire. Not only were they badly burned, but the invisible gamma radiation had invaded their bloodstreams and condemned them to a certain death. The wounded asked continually for water.

Nearly half of the medical personnel in Nagasaki were dead or wounded; as a result, casualties received little, if any, relief. Those suffering from burns continued to scream, the lacerated bled to death, and those with radiation poisoning died slowly. One of the doctors who died was Dr. Tsunoo, the man who had just returned from Hiroshima. Some doctors and nurses were so overwhelmed by the enormity of the catastrophe that they concerned themselves with their own safety, forgetting their medical vows.

Many of the casualties lay for a time where they fell. Not only were they too weak to continue, but many were dazed and their memory a blank after the initial explosion, flash, and fire. As they regained their senses, they began a mass migration toward the sea. The wounded were clothed in shreds or not clothed at all, victims of the terrible heat and fire. Their skin was seared and blistered, and they sought only to escape the horrifying fire that was consuming the city.[6]

According to author William Craig, all firefighting equipment was destroyed, and water mains leaked everywhere. By one o'clock, refugees began to straggle down to the less-damaged portion of the city near the water.[7] Most had lost their clothing and hair to the intense heat and fire. Their burns had begun to swell and turn black. Faces were indistinguishable, just indentations where eyes and noses had once been. The mass of survivors vomited continually and suffered from diarrhea as they inched along.[8]

Not all the dead and dying were Japanese. There were about 350 Allied prisoners in and around Nagasaki. Many of those who were forced to work in the steel and arms factories perished as did many Korean laborers. Sixty to 80 prisoners in the POW camp at Saiwaimachi, a mile away, were also killed by the blast.[9]

Governor Nagano had survived the holocaust, thanks to the tips given him by publisher Nishioka. Now he acted quickly to avert sanitation problems and ordered mass cremations for the thousands of cadavers lining the streets. As twilight came to the Urakami Valley, volunteers began the gruesome job of collecting corpses by the light of burning trees and buildings.

Three days later, fires still raged, and on all sides lay the dead. Many buildings smoldered, and a putrid, decaying smell clogged the nostrils and made members of the disaster team wretch. One mile from ground zero, the bodies showed evidence of multiple burns and wounds about the head and extremities. Inward, toward the blast center, the bodies were roasted black.

Survivors were sent to surrounding towns for treatment. The appearance of the patients was horrifying. Their hair was burned, their clothing torn to pieces and stained by blood, and the exposed parts of their bodies burned and inflamed. Many had jagged pieces of glass, wood, and metal driven into their bodies. Few of the survivors resembled human beings.

It was on the third day following the explosion that survivors started to die in increasing numbers. The physicians who treated them for burns and wounds could not believe it. They were at a loss to explain why their patients were dying rather than recovering.[10]

The situation was the same in Hiroshima. Diarrhea, vomiting, lack of appetite, and anemia were early symptoms. Now we know that their blood streams were being ravaged by radiation. The *genshibakudansho*, the "*atomic bomb sickness*," was just starting to take its toll on the initial survivors.

28

JAPAN CONDITIONALLY SURRENDERS: AUGUST 10, 1945

Late on the evening of August 10, (US time) a small group of very important conferees began arriving at the Imperial Palace grounds in response to the emperor's unexpected call for a meeting. As the conferees arrived, they were escorted down a steep stairway to a tunnel that led to the emperor's underground command center and conference room.

Even without air conditioning, the room was the finest air raid shelter in Japan. Small in size, measuring 18 by 30 feet, the shelter had steel-beamed ceilings and its walls were panelled in dark wood.[1]

As the 11 conferees waited for the emperor, they perspired heavily due to the complete lack of ventilation and their high-collared uniforms and formal attire. They were kept busy swatting the hordes of ravenous mosquitoes that seemed determined to take advantage of their captive audience.[2]

Four of the conferees were aides or secretaries. One man, Baron Kiichiro Hiranuma, was a guest. The others were Japan's Big Six, or "inner cabinet," with the formal name of "The Supreme Council for the Direction of the War." These six men, four cabinet ministers and two military chiefs of staff, had formulated the policies that directed the lives of 80 million Japanese citizens.[3]

At 10 minutes before midnight, the emperor entered the room through a door partially hidden by a screen. He seemed tired and sat quietly at his place in front of the screen. After bowing, the conferees sat down at long tables facing each other and took care not to look directly towards the emperor.[4]

Although the inner cabinet had titular authority to formulate policy, it functioned very cautiously. Actual power belonged to the army and navy general staffs who could resign when things did not go their way and topple the cabinet. There was also the constant threat of violence on the part of the young army officers who would take matters into their own hands. The other organs of government, the Diet and Privy Council, functioned only as rubber stamps to approve matters after the fact.[5]

Meeting of the Supreme Council for the Direction of the War in the presence of the emperor on August 9th (Japan time). From left, clockwise: Lt. Gen. Sumihisa Ikeda, director of the Cabinet's Overall Planning Bureau; Vice-Adm. Zenshiro Hoshina, director of the Bureau of Naval Affairs; Adm. Soemu Toyoda, Navy chief of staff; Shigenori Togo, foreign minister; Adm. Mitsumasa Yonai, Navy minister; Baron Kiichiro Hiranuma, president of the Privy Council; Gen. Shigeru Hasunuma, chief aide-de-camp (behind Hiranuma); the emperor; Baron Kantaro Suzuki, prime minister; Gen. Korechika Anami, war minister; Gen. Yoshijiro Umezu, Army chief of staff; Lt. Gen. Masao Yoshizumi, director of the Bureau of Military Affairs at the War Ministry; and Hisatsune Sakomizu, chief cabinet secretary.

Mainichi

Prime Minister Kantaro Suzuki, by title, was the head of the Big Six. As a young officer, Suzuki had led a suicide charge against the Russian Czarist fleet at Tsushima, thereby earning for himself a hero's reputation within Japan. Many years later, during a rebellion of young army officers who were assassinating persons of importance, Suzuki was shot three times and still carried the mental and physical scars of that encounter.[6] Suzuki had been appointed premier to find a way to end the war. At age 81, he seemed both deaf and drowsy to the other members of the cabinet. Suzuki often reversed his position on issues and dozed through many of the long cabinet discussions.[7]

It was Suzuki, who, through his bumbling use of the word *mokusatsu* at a press conference on July 27, doomed hundreds of thousands of Japanese to death from the atomic bombs. In his announcement of Japan's response to the Allied Potsdam Proclamation, Suzuki said Japan would *mokusatsu* it (kill it with silence). The *Asahi Shimbun*, the Tokyo daily paper, characterized Suzuki's statement as meaning that the Potsdam Proclamation was "a thing of no great value."[8] The Allies, upon learning that Japan would not even bother to reject or negotiate the Potsdam Proclamation, prepared for "the complete destruction of the Japanese Armed Forces,"[9] and, as a consequence, the devastation of Japan and its people.

Aligned with Suzuki in the emperor's shelter as part of the peace faction, sat Foreign Minister Shigenori Togo, 63 years old and a strong supporter of peace. After the war, the Allies would try him as a war criminal for his role as foreign minister at the time of the attack on Pearl Harbor. Actually, Togo argued against war with the United States and was able to delay commencement of Japan's attack on Pearl Harbor. Togo ran afoul of Premier Tojo's timetable and was brushed aside.[10] Togo had been retired until 1945 when he agreed to join the cabinet to end the war as soon as possible.

A third member of the peace faction, Navy Minister Adm. Mitsumasa Yonai, was a quiet, pleasant man with a ready smile.

Yonai had been premier in 1940, but was forced to resign because he opposed Japan's alliance with Germany and Italy. He had been active among top circles in the government for nearly 20 years, and was brought back as navy minister when Tojo resigned in July, 1944.

Now at age 65, Yonai had developed many enemies among the military who resented his overtures for peace. Still conscious of the danger of assassination at the hands of the young officers, he continually pressed for a discussion of the issues in hopes of resolving the impasse.[11]

Against Suzuki, Togo, and Yonai were the other members of the Big Six, led by Gen. Korechika Anami, war minister, spokesman for the army and the single-most powerful person in Japan. Anami knew that Japan could not win the war, but insisted upon bleeding the enemy on the beaches of Kyushu and at sea so that Japan could obtain honorable peace terms from the Allies. The 57-year-old general insisted on one last decisive battle.[12]

The army chief of staff, Gen. Yoshijiro Umezu, sat next to Anami. He had been arguing against the Allied surrender terms since they were received. "With luck we will be able to repulse the invaders before they land," Umezu had stated at an earlier cabinet meeting.[13] He argued that the army would be able to destroy the major part of an invading force and "inflict extremely heavy damage on the enemy."[14] Umezu now rose to state that it would be unthinkable to surrender unconditionally after so many brave men had died for the emperor.

Umezu, unlike Anami, was a stereotype military officer. He was a product of the fanatical Kwangtung Army which used similar arguments to prevent Japan from withdrawing from China. From his shaven head and visored cap to the spurs on his shiny boots, he epitomized the dilemma facing Japan. The army must have peace with honor or no peace at all.[15]

The sixth member of the council was Adm. Soemu Toyoda, the navy chief of staff. The 60-year-old Toyoda had argued to reject the Potsdam Proclamation and vigorously defended the army's ultimatum of one final battle. Although without a navy, Toyoda continued to speak eloquently for the continuation of the war which ensured that the cabinet remained deadlocked over the surrender issue.

The guest, Baron Kiichiro Hiranuma, had no right to be there, and the war faction resented his presence. Suzuki had invited him, since Hiranuma was president of the Privy Council and the council was required to ratify all foreign treaties.[16] Actually, the Privy Council was only an advisory body to the emperor, and Hiranuma approved decisions after they had been decided by the full cabinet.

Hiranuma, now 80 years old, had been involved in Japanese politics since before World War I. In 1927, he caused the overthrow of a reform-minded cabinet and was instrumental in the appointment of army Gen. Gi-ichi Tanaka as premier.

Hiranuma had become premier in 1939 and tried without success to slow the army's expansion in China. Terrorists tried to assassinate him in 1941, and he disappeared from public service when Tojo came to power. Hiranuma was present to ensure that the emperor system remained intact in any surrender response that the council was able to develop. He also planned to ask the hard questions that the war faction would prefer not to answer.

The Big Six, their aides, and Hiranuma waited 25 minutes before the door to the emperor's quarters opened and the Divine Ruler entered. The time was 11:50 P.M. When the emperor was seated, Premier Suzuki stood at the emperor's left side and asked the chief cabinet secretary to read the Potsdam Declaration once more. The secretary, Hitatsune Sakomizu, read the terms of surrender laid down by the Allies, the same terms that everyone in the room knew so well. Suzuki then described the discussions that had led to a 3-3 vote and a deadlock over the issue of surrender. Included in his review were the four conditions attached by some members of the cabinet to the acceptance of surrender: one, Japan must retain the emperor system of government; two, Japan must be allowed to try its own war criminals; three, Japan must be permitted to disarm its own military; and four, the Allies must not occupy the home islands of Japan.

Next, Suzuki called upon each of the cabinet members to explain his position. Foreign Minister Togo stated that the Potsdam Proclamation should be accepted so long as *kokutai* (the national essence) could be maintained.[18] Admiral Yonai stated his agreement with Togo. General Anami jumped to his feet and, pointing at Yonai, angrily shouted: "Absolutely not!"[19] Unless all four conditions are met, Japan must fight. General Umezu agreed with Anami and insisted upon the four conditions for surrender.

Suzuki then called upon Baron Hiranuma for his opinion. Hiranuma asked many questions of both sides concerning the readiness and ability of the military to defend the nation. Finally, he turned to the emperor and reminded him that he was also responsible for the welfare of his subjects. "I should like to ask His Majesty to make his decision with this point in mind."[20] Admiral Toyoda spoke next but added nothing new.

Prime Minister Suzuki then rose from his seat and explained that, for two hours, they had discussed the issue of surrender and had not come to a conclusion. "I now propose to seek the Imperial guidance and to come to a decision on that basis. His majesty's wish should decide the issue, and the government should follow it."[21]

Without a pause, Suzuki stepped towards the emperor. There was a gasp of surprise at his audacity. "Mr. Prime Minister," Anami cried in stunned disbelief.[22] "We have no precedent for this procedure" Suzuki explained, "and I find it most difficult to do, but I must now ask the Emperor to express his wishes."[23] "Which proposal should be accepted, the foreign minister's or General Anami's proposal with the four conditions?"[24]

Suzuki had truly trumped the war party. No one expected the emperor to speak. The emperor never spoke at such meetings. Suzuki had taken the matter out of the cabinet's hands and asked the emperor to make the decision. Hirohito rose and spoke slowly. "I agree with the Foreign Minister's plan . . . to accept the Potsdam Declaration. . . . I cannot bear to see my innocent people struggle any longer . . . . the time has come when we must bear the unbearable."[25]

Hirohito did not wait for a reaction. He turned and walked through the door opened by his aide. There was no sound in the room. Eleven men remained with their private thoughts. No one raised his voice in protest or argument. Finally, Suzuki rose and stated, "His Majesty's decision should be made the decision of this cabinet as well."[26] No one disagreed. Suzuki adjourned the group to a full cabinet meeting the following morning.

The full cabinet assembled shortly thereafter at Suzuki's home to phrase the sentence dealing with preservation of the emperor's status. Hiranuma insisted that the sentence be changed to: "With the understanding that the said declaration does not compromise any demand which prejudices the prerogatives of His Majesty as a Sovereign Ruler." The sentence was approved by the full cabinet, and, early the following morning, wireless operators began clicking the news to neutral Sweden and Switzerland for subsequent transmittal to the Allied capitals.

Adm. Chester W. Nimitz, commander of the Pacific Ocean area (left), Adm. Ernest J. King, chief of naval operations (center), and Adm. Raymond A. Spruance, Fifth Fleet commander, in July 1944.

US Navy / National Archives

29

THE ALLIED RESPONSE

Later in the day of August 11, Saiiji Hasegawa, foreign news editor of Domei news agency, broadcast the uncoded news of the conditional acceptance directly to the United States in English in Morse code. Hopefully, the message would be received before the military could prevent its transmission.

The message was received early on the morning of August 10 (U.S. time.) President Harry S. Truman scheduled a 9:00 A.M. meeting of his "war council" to discuss the message.[1] Truman's inner circle of advisors included Secretary of the Navy James Forrestal, the president's personal chief of staff, Adm. Bill Leahy, Secretary of War Henry Stimson, and Secretary of State James Byrnes.[2]

Forrestal had been in and out of politics since 1940. He accepted the navy's top position in 1944. An intense man, he drove himself and others unmercifully. Slighted at not being invited to the Potsdam Conference, which Byrnes and Leahy did attend, he started appearing unannounced at the "big three" sessions and resolved the issue to his satisfaction, if not President Truman's. The "big three" sessions became, de facto, the "big four," though their meetings were never announced as such.[3]

Adm. William D. Leahy, a veteran of 52 years of naval service, tended toward blunt assertions and a cynical outlook. Leahy had served on the frigate *Constellation* in his younger days and "was there" during the Boxer Rebellion in China and in World War I. Bill Leahy was a bachelor who loved tobacco and hard work. He is reported to have averaged 60 cigarettes per day while assisting the president.[4]

Henry Stimson had served the U.S. since 1931, when he was secretary of state under President Herbert Hoover. He was a mild and highly moral gentleman who wrestled at length with the morality issue of the atomic bomb, deciding finally that, since "war is death," the atomic bomb was just one more in a series of weapons to be used on human beings.[5]

Byrnes was the only Truman appointee in the room and had come very close to being the acting president. Both Byrnes and Truman were shocked at the national convention when Truman was nominated as Franklin Delano Roosevelt's running mate. Truman acted quickly, when Roosevelt died, to recall Byrnes from retirement to head the state department. Truman and Byrnes worked well together as demonstrated by their work with the intransigent Russians at the Potsdam Conference.[6] Now they were meeting to specifically discuss Baron Hiranuma's conditional-acceptance portion of the surrender message.

President Truman asked his advisors if the Allies should let the emperor continue to reign. His cabinet seemed not to be concerned with continuation of the emperor.[7] Secretary of War Stimson argued for retention of the emperor as a practical matter. Without the emperor's directive, the scattered Japanese armies would be unlikely to surrender. Leahy and Forrestal concurred. Forrestal was more concerned with Russia's designs in the Far East. If keeping the emperor would end the war quickly, he was for it. James Byrnes was against retreating from the Allied unconditional surrender demand. Wasn't unconditional surrender what the Japanese demanded and received on Bataan and at Singapore? If there were to be conditions attached to the surrender, it should be the Allies who would state such conditions. Forrestal suggested that their response could be written to indicate that surrender was in accordance with the Allied proclamation.

Both the state and war departments had drafted replies to the Japanese surrender message. The state department draft was considered most appropriate; after a slight modification to the second paragraph, it was approved by the president and his cabinet. "From the moment of surrender the authority of the Emperor and the Japanese Government to rule the state shall be subject to the Supreme Commander of the Allied Powers who will take such steps as he deems proper to effectuate the surrender terms."[8]

At two o'clock, the official Japanese message arrived from the Swiss embassy. By four o'clock, the draft allied response had been sent to London, Chungking, and Moscow for approval. Britain and China agreed quickly to the terms. Predictably, Russia balked. Ambassador Averell Harriman refused to transmit the Soviet's acceptance conditions to Washington and called the Soviet's bluff. By the end of the day they agreed, and the Allied response was ready for transmission.[9]

Secretary-General of the Soviet Communist party, Josef Stalin (left) and President Harry Truman (right) meet at Potsdam in July, 1945, to map out the future of Germany and Japan. Prime Minister Winston Churchill, representing Great Britain, also participated in the Potsdam conference.

National Archives

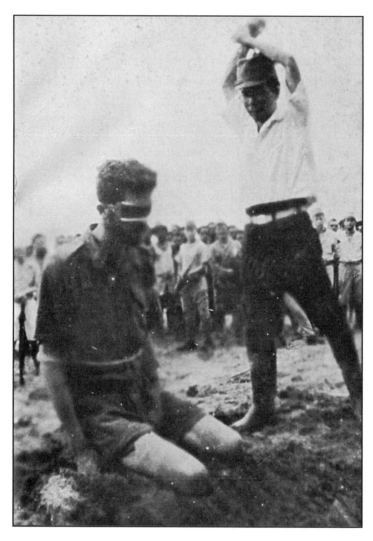

Sergeant Leonard Sifflett, Australian Army, is being beheaded by Yasuno Chickao, Japanese Army. The picture was taken in New Guinea on October 24, 1943.

US Air Force

30

RETRIBUTION: AUGUST 11, 1945

By August 11, Japan's major cities were in ruins, the result of Gen. Curtis Lemay's firebombing campaign and the devastation caused by the atomic bombs on Hiroshima and Nagasaki. Many of the people were homeless and hungry, and frustration within the military had become a major problem.

Gen. Korechika Anami, Japan's minister of war, continued to argue for a final battle against the Allies and against unconditional surrender. Anami was supported by Gen. Yoshijiro Umezu, army chief of staff, and by Adm. Soemu Toyoda, navy chief of staff. Their opposition to the emperor's desire to accept the Allied surrender demands frustrated the peace process and provided support to a small number of military zealots who were plotting a coup to isolate the emperor and continue the war.

Outside of Tokyo, there was confusion and frustration. Unaware of the results of the cabinet meetings and the emperor's desire for peace, many members of the army took out their frustrations on the allied prisoners, especially on the American B-29 crewmembers who were identified as being responsible for much of Japan's plight. Organized execution of prisoners, and especially airmen, was nothing new. During the May 24-25 firebombings of Tokyo, 62 captured American airmen were found murdered in their cells following the bombing.[1] In Sendai, in northern Japan, 250 prisoners were buried alive.[2] At Hatensho, on Kyushu, large crowds would assemble to watch captured airmen being beheaded.[3] Such murders would continue even after the emperor's announcement of surrender.

In Fukuoka, Japan, about 100 miles north of the devastated city of Nagasaki, frustrations and emotions were at a fever pitch. Two days after the bomb was dropped on Nagasaki, a group of army officers and non-commissioned officers arranged for the murder of eight captured B-29 crewmen.[4] The arrangements were similar to an earlier execution on June 20, when eight crewmen were similarly murdered. The prisoners, under heavy guard, were bound, forced into the back of a military truck, and transported several miles to a vacant field in a place called Aburiyama.[5] There the prisoners were stripped to their underwear and made to watch as several large holes were dug in the ground.

One of the airmen was pushed forward and forced into a kneeling position near one of the holes. A lieutenant drew his sword and, after a few preliminary motions, swung the sword with all his might, severing the flier's neck. His body was pushed into the pit.[6] The remaining seven prisoners were given ample time to contemplate what was in store for them. Then four of them were executed in a similar manner.

The next two prisoners were held on their feet with their arms tied behind their backs. Again and again, one of the officers trained in karate would run toward the prisoner and deliver karate blows to the body. When the flier staggered from the blow, he would be pulled back upright for another assault. When the first flier failed to die from such treatment, he was decapitated.[7] Another karate expert, angered because his smashes to the stomach, kidneys, and throat failed to kill the second prisoner, kicked him in the testicles. The airman fell to his knees and was killed by a method called *kesajiri*, a sword cut down and through the left shoulder and into the lungs. He died in his own froth of blood.[8]

The final prisoner, who had been forced to watch his friends slashed to death, was made to sit on the ground with his hands tied behind his back, facing an archer who stood only ten feet away. Slowly, the archer placed an arrow on his bow, took careful aim at the pilot, and loosed the arrow. On the third attempt, the arrow impacted just over the left eye. The prisoner, with blood spurting down his face and body, was kicked into the kneeling position and decapitated.[9]

In the next few days, 16 more airmen were murdered at Fukuoka and the last five airmen at the Osaka POW camp would suffer a similar fate.[10]

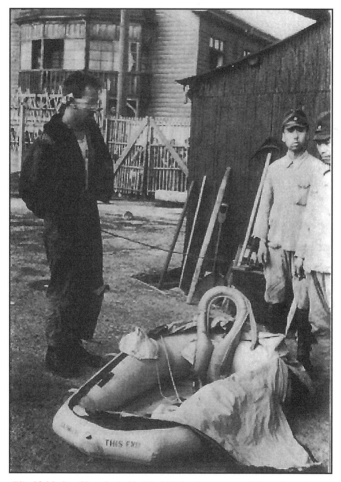

Blindfolded and hands tied behind his back, a captured American airmen is photographed before being paraded through the village. Villagers would hit, kick, and try to hack the airman with swords and knives. If he survived, he would likely be executed by the *Kempeitai*.

Mainichi Shinbun

Australian survivors at Changi POW camp display artificial limbs of scrap metal and rubber, made by POW medics to replace legs that had turned gangrenous as a result of skin ulcers.

Australian War Memorial

31

DAY OF CRISIS: AUGUST 12, 1945

Just before 1:00 P.M. on August 12, the Allied response to Japan's conditional acceptance of surrender arrived in Tokyo. Prime Minister Kantaro Suzuki's secretary, Hisatsune Sakomizu, read the first draft and made special notice of three points:

> . . . from the moment of surrender the authority of the Emperor and the Japanese Government to rule the state shall be subject to the Supreme Commander of the Allied Powers. . . . The Emperor will be required to authorize and ensure the signature by the Government of Japan and the Japanese Imperial General Headquarters of the surrender terms. . . . The ultimate form of government of Japan shall . . . be established by the freely expressed will of the Japanese people.[1]

Sakomizu was crushed by the severity of the language. He was joined by his friend, Shunichi Matsumoto, who was the aide to Foreign Minister Togo, and the two of them sat down in the predawn darkness to try to fully understand the words.

To the two aides, the American reply was discouraging and inconclusive. It neither promised the emperor's sovereignty nor denied it. They were particularly alarmed by the clause, "The ultimate form of government of Japan shall. . . ." Regardless of their concern, however, the aides saw no recourse other than to force the response through their superiors in its present form.[2]

Sakomizu confronted a sleepy Admiral Suzuki and convinced him that Secretary of State James Byrnes' note was acceptable.

Without bothering to read the draft, the aged prime minister said seriously, "In any case we must end the war."[3] Matsumoto had little trouble with Togo. The frustrated foreign minister realized the pitfalls in the reply but agreed that there were no other options. It had to be forced through for acceptance.

The aides returned to their offices believing that they had stolen a march on the war party. They were wrong. On the same morning, young officers in the war ministry were in the office of Gen. Ushijiro Umezu demanding that he denounce the Allied reply. At naval headquarters, Admiral Soemu Toyoda was confronted by angry naval officers who demanded that he reject the Allied response. Both Umezu and Toyoda were in a difficult situation. Each was bound to support the emperor's desire for peace, and each somehow had to convince his subordinates that surrender was the proper action.

Gen. Korechika Anami had gone to the residence of Premier Suzuki. With him went Baron Hiranuma whose chief worry was the fate of the emperor. Anami and Hiranuma had decided that the Allied terms were unacceptable and that Suzuki could be brought to their side. Suzuki was no match for the arguments of Hiranuma and Anami. He agreed that the terms of the surrender, insofar as the sovereignty of the emperor was concerned, were unacceptable and promised to stand firm in defense of the throne.[4]

Anami then went immediately to meet with Prince Mikasa, the emperor's youngest brother, the so-called Red Prince. Mikasa listened politely to Anami and then turned on him: "Since the Manchurian incident, the Army has not once acted in accordance with the Imperial wish. It is most improper that you should still want to continue the war at this stage."[5] Anami was stunned. Mikasa's words were true and would continue to bother Anami even up to his death.

The fiery young officers of the army and navy forced General Umezu and Admiral Toyoda to go to the palace and ask for a prompt and total rejection of the Allied terms. Emperor Hirohito listened to them, thanked them for their concerns, and dismissed them. Within minutes, the emperor summoned Marquis Koichi Kido to help him analyze the trend developing at military headquarters. His suspicions were well-founded. At noontime, the conspirators had assembled at war minister Anami's office and were waiting when he returned. A shouting match quickly developed between Maj. Kenji Hatanaka, a coup leader, and members of Anami's staff. It was necessary for Anami to intervene and suggest that Hatanaka come to his home later to discuss the issue. Anami had forestalled the plotters momentarily, but he knew he would have to meet with them later and listen to their plans.[6]

Prior to the afternoon cabinet meeting, the emperor met with his advisors and family members to discuss the Allied note. To the amazement of Baron Hiranuma, the privy seal, Marquis Koichi Kido, Prince Mikasa, and others, the emperor had no problems with the terms of the note. He stated that it was all right to leave the form of government to the people. If the people did not want an emperor it would be useless to try to argue for the continuance of one.[7]

The full cabinet met at 3:00 P.M. Following a reading of the unofficial Allied note, Admirals Togo and Yonai spoke for acceptance. Generals Anami and Hiranuma reiterated their fears for the emperor and Anami his demands for additional conditions.

Togo, frustrated by the silence of Suzuki and the same old arguments of the war party, lost his temper. He snapped, "To add issues at this moment would make the Allies wonder at the integrity of the Japanese government and at its sincerity in negotiating at all."[8] He strode from the room and slammed the conference door hard behind him. Togo returned to the meeting just in time to hear Suzuki support the arguments of the war party. Crushed by Suzuki's vacillation and failure to support the wishes of the emperor, Togo proposed that the meeting be adjourned and that the issue be reopened after the official response from the Allies has been received. There was agreement and the meeting was adjourned. Togo was

189

furious. He followed Suzuki to his office and took out his frustration on him. Didn't Suzuki understand that the emperor wanted to accept the Allied response? Togo wanted to know why Suzuki changed his position, and threatened to go to the emperor himself if Suzuki did not support acceptance of the note.[9]

Suzuki, too tired to argue and confused by the issues, did not mention the conversation that he had with Anami and Hiranuma. He offered no defense for his actions. Togo stormed out, seriously considering resignation. He then went to report the turn of events to Marquis Kido who quickly arranged a meeting with Suzuki. About 9:30 P.M., Suzuki visited Marquis Kido at the palace in response to his request. Kido was blunt and to the point. "If we do not accept the Allied position now, we will be sacrificing hundreds of thousands of innocent people to the continued ravages of war. . . . Furthermore, it is his Majesty's wish that we advance on the basis of the views held by his Foreign Minister."[10] Once again, the old admiral changed his position and promised to support Togo's acceptance of the surrender document.

32

THE COUP DEVELOPS

On the evening of August 13, Japan's minister of war, Gen. Korechika Anami, left the cares of state for a brief time to visit with his family and wish them farewell. Still pained by the rebuke of Prince Mikasa and under increasing pressure from the rebellious young officers, Anami had formulated a scenario that did not include him in the future of Japan. He could not go against the emperor's decision to surrender, but neither could he accept it. There would only be one way out for the war minister.

After returning to his official quarters, Anami continued to dwell on his dilemma. About 4:00 in the morning, he sent his adjutant, Maj. Saburo Hayashi, to the home of General Yoshijiro Umezu, army chief of staff, to ask Umezu to help change the emperor's decision to surrender. Umezu realized that if he did not cooperate, the burden of guilt would fall on him. He agonized over the request for a time, then turned to Hiyashi and said, "You must forgive me— I favor acceptance of the Potsdam Declaration."[1]

Hayashi's subsequent report was another shock to Anami. Without Umezu's support, Anami was momentarily stymied. He rested briefly and then went to the palace to seek the assistance of the privy seal. Kido had just sat down to breakfast but received Anami cordially. After some preliminary discussion, Anami asked Kido to "just once more request the emperor to reconsider acceptance of the note."[2] Kido responded that he could not do that and explained that the emperor was comfortable with the Allied conditions. "We must abide by the wishes of his Majesty. We must accept the Allied reply in its present form," continued Kido.[3]

Anami had run out of options. He was well aware that Kido and the other advisors to the emperor were committed to support the decision to surrender, but he was also the leader of the military, and he was not at all certain that he could retain control if the cabinet accepted the terms of the surrender. Anami did not push the issue further. He rose quietly and said goodbye to Kido. Anami had managed to avoid the young officers who were involved in the planning for a coup and hoped to do so for a while longer. Instead of returning to the war ministry where the coup plotters were waiting for him, the general went directly to the 9:00 A.M. meeting of the Big Six.

The cabinet was back to its previous deadlocked position with Prime Minister Suzuki, Foreign Minister Shigenori Togo and Navy Minister Adm. Mitsumasa Yonai favoring acceptance of the Allied surrender terms. Aligned against them remained the war minister, General Anami, the navy chief of staff, Adm. Soemu Toyoda, and the army chief of staff, General Umezu, who wanted better terms or a continuation of the war.

At noon, with the group still hopelessly split, Suzuki adjourned the group for lunch. When they resumed, the same division existed. Once again, Suzuki was unable to get a consensus. He adjourned the meeting with the warning that he would ask the emperor for a decision.[4] Anami asked Suzuki for two more days before he went to see the emperor, but Suzuki was adamant that the cabinet had to act at once.

General Anami knew that when the cabinet met again the emperor would direct an unconditional surrender. His immediate problem was to delay the rebel officers until the acceptance had been formally communicated. Then a coup would serve no purpose. At 8:00 P.M., the rebels arrived at his residence: Lt. Col. Masahiko Takeshita, Lt. Col. Masao Inaba, Maj. Kenji Hatanaka and Lt. Col. Jiro Shiizaki, plus six others.[5] They wanted Anami's approval of their plan for a coup d'etat. Col. Okitsugu Arao, a senior officer from the war ministry, acted as their spokesman and handed Anami a paper containing the outlines of the projected coup. The rebellion was set for 10:00 A.M. on August 14.

The rebels' plan called for a rejection of the Allied proclamation until there was assurance that the emperor system was to be retained. Kido, Suzuki, Togo, and Yonai were to be imprisoned, martial law was to be put into effect, and the palace was to be isolated until it was possible to determine the emperor's true feelings.[6] Arao reported that Lt. Gen. Takeshi Mori, commander of the First Imperial Guards Division, had promised to consider the plan, but that, even if he refused, most of General Mori's regimental commanders had agreed to support the coup.

In addition to General Anami's approval of the plan, his help was needed to gain the support of Gen. Shizuichi Tanaka, commander of the Eastern District Army. This was, perhaps, the most fateful moment of Anami's career. His response could mean life or death for himself, the emperor, and of millions of Japanese. Anami waffled! "The plan is very incomplete," he stated, without saying whether he was for or against the idea of revolt.[7] The rebels begged for an answer, but Anami told Colonel Arao to come to his office at midnight to discuss it further. The rebels finally left confused, which is precisely what Anami wanted.

At midnight, Arao came to Anami's office where Anami told him that he doubted that the coup could succeed but promised to give a final statement for or against the coup in the morning. Arao left more confused than ever, which is exactly what General Anami had intended.

By 2:00 A.M., Anami was in bed for a much-needed rest. Togo had spent several hours in a heated argument with pro-war figures General Umezu and Admiral Toyoda, and with Adm. Takajiro Onishi, who had burst in and demanded that Japan fight to the death of every inhabitant of the nation. Togo rejected his plea, said goodnight to his visitors, and now he slept.

Prime Minister Suzuki would have to visit the emperor in a few hours to request his imperial guidance on the deadlocked issue of surrender terms. At age 80, he could not keep the pace maintained by Anami and others. Now, he, too, slept.

Funerals such as these become common after 1943. Here a soldier's ashes and personal effects are being returned to the family.

Imperial War Museum

194

33

THE EMPEROR'S DECREE: AUGUST 14, 1945

Japan's minister of war, Gen. Korechika Anami, was up early on the morning of August 14. After only three hours sleep, he was having breakfast with Field Marshall Shunroku Hata, who had just arrived from Hiroshima to personally brief Anami on the devastation of the city. Hata described in some detail the effects of the blast, fire, and radiation. Then, almost as an afterthought, he mentioned that the troops and equipment that had been underground survived. Anami focused on this remark and told Hata, "Be sure to tell the Emperor that the bomb is not so deadly."[1]

Following breakfast, Anami went to his headquarters at Ichigaya. It was only 7:00 A.M., but the coup plotters were waiting for him. The young officers were extremely agitated since the coup was scheduled to take place in three hours and they still had no statement of support from General Anami. They demanded to know, did the general support the coup or not?

Anami made a bold move. Without answering the question, he told Col. Okitsugo Arao, spokesman for the plotters, to come with him. The two men walked down the hall to the office of the army chief of staff, Gen. Yoshijiro Umezu. Anami asked Umezu if he would support a coup against the emperor's decision to surrender. "Absolutely not," responded Umezu.[2] Anami looked at Colonel Arao who nodded and went to a telephone to notify the conspirators that they had no support. Arao's job as spokesman for the rebels was over.

Earlier, while Anami was being briefed by General Hata, a single B-29 from Tinian had dropped millions of leaflets over the center of Tokyo. The leaflets, in Japanese, were addressed to the Japanese people.

TO THE JAPANESE PEOPLE

These American planes are not dropping bombs on you today. They are dropping leaflets instead because the Japanese Government has offered to surrender, and every Japanese has a right to know the terms of that offer and the reply made by the United States Government on behalf of itself, the British, the Chinese, and the Russians. Your Government now has a chance to end the war immediately.[3]

In addition, the leaflet also contained the verbatim words of the Japanese conditional acceptance of the surrender proclamation and the Allied response.

Marquis Koichi Kido, lord keeper of the privy seal and confidante of the emperor, was shown one of the leaflets that had been dropped all over Tokyo. Kido needed only a quick reading to comprehend the disaster that the leaflets could create if they were read by the military who had no idea that Japan planned to surrender. If the troops suddenly became knowledgeable, they might revolt.

Kido was able to see the emperor at 8:30 A.M. Hirohito quickly grasped the significance of the danger and directed Kido to take such steps as necessary to end the war. As Kido left the emperor's library, he found Suzuki waiting for him. The prime minister was on his way to ask for the emperor's guidance on the same matter. The two men went to see the emperor together, and from their meeting came a summons for the cabinet ministers to meet with the emperor at 10:30 A.M., in less than 30 minutes. If the deadlock over the surrender terms continued, his majesty would "command" the cabinet to accept the Allied terms.[4]

The call for a meeting with the emperor on such short notice created panic in the various offices of the cabinet members. Clothes were borrowed and minor alterations quickly made by staff members. Trousers were pressed and the necessary papers quickly put together. Normally, a meeting with the emperor was a formal affair, but not this time. A procession of assorted vehicles was quickly arranged and made their way to the palace.

Once again, the cabinet members sat in the hot, humid shelter waiting for the emperor. At 10:55 A.M., the door to the underground conference room opened, and the emperor of Japan entered the room. He was dressed in his army military uniform and moved directly to the front of the room where he sat down on a simple wooden chair behind a small table. His audience, who rose and bowed when he entered, sat down and diverted their gaze from looking directly at the emperor.[5]

In the front two rows were Adm. Mitsumasa Yonai, minister of the navy; Prime Minister Suzuki; Shigenori Togo, minister of foreign affairs; General Umezu, Admiral Soemu Toyoda, and General Anami. Also present were Baron Kiichiro Hiranuma, president of the privy council, and Hisatsune Sakomizu, chief cabinet secretary, who was concerned that Suzuki was unprepared for the meeting and might not be able to guide the conversation so as to avoid the military opposition to the emperor's decision to surrender.[6]

Prime Minister Suzuki arose, faced Hirohito, and apologized for his need of guidance. He then explained the different viewpoints that had brought the cabinet to their current deadlocked situation. When he finished, he turned to the three dissenters, Anami, Toyoda, and Umezu, and asked them to state their positions.[7]

Anami and Umezu, in a highly emotional state, argued for a continuation of the war in order to obtain better surrender terms. Adm. Toyoda made an excellent presentation, but his arguments contained nothing new: "Japan must not be occupied. . . . The Emperor's sovereignty must be maintained. . . . The surrender clause, determined by the free will of the people is most

197

dangerous."[8]

When no one else rose to speak, the emperor began to express his opinion. "My views are unchanged from those expressed at the conference on the ninth," he stated. "I consider the terms of the Allied response to be acceptable." At this point, according to author William Craig, the emperor became quite emotional.[9] He wiped his tear-filled eyes, and then continued: "I appreciate how difficult it will be for the officers and men of the Army and Navy to surrender their arms to the enemy and to see their homeland occupied. . . . In spite of these feelings. . . . I cannot endure the thought of letting my people suffer any longer."[10] The emperor concluded with a request that his ministers accede to his wishes and speedily accept the Allied terms. "Therefore as the Emperor Meiji once endured the unendurable, so must you."[11] Hirohito asked each of the ministers to accept and support his decision.

Suddenly it was done. The emperor had accomplished what his cabinet had been unwilling to do. Everyone in the room knew that the war was over. Men sobbed, and, according to author John Toland, two of the ministers collapsed uncontrollably to the floor.[12] Japan had lost its honor.

Prime Minister Suzuki stepped toward the emperor, bowed, and once again apologized. Hirohito arose and walked back through the door he had entered less than an hour ago. Few actually noticed his departure.

Following the cabinet meeting, General Anami assembled his staff and told them of the emperor's decision. His news created a mixture of emotions. Many members of his staff cried. Some shouted that the war should continue. Several pulled papers from drawers and started to burn them. Anami finally stilled the group by stating that the will of the emperor would be obeyed. "Anyone who disagreed, would have to do so over my dead body!"[13] Nevertheless, certain angry men left the conference vowing that it was not too late for a coup and that they would prove Anami wrong.

It was nearly midnight when the emperor finished the radio recordings of his surrender announcement. The records were taken by the court chamberlain, Yohiro Tokugawa, who secured them in his wall safe for the night.[14] Then, with no worries, the emperor went to bed and slept soundly. The next day the cabinet would sign the documents approving the surrender, and public radio would use his recording to announce the surrender to his loyal subjects.[15]

On Okinawa and Guam, preparations for the invasion of mainland Japan continued. On Tinian, B-29s were being loaded for firebombing missions against two more Japanese cities. The use of a third atomic bomb was put on hold. In China, the Soviet Union continued to overwhelm the feeble Japanese resistance as the Soviets, ahead of their timetable, moved quickly to obtain a share of the spoils.

Chief Cabinet Secretary Sakomizu (in black jacket) announces the emperor's surrender to the press, August 15, 1945.

Asahi Shimbun

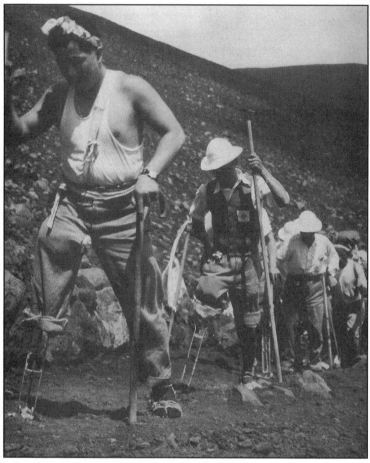

One-legged Japanese war veterans hobble up the lower slope of Mount Fuji to show their respect for the emperor and the greater glory of Japan.

Imperial War Museum

34

COLLAPSE OF THE COUP

About 11:00 P.M. on August 14, while the emperor of Japan was recording the radio announcement of Japan's surrender, Maj. Kenji Hatanaka obtained the assistance of several other young officers for his coup attempt. Lt. Col. Jiro Shiizaki and Maj. Hidemasa Koga, son-in-law of deposed Premier Hideki Tojo, both promised to help. Koga's help was especially important because he served in the Imperial Guards Division which protected the emperor.[1]

The plotters then went to the military affairs section of the ministry of war to secure the assistance of Col. Masataka Ida. Ida was known to be close to the minister of war, Gen. Korechika Anami, whose support would be essential for the coup to succeed. Ida was reluctant to join the plotters. "Eventually, it will be necessary to persuade Gen. Shizuichi Mori, commander of the Imperial Guards, to support you," stated Ida, "and that will be most difficult. What will you do if he refuses?" To Ida's question, Hatanaka replied, "If Mori doesn't agree with us, I'll kill him."[2]

Ida was shocked at the determination of the rebels. He stalled by asking about the position of Gen. Shizuichi Tanaka, commander of the Tokyo area military forces, but Hatanaka dismissed the issue by saying that all of the army would follow the Guards Division. Ida finally relented and agreed to accompany Hatanaka to the palace to see General Mori and gain Mori's support for the coup.

General Anami was both weary and despondent. Following the meeting, wherein the cabinet officially approved the emperor's decision to surrender unconditionally, he spent many hours trying to change the wording of the Imperial Rescript to save face for the army. At issue was the phrase, "the war situation is growing more unfavorable for us every day."[3] During one of the numerous arguments between Anami and the navy minister, Adm. Mitsumasa Yonai, Chief Cabinet Secretary Hisatsune Sakomizu suggested that the phrase could be changed to, "The war situation has developed not necessarily to Japan's advantage." Anami liked it; Yonai did not. Several more hours of debate ensued before Yonai suddenly changed his mind and agreed to accept the change.

Anami hurried home, changed into his best uniform, and went to pay his final respects to Prime Minister Suzuki. Anami asked Suzuki to accept the box of cigars he proffered and then apologized for having made the prime minister's job so difficult during the surrender discussions. Anami went on to say that his primary purpose had always been to preserve the emperor system of government and asked Suzuki to "please believe me."[4] The two gentlemen grasped hands. " I am aware of that," responded Suzuki.[5] Anami bowed and left the prime minister's office.

At his official residence, Anami enjoyed a hot bath and changed into a comfortable kimono. Finally at peace with himself, he settled himself on the tatami and began to write his farewell and apology to the emperor. His servants would enter the room periodically to refill his heated saki pitcher or to pass along a few bits of information.[6]

Hatanaka and Lieutenant Colonel Ida arrived at the headquarters of the Imperial Guards Division about 11:30 P.M. General Mori was inside his office discussing the Hiroshima bombing with his brother-in-law, Lt. Col. Michinori Shiraishi. Ida and Hatanaka, along with fellow conspirators, Lt. Col. Jiro Shiizaki, Maj. Hidemasa Koga, and Maj. Sadakichi Ishiharo, a highly emotional man who wholeheartedly supported the coup, were told to wait.

It was 30 minutes after midnight on the morning of August 15 when General Mori agreed to see them. As they started to enter Mori's office, Hatanaka suddenly remembered something else he had to do and left, telling Ida to go ahead. The fate of the coup might now hinge upon Mori's reaction to Ida's request. Ida came directly to the point and asked for General Mori's support for the coup.[7] Mori began a long monologue on his life, obviously stalling for time. When he ran out of things to say, he announced that he was going to go to the Meiji shrine and ask God's will.

Hatanaka had hurried to the room of Lt. Col. Masahiko Takeshita, another of Anami's subordinates, where he was successful in persuading Takeshita to visit Anami to gain the general's support for the coup. Hatanaka returned to Mori's office about 1:00 A.M., just in time to hear the general say he planned to visit the shrine for guidance.[8] Hatanaka had little interest in God's will at this point. It was nearly 2:00 A.M., and his patience had run out. He pulled his revolver from its holster and fired directly into Mori. Another rebel, Capt. Shigetaro Uehara, reacted almost simultaneously and slashed downward through Mori's left collarbone with his sword. Mori died within seconds. The horror-stricken Shiraishi grappled with the conspirators and was cut down with a sword slash that entered the right side of his neck and continued through to his left ear. He died instantly.[9]

Following the assassination of General Mori, the attackers used Mori's personal seal to forge orders for the guards to isolate the palace and emperor, and to locate and destroy the recording of the radio broadcast scheduled for noon that day.[10] Ida was sent to General Tanaka's office to obtain his support now that the Imperial Guards were cooperating.

Ida's subsequent request for support from Tanaka was answered with a flat, "Absolutely not."[11] Although the rebels now controlled some units of the Imperial Guards, their coup was doomed to failure if they could not gain the support of the army through either Generals Anami or Tanaka. Hatanaka sent Ida on a hurried trip to find Anami. In the meantime, the rebels began to search the palace for the surrender recording.

Ida arrived at the home of General Anami about 4:00 A.M. He found Anami and Lt. Col. Takeshita in the bedroom drinking saki and was immediately aware of what was about to happen. Anami had wrapped a white cloth about his abdomen and put on a white shirt given to him by the emperor. Ida burst into tears and cried, "Let me die with you."[12] Anami gazed at his young protege and told him to live on and save the country. Together, the three men toasted each other for about 30 minutes until Ida realized he must leave. Colonel Takeshita also excused himself to go to the front door to speak to a messenger.

Inside, Anami moved quickly. There had been too many people for too long. His action needed privacy. He walked out to the corridor, knelt down, and with a short, single movement, plunged his knife into his stomach, cut from left to right, and then sharply upward. Takeshita found him a few moments later. The general was still conscious and in terrible pain. Despite his own pain and loss of blood, Anami was able to plunge his dagger into his neck just below the right ear in an effort to end his life. He remained kneeling in a spreading pool of blood.[13]

Elsewhere in Tokyo, small groups of disorganized soldiers, loosely supportive of Hatanaka's coup plans, roamed the streets and struck out at officials of the government in haphazard fashion. Attempts were made to assassinate Suzuki, Baron Hiranuma, and Marquis Kido.[14]

The rebels' primary target was Prime Minister Suzuki, considered to be the man most responsible for the surrender. Warned, Suzuki escaped with his wife and spent the remainder of the night riding in a chauffeured automobile through the back streets of Tokyo.[15] The rebels also narrowly missed Baron Hiranuma, who watched from hiding while the would-be assassins burned his home down.

By 5:00 A.M., Hatanaka's authority had collapsed. The Japanese surrender acceptance was on the way to neutral Switzerland. General

Anami lay on the floor of his bedroom, still conscious and bleeding to death. General Mori and Colonel Shiraishi were dead. The emperor slept on, never having been disturbed by the frantic searching for the surrender broadcast or the violence. Hatanaka wiped tears from his eyes and started to walk away. "We've done everything we could, let's go,"[16] he told his cohorts.

At 7:00 A.M., Gen. Shizuichi Tanaka reported to the emperor that the rebellion was over. Hatanaka, Shiizaki, and Koga eluded arrest, and General Tanaka did not have them pursued, assuming that they would commit suicide.

At the war minister's home, little had changed. General Anami was unconscious but still alive. Shortly thereafter, a Colonel Kobayashi from the staff of Gen. Hajime Sugiyama, commander of Japan's First General Army, came to visit Anami. Sickened at the prolonged struggle, Kobayashi ordered a physician to put Anami's struggle to an end. Under Anami's body was found the bloodstained paper which he had composed earlier. The paper read, "Believing firmly that our sacred land shall never perish, I . . . with my death . . . humbly apologize to the Emperor for the great crime."[17] Anami's death by ritual suicide served as an inspiration for the army, and saved face for the entire military. Now, the defeated military could face the enemy with self respect.

Throughout the morning, radios informed the citizens that a most important radio message would be broadcast at noon. Rumors circulated that the emperor, for the first time in history, would speak to his subjects.

Prime Minister Winston Churchill of Great Britain, President Franklin Roosevelt of the United States, and Secretary General of the Soviet Communist Party Joseph Stalin of the USSR. The Allied leaders met at Yalta in the Crimea from Feb. 4-11, 1945, the final great wartime summit conference.

A. Gross

206

35

THE EMPEROR SPEAKS

At exactly noon on August 15, Chokugen Wada, a Japan Broadcasting Corporation (NHK) radio announcer, spoke these words: "This will be a broadcast of the gravest importance. Will all listeners please rise. His Majesty the Emperor will now read his imperial rescript to the people of Japan."[1]

Japanese subjects listen to the emperor's announcement of surrender on August 15, 1945.

Mainichi

Kimigayo, the Japanese national anthem was then played as all traffic in Japan came to a halt. Perhaps everyone in Japan except the emperor was standing. Most people bowed their heads in total silence. "To our good and loyal subjects," the emperor began. "After pondering deeply the general trends of the world, and the actual conditions obtaining in the Empire today, we have decided to effect a settlement of the present situation by resorting to an extraordinary measure." The years and the situation had not necessarily developed to Japan's advantage, and since the enemy had developed a new and cruel bomb, "This is the reason we have ordered the acceptance of the provisions of the Joint Declaration of the Allied Powers."

The emperor's voice was high-pitched and quavered. His imperial language was foreign to most of the people, and the reception quality was generally poor. As a result, few listeners understood exactly what was being said, but everyone understood that Japan had been defeated. Saving face was never more important than in the hour of defeat. Although the emperor never used the term surrender, the people understood full well what had occurred, and the shock was felt throughout Japan. For the first time in 2,600 years, the Japanese would bow to a conqueror.[2]

Even after the emperor's announcement, surrender did not come easily. Hirohito had to send members of the Imperial family to the major military commands to ensure that his rescript was followed. At the Atsugi airfield near Tokyo, kamikaze pilots were boasting that they would sink *Missouri* when the battleship entered Tokyo Bay. Navy Capt. Yasuna Kozono told members of his air group at Atsugi Air Base, that surrender would be treason.[3] Hirohito's younger brother, Prince Takamatsu, had to be sent to Atsugi to enforce the rescript. Just to be certain that the airmen obeyed orders, the propellers were removed from the aircraft.[4] At Oita Air Base on northern Honshu, the final kamikaze mission against naval forces off Okinawa was flown by 11 torpedo bombers led by Adm. Matome Ugaki. The flight departed in late afternoon, well after the emperor's announcement.[5]

Over 3,000,000 Japanese forces were scattered throughout the Pacific at the time of Japan's surrender. Their reaction ran the gamut of emotions. At Osaka, where the Japanese had been killing captured

American airmen for some time, the last five captives were taken to a cemetery where three were shot and the remaining two beheaded.[6] In Fukuoka, 16 captured airmen were trucked to a field in Aburayama, where eight of their comrades had been beheaded four days earlier. The airmen were stripped and executed in various ways while the supervisor and his girlfriend watched.[7] On Celebes, two Australian airmen were strangled, and on Borneo, the last 30 Allied prisoners were massacred.[8]

In Manchuria, at the infamous Unit 731 laboratory, 600 Chinese laborers were machine-gunned to death, and all surviving human experimental patients were gassed.[9] On Okinawa, where individuals and small bands of guerrillas continued to fight, there was relief in the knowledge that they could stop fighting. In Manchuria, some members of the military changed to civilian clothing and tried to mingle with the populace to escape the retribution of the Chinese and Russians. On mainland Japan, millions wept and sought privacy in their homes or whatever shelter they could find. Despite the humiliation of defeat and the concern for not having done enough, the people were relieved that the war was over and seemed content to just wait for the enemy to arrive.

Hundreds of subjects gathered in front of the Imperial Palace to pray and offer allegiance to the Divine Ruler. In the crowd were military officers who had come to commit suicide. A shot would be heard followed by the sound of a falling body. There was no panic as people walked around the dying men and went about their business.[10]

A total of 526 suicides were reported in the Tokyo area during the first week after the surrender.[11] The suicides included Prince Fumimaro Kanoye, the pre-war prime minister, who poisoned himself; General Sugiyama, the former war minister, who shot himself, and Mrs. Sugiyama, who took poison and fell on a small dagger; Gen. Korechika Anami, the current minister of war, who committed ritual *seppuku*; Adm. Takijiro Onishi, father of the kamikazes, also a *seppuku* victim; Col. Tomomi Oyadomari, from the ministry of war; Mrs. Oyadomari and their two children, dead from poisoning; plus the coup leaders, Maj. Kenji Hatanaka, who killed himself with the same pistol that he used to kill General Mori; Lt. Col. Jiro Shiizaki, who used both a sword and a pistol to kill himself; Maj. Hidemasa Koga, who committed *seppuku* beside the coffin of General Mori; and Capt. Shigetaro Uehara.[12] Gen. Hideki Tojo, prime minister at the time of the Pearl Harbor attack, attempted suicide by a pistol bullet to the heart but survived and was tried as a war criminal.

Following the emperor's announcement, Prime Minister Suzuki resigned his cabinet. The admiral had done what the emperor asked him to do. He saved the Japanese people from possible annihilation, and, as a result, was branded a traitor by the military. Wanting only to live out the remainder of his life in peace, Suzuki and his wife were followed by military fanatics wherever they went. After several months of Allied occupation, the young Army officers lost interest, and the Suzukis survived.[13]

Allied prisoners near *Yokosuka*, Japan, welcome U.S. military rescuers.

US Coast Guard

210

36

ALLIED PRISONERS IN CHINA

During the period of August 11-14, 1945, as the cabinet of Japan wrestled with the issue of surrender, Gen. Albert Wedemeyer, who had relieved General Stilwell as Chiang Kai-shek's chief of staff, was wrestling with a staggering assignment of his own: how to reach and save allied prisoners in several POW camps in the event of a Japanese surrender. Chinese divisions would not be able to reach them. Tanks could not get there in time, since some of the camps were in Manchuria, thousands of miles from Chungking. The Russians could probably reach them first, but could they be trusted? Wedemeyer asked for opinions from his staff, and Col. Arthur Dobson suggested sending in special teams by parachute. Once on the ground, the teams would demand access to the prisoners on the basis of the Japanese surrender.[1]

Dobson's idea was adopted as having the best chance of success. Gen. George Olmstead, Wedemeyer's assistant, was given overall responsibility for the project, and organization of the teams was passed to Col. Richard Heppner in Kunming. Heppner and his staff, including Col. Ray Peers, began identifying personnel for the teams that would jump into Manchuria, Korea, and Hainan.[2]

The Office of Strategic Services (OSS) had more than 70,000 men in China at this time. The men were specialists in many different occupational fields and came from all branches of the military services. The prisoner-rescue project would be their most difficult assignment.

On August 12, Maj. Jim Kellis infiltrated his team into an apartment in Peking. The apartment was located next to the building that housed a section of the Japanese general staff in North China.[3] The following day, the OSS teams were notified of the "Peace Warning" and Colonel Ray Peers in Kunming was tasked to move his team to Hsian.

On August 16, immediately following the emperor's surrender announcement, Major Kellis visited General Takahashi at the Japanese headquarters in Peking to inform him that he had come to effect the prompt release of all Allied prisoners in the area. Takahashi agreed to cooperate completely.

As Major Kellis and General Takahashi discussed plans for the prisoner release, a single American B-24 was en route to the Hoten prison camp at Mukden, Manchuria. The camp housed more than 1,700 men who had managed to survive, some for the entire war.[4]

Only six parachutes spilled into the sky over the Hoten camp. Maj. James Hennesy led the OSS rescue team that included Maj. Robert Lamar, a combat doctor; Sgts. Ed Starz and Harold Leith; Maj. Cheng Shi-Wu, a Chinese guide; and Fumio Kido, a nisei interpreter.[5]

Once on the ground, Hennesy and his men started immediately for the Hoten camp. They were shortly intercepted by a company of Japanese troops who ordered them to stop and kneel down. The Japanese moved in among the kneeling group and made menacing gestures with their bayoneted rifles.[6]

Kido translated the news of the surrender to the Japanese who sneered at the idea. Hennesy guessed correctly that the Japanese did not know that the war was over. So much for General Takahasi's complete cooperation. Starz, Cheng, and Lamar were forced to strip and kneel down. One of the Japanese pulled his sword from its scabbard, causing Starz to tense for what was about to come. Lamar tried to protest and was smashed in the mouth. All communication amoung the team members was prohibited.[7]

Lamar was finally able to produce a paper signed by General Wedemeyer which stated that the team members were an advanced unit bringing relief to the Allied prisoners. The Japanese thought the note was very funny but refused to consider that the war might be over. Shortly, a Japanese officer approached on horseback and spoke to the guards. A subtle change took place. A few minutes later, another officer arrived and apologized to the OSS team. News of the surrender had just reached Mukden. Still, the Japanese were cautious. Starz, Lamar, and Cheng were blindfolded and guided to a truck. Hennessy, Leith, and Kido were allowed to join them after a short while. They were driven to the local military police headquarters but refused access to Hoten.[8]

After an hour of arguing, the Americans were taken to the main prison camp, but once there, Colonel Matsudo, commandant of the prison, denied the team access to the prisoners. Hennessy protested vigorously to no avail, so the team agreed to be taken to a hotel in town for the night while Matsudo contacted his superiors for instructions. What those instructions might be weighed heavily on the minds of the team members.[9]

On August 17, after a surprisingly pleasant night at the Yamata hotel in Mukden, the OSS team was driven to the Hoten POW camp and allowed to meet the Allied prisoners. The team left the hotel without Maj. Cheng Shi-Wu, who deserted due to his fear of the Japanese. It was a joyous reunion. The prisoners had hundreds of questions. One bit of upsetting news for the team was that Gen. Jonathan Wainwright, hero of Corregidor, was not at the camp. They learned that he was kept at Mukden Camp Two, at Sian, 100 miles to the northeast.[10]

In the midst of the excitement associated with the unexpected liberation of the prisoners, a chauffeured Japanese staff car drove up to the main gate. From the car stepped Capt. Roger Hilsman, an American soldier from Burma. Hilsman had hitched a ride to Kunming. From there he caught a flight to Hsian and then a ride to Mukden. Arriving at Mukden, he asked a Japanese general for a ride to Hoten. The general willingly provided his staff car.[11]

Hilsman received instructions from the guard at the gate, ran to the designated barracks, flew up the stairs to the second floor, and scanned the rows of beds. A middle-aged man sat on one of the beds. He had been captured in the Philippines in 1942 and had last been reported to be at Mukden. "My God, My God," Colonel Hilsman, the father murmured. Capt. Roger Hilsman's long search for his father had ended.[12]

So far all of the OSS units dropped behind enemy lines had been successful in their mission to free the Allied prisoners. At Weischen, China, team members found their greatest obstacle to be the female civilian internees. Their affection at the sight of the healthy Americans was almost more than their liberators could handle.[13] Prisoners would also be liberated in Peking and Sian China, Hainan, and Keijo, Korea.

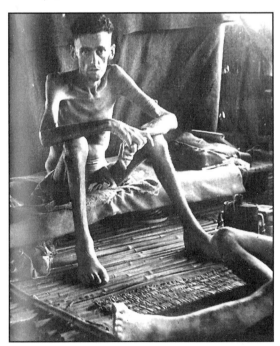

A liberated British POW in a Japanese hospital camp in Thailand.

Imperial War Museum, London

37

THE DOOLITTLE POWs

Early on the morning of April 18, 1942, 16 B-25 bombers launched from the pitching deck of the U. S. carrier *Hornet*. The aircrews flew 650 miles across the ocean to attack Tokyo and surrounding cities, and then flew low-level for another 1,200 miles across the China Sea toward Kiangsi province in China. When their fuel was exhausted, 15 of the B-25 crews either bailed out or crash-landed at sea.

The fact that only eight of the 80 airmen involved were captured by the Japanese is a miracle. Under perfect launch conditions, clear weather enroute, and complete cooperation from allied China, the Doolittle Raid would have been a long-odds gamble for the crews. Instead, the B-25s were forced to launch 150 miles further from Tokyo than planned due to early discovery of the *Hornet* Task Force by Japanese picket ships. The greater distance lessened the chances of reaching the few airfields in China still under control of Chiang Kai-shek's forces.

Weather enroute to Tokyo was clear, but became a low ceiling with rain and a headwind as darkness approached and fuel ran out. There were no radio beacons to guide the B-25s to the airfields since the U. S. military did not trust the Chinese to keep the raid a secret. Consequently, Chiang Kai shek was not told that the bombers were coming.

Each B-25 flew to Tokyo and on to China independently. Now, as their engines quit due to fuel starvation, each crew made a decision to bail-out or crash-land. Ten of the crews, including the crew of lead pilot, Jimmy Doolittle, bailed out. Only one of those who parachuted suffered serious injury, Cpl. Leland Faktor's body was found on the ground with an unopened parachute.[1] Four crews decided to crash-land, three ditched in the ocean, and one landed in a rice paddy. The crew of one B-25, realizing that they could not make the designated airfields in China, diverted to an airfield near Vladivostok, Soviet Union. The plane was promptly confiscated and the crew imprisoned for 13 months until they managed to escape to Iran.

Japanese reaction to the bombing was immediate. Fifty-three Japanese army battalions were ordered into Kiangsi and Chekiang provinces to search for the American flyers and to "scorch the earth." Chinese were murdered in every conceivable way. Homes were destroyed, usually by burning, inhabitants included. Wells were fouled with human carcasses, graves and ancestor tablets were desecrated and destroyed. Anyone even suspected of assisting the American airmen died a horrible death.

As part of their retribution, the airfields at Chuchow, Lishui, and Yushan, the hoped-for destination of the raiders, were so destroyed that Gen. Claire L. Chennault, leader of the Flying Tigers," later stated that ". . . it was easier to build new airfields than to restore the damage."[2]

The Japanese took three bloody months to teach the Chinese the consequences of befriending Americans. In the process, they captured eight of the Doolittle Raiders and massacred 225,000 Chinese. The captured airmen were from two separate B-25s. The aircraft piloted by Lt. Dean Hallmark bombed a steel mill in Tokyo, flew low-level towards China, and approached the coast at dusk, some 60 miles north of Wenchow. When the engines quit, the aircraft was still several miles from shore. The crew voted to ditch the aircraft in the ocean.

Sgt. William J. Dieter (bombardier) and Sgt. Donald E. Fitzmaurice (engineer-gunner) were seriously injured during the ditching and became separated from the rest of the crew in the darkness and confusion caused by 15-foot waves which swept the men off the wing of the aircraft.

Lt. Chase J. Nielson (navigator) swam and floated for three hours and finally reached the rocky shore. As he moved inland, he accidently fell into a crevasse and lay unconscious until morning. With the first rays of daylight, he was able to climb from the crevasse and reach a tree line where he could observe the happenings on the beach. Shortly thereafter, he was captured by a Chinese soldier. After some questioning in pidgin English, Nielson was led by his captor to see the chief.

They hiked for more than an hour before coming to a humble wooden building distinguished from several others by a Chinese nationalist flag flying from a tall pine pole. The senior Chinese official informed Nielson that two of his crew (Dieter and Fitzmaurice) were found dead on the beach and would be given a soldier's burial. As Nielson was eating some boiled eggs, rice, seaweed soup, and some foul-smelling fish, a messenger brought news that another crewmember had been found by the Chinese and that the Chinese "guerrillas" would take them both to "free" China.

That afternoon Nielson was led over a rough trail to a shanty where he was reunited with Lieutenant Hallmark. Jim Hallmark's knee was badly cut and he had bruises over most of his body, but he pronounced himself ready to travel. The two airmen were led to a compound where they were joined by Lt. John Meader (co-pilot). Meader explained how he had found and pulled the unconscious Fitzmaurice to shore where he subsequently died, and how he found Dieter's body in the surf and pulled him to shore.

The following morning, the Americans were taken by sampan to the walled city of Wenchow. Whether they were betrayed to the Japanese by their guides or simply discovered by one of the Japanese search parties is not clear. The airmen were tied and dragged to a

Japanese headquarters building where they were handcuffed, told they would be shot if they did not answer the questions, and were then questioned separately. Later in the day, the men were flown to Shanghai and put into separate cells. Shortly after midnight, the questioning began. By now the Japanese had learned that the airmen were the ones that had bombed Tokyo, that Doolittle had led the raid, and were quite certain that the planes had come from the carrier *Hornet*.

Lt. William Farrow's aircraft was the last B-25 to takeoff from *Hornet*. The crew dropped their bombs on an aircraft factory and oil storage area in Nagoya and then flew at 500 feet across the China Sea. Approaching the coast of China, they climbed to 11,000 feet, tried without success to contact the airfield to obtain navigation assistance, and then bailed out when their fuel-warning lights came on. The entire crew landed safely near Nanching, China, which was controlled by the Japanese.

By the following afternoon, all five crewmembers were captured. Interrogation of Farrow, Lt. George Barr (navigator), Cpl. Jacob DeShazer (bombardier), Sgt. Harold A. Spatz (engineer-gunner), and Lt. Robert L. Hite (co-pilot), began immediately.

The initial questions were routine but quickly turned to specifics about *Hornet*. "How long was the flight deck? How many bombs had they carried? How many aircraft were on the raid?"[3]

The prisoners were not allowed to sleep, and, if they did fall asleep, were kicked and jabbed to keep them awake. Their will to resist weakened from fatigue and hunger. They were kicked in the groin and shins, their faces were smashed, and, when sufficiently softened up, were subject to the *Kempei Tai* (secret police) water, knee spread, and finger methods of torture. In time, the Japanese got the answers they wanted.

Next morning, the five airmen were blindfolded and flown to Tokyo where they were treated to even more highly skilled torture methods of the secret police. The questioning went on continuously for several days.

While Farrow's crew was being tortured in Tokyo, Hallmark, Meader, and Nielson were receiving similar treatment in Shanghai. After all the barbaric torture methods had been used on him, including the medieval "human stretcher" device, Chase Nielson still refused to answer the questions of his captors. He was blindfolded, taken outside, and turned to face a firing squad. The command was given to the firing unit to raise rifles. Nielson, weak from starvation, beatings, and torture was kept in the standing position waiting for the volley that would end his life. Finally, an interpreter announced to Nielson that he would be executed at sunrise, unless he decided to answer the questions in the meantime.

Nielson was taken to his cell and hung from a peg in the wall. The guards were careful to ensure that his feet did not touch the floor, so that his entire weight was supported by his arms, wrists, and handcuffs, which were attached to the peg. Mercifully, Nielson passed out after a few hours.

Next morning, Nielson, Hallmark, and Meader were blindfolded and flown to Tokyo. To this point, the two aircrews were not aware that they were in the same prison or that other Raiders had survived. They were kept there until June, when they were forced to sign confessions that they could not understand. Once they signed the confessions, the interrogations and torture stopped, and the prisoners were able to see the other crewmembers for a brief period each morning as they were taken from their cells. All eight men were taken to a train and, under heavy guard, were moved to Nagasaki. From Nagasaki, they were moved by ship back to Shanghai, arriving there on June 19.

Talking among the prisoners was prohibited, but the crewmembers were able to devise a code which allowed them to communicate in a limited way. In this manner they learned of the death of other crewmembers, the events of their capture, and compared interrogation and torture methods.

Japanese legal experts had not been able to establish a precedent, under law, whereby the Doolittle Raiders could be charged as war criminals. Therefore, they decided to enact such a law, and make it retroactive. On July 28, 1942, Heitaro Kimura, vice-minister of war, dispatched Secret Order No. 2190 to Tokyo. The order said that, "An enemy warplane crew who did not violate wartime international law, shall be treated as prisoners of war."[4] Aircrews that acted against the law, shall be punished as wartime capital criminals. Airmen who bombed other-than-military targets or killed other-than-military personnel were in violation of the law. The signed confessions of the airmen admitted such crimes.

General Seibu Tanabe, assistant chief of staff of the Grand Imperial Headquarters, quickly sent the order to General Sunao Ushiromiya, chief of staff of the Kwantung Army in China. General Tanabe included a memo which directed Ushiromiya to schedule the trial and execution of the American airmen.

On August 28, the men were moved by truck to the Kiangwan military prison where they were tried as war criminals. The record of trial indicates that the airmen were found guilty as charged and sentenced to death. The airmen knew nothing of the findings or the sentence. Since their capture, the men had not been out of their cells. They were not permitted to wash, shave, or take off their clothes, which were infested with lice and bedbugs. They all lost at least 25 percent of their body weight. Hallmark, who weighed 200 pounds when he was captured, was down to 140 pounds at most.[5]

Following the trial, conditions gradually began to improve. The men were able to bribe certain guards with paper money that was exchanged on the black market. When they were captured, the prisoners' watches, rings, and wallets were confiscated, but they were allowed to keep their small amounts of paper money. After 120 days of captivity, they used this money in exchange for a bath, haircut, and clean clothes. The few dollars greatly improved their morale.

On the afternoon of October 13, Hallmark, Farrow, and Spatz were informed that they had been sentenced to death and would be executed the next day. Just after 4:00 P.M., on the 14th, the three Americans were handcuffed, put into trucks with heavily armed guards, and taken to Kiangwan Public Cemetery number one. Three short wooden crosses were placed into the ground and the men were forced to kneel while they were tied to the front of the crosses. They now faced the firing squad.

The firing squad consisted of nine members, three of which were posted as security. The remaining six members were divided into two ranks facing the prisoners. The rear rank would be used if the front rank did not kill the three prisoners. On the command of 1st Lt. Goro Tashida, the first rank raised their bolt-action rifles. On Goro's next command, a bullet was fired into the forehead of each of the airmen. Their heads snapped back from the impact of the bullets, and then fell forward, blood gushing through the blindfolds. Death was instantaneous. There was no need for the second rank of the firing squad.

The bodies were placed in three coffins and taken to the Japanese Residents Association Crematorium where they were reduced to ashes. The ashes were placed in small boxes and taken to the International Funeral Home in downtown Shanghai.[6]

Barr, DeShazer, Hite, Meader, and Nielson were not aware that their friends had been executed. Each were in solitary confinement until the following morning when they were marched together into a room and told that they had been found guilty and were sentenced to death. After the sentence had been interpreted, the interpreter added, ". . . through the graciousness of His Majesty, the Emperor, your sentences are hereby commuted to life imprisonment . . . with special treatment.[7]

The remaining prisoners were kept in solitary confinement for

23-and-one-half hours per day, leaving their cells for 30 minutes to wash each morning (special treatment). On April 17, 1943, they were blindfolded, handcuffed, tied with ropes, and loaded aboard a plane with three guards assigned to each prisoner. Their unknown destination proved to be Nanking.

The prison at Nanking was a substantial improvement. The individual cells were larger. There was some furniture, and food was a bit more plentiful. The onset of winter, however, contributed to a number of serious diseases. Bob Meader developed severe dysentery which caused even more weight loss. In November, his legs began to swell, the first outward signs of beri-beri, and an obvious prelude to death without medical care. On December 1, 1943, Meader, who was a strong and healthy track star in school, died. He became the seventh member of Doolittle's volunteer mission to give his life for participating in the raid.

Medical 1st Lt. Soshi Yasuharu certified that Lt. Robert J. Meader died of heart failure. Meader's body was cremated, and the ashes brought back to the prison.

During 1944, the four surviving crewmen learned that there were other Americans in the prison, including navy Cdr. W. S. Cunningham, commander of the forces on Wake Island when the garrison surrendered. A Morse code system of communication was developed so that the men could talk to one another around and through the thick walls.

Bob Hite developed a high fever during the hot summer of 1944 and lay near death in his cell. Suddenly, the Japanese, who knew full well that the war was going against them, began to realize that they might be held accountable for the treatment of the Americans. A medical assistant was moved to the prison and gave Hite sponge baths, shots, and extra food. For the first time since their capture, one of the prisoners was actually receiving medicine and medical care. As a result, Hite recovered before the winter season.

Heavier clothes were issued to the men after the first snow-fall. On Christmas day, the men witnessed the first American aircraft bombing of Nanking. It was the best Christmas present they could have received. On June 15, the prisoners were handcuffed, blindfolded, and loaded aboard a train. Each prisoner was tied to an armed guard. After travelling for three days, they arrived in Peking, their final destination.

Their treatment in the prison at Peking was much worse than at Nanking. They were forced to sit on a tiny stool, in solitary confinement, facing the wall, which was three feet away.[8] They were allowed out of their cells for only five minutes a day to wash, and the guards accompanied orders with slaps and kicks. The quantity and quality of their food declined appreciably so that little nutrition was received.

On August 20, 1945, the door to DeShazer's cell was opened by a prison guard who announced, "War over, you go home now." The scene was repeated in many cells throughout the prison, including the cells of Nielson and Hite. George Barr was too sick to leave the prison on his own power and was carried to the hotel that functioned as a temporary hospital. DeShazer, Nielson, and Hite left Peking the following day and arrived in Washington, D. C., on September 5.

As result of the Raiders' testimony, Lt. Gen. Shigeru Sawada; Capt. Ryuhei Okada, a member of the court that tried the Americans; Lt. Yusei Wako, the prosecutor; and Capt. Sotojiro Tatsuta, the warden at Kiangwan prison and executioner of Hallmark, Farrow, and Spatz, were brought to trial. Others who would have been tried had either died or were being held in Tokyo by the War Crimes Commission for trial on more serious charges.[9]

The trial of the four Japanese began on the morning of March 18, 1946, after two postponements by the defense counsels to allow more time to prepare. There was no comparison between the trial of the Americans and the Japanese. The Japanese were provided all the time they wanted to prepare their defense. They were assigned a qualified American defense counsel and three Japanese attorneys if they so desired. All testimony was interpreted at the time it was given, and all essential safeguards for the rights of the prisoners were observed. Only Chase Nielson felt strong enough to return and testify at the trial. He did so for two full days. The court adjourned on April 12, and pronounced the verdict two days later.

Sawada, Okada, and Tatsuta were found guilty and sentenced to five years at hard labor. Wako, the lawyer, received a nine-year sentence. General Albert C. Wedemeyer, the reviewing authority, disagreed with the light sentences but lacked authority to increase them. The prisoners were transferred to Sugamo Prison in Tokyo where all, except Yusei Wako, were released on January 9, 1950 (four years and three months). Following the Shanghai trial, Wako was tried on other charges and received an additional sentence of life imprisonment at hard labor. He was released in December, 1958, after 13 years in prison.

George Barr, who was too ill to return to the states with his fellow crewmen following their release from prison, became a prisoner of medical bureaucracy. Still suffering from flashbacks of his beatings and torture, and weak from his years of starvation, Barr alternated between reality and supposition. He was moved from one hospital to another, sometimes in a strait jacket, and always with people he did not know. He finally reached San Francisco on October 12, and, only after being visited by General Jimmy Doolittle, did he respond to psychiatric treatment. Barr married on December 14, 1946, retired for physical disability as a captain in 1947, and completed his bachelors and masters degrees.

Finally, in 1965, at the Tokyo Raider reunion in Dayton, Ohio, Gen. Jimmy Doolittle presented George Barr with the purple heart for wounds received at the hands of the Japanese. The medal Barr earned in 1942, had taken a long time to come home.

224

38

THE SIAN PRISON CAMP

In the early morning light of August 16, 1945, a military truck drove slowly through the deserted streets of Tokyo. The truck bounced over the rough road and jostled a pine box lying in the rear. Inside the box lay the body of warrior Takajiro Onishi, architect of the air attack on Pearl Harbor and the founder of the kamikazes.[1] In the last hours of the war, Admiral Onishi had tried desperately to avert surrender. His attempts were rebuffed by contempt and ill-concealed hatred by those whom he had scorned for so long. Onishi had retreated to his official residence and committed hara-kiri. Refusing all help, he had lain on the bloody floor for nearly 18 hours. Now his body was on the way to the crematorium.[2]

At the Sian POW camp, 100 miles north of Mukden, China, Gen. Jonathan Wainwright and 35 other prisoners had survived. Many were senior officers and civilian officials such as the former governor-general of Singapore, Sir Shelton-Thomas; British Gen. Arthur Percival, who surrendered Singapore to Gen. Tomoyuki Yamashita; governor-general of the Dutch East Indies, Tjarda V.S. Stachouwer; governor of Hong Kong, Sir Mark Young; and governor of Sumatra, A.I. Spits.

The prisoners had been forced to work in the gardens and to herd goats. If the goats were not precisely where the Japanese wanted them, the high-ranking goat herders were beaten. General Wainwright had been moved to this remote Manchurian area from Formosa the previous fall to keep him from the Allies as long as possible. Many of the prisoners had died as the result of the cruel and vicious treatment of their captors.[3]

The worst treatment had always come from the lower-ranking Japanese guards. The beatings and the hours of standing at attention in the freezing cold wore down the captives' morale. Perhaps worse than the physical torture was the mental frustration of seeing an infrequent shipment of Red Cross food packages arrive at the camp, only to learn that the boxes were always somehow lost in the system, never to be distributed to the prisoners.[4]

During Wainwright's three years of captivity in Formosa and Manchuria, he had kept his mind active by reading what books he could and playing solitaire. Besides the forced labor, much of his energy was expended in staying alive during the unbelievably cold Manchurian winters when the temperature would drop to 45 degrees below zero. The entire time of his captivity he worried that America might blame him for his surrender of Corregidor on May 6, 1942, and the horrible events of the Bataan Death March. Day in and day out, the monotonous, barren existence, lack of food, and cruel treatment took a toll of all the prisoners.[5]

After 1,200 days in captivity, Allied POW Cpl. James Willard approached General Wainwright and said, "I congratulate you General." "Really, for what?" asked Wainwright.[6] Willard explained that he had heard from a Japanese interpreter that the Russians had invaded Manchuria and the war was over. Dazed, Wainwright asked if the Japanese was drunk or sober. "Well," Willard answered, "he'd had some sake."[7] Although not convinced, Wainwright would not sleep that night.

Maj. Robert Lamar and Sgt. Harold Leith, from the OSS team that had parachuted into the Hoten prison camp at Mukden on August 17, arrived at the gates of Sian on August 19. When they demanded to see the prisoners, the commandant, Lieutenant Marui, refused. After a prolonged argument, Marui sent for General Wainwright. When the emaciated general arrived a few minutes later, he did not enter the room but stared at Lamar and whispered, "Are you Americans?"[8] Lamar assured Wainwright that he was an American and identified himself.

226

Wainwright waited until Marui signalled him to enter and then bowed from the waist to his captor. Major Lamar jumped quickly to his feet and offered a chair to the general. Marui objected shouting "No," and insisted that Wainwright must stand. Another argument began which Lamar also won. General Wainwright took his seat.[9]

Lamar informed Wainwright that he was no longer a prisoner and was going back to the states. Wainwright considered the news for a long moment and then asked the question that had been foremost on his mind for his entire captivity, "What do the people in the states think of me?"[10] As author William Craig reports, Wainwright's eyes bore into Lamar's as the major responded that Wainwright was a hero in the states, his picture even appearing in *Time* magazine.[11]

There was no transportation for the prisoners at Sian, and Major Lamar was unable to contact Maj. James Hennessy at Mukden to request assistance. Lamar was concerned that this special group of prisoners might be used by the Japanese or invading Russian forces as hostages and wanted to move them as quickly as possible. After a short conference, Lamar made the decision to go to Mukden to make the necessary transportation arrangements for the prisoners.[12]

After Lamar left for Mukden, four days went by without the vehicles arriving or any information from Lamar. The prisoners were beginning to worry, but, at least, they had the freedom of the camp.

The arrival of the Soviets at Sian on August 24 lacked the suspense of the American parachute drop. The Russians simply drove a tank through the prison wall and gave the Japanese five minutes to surrender all weapons and start cooking food.[13] A huge, black-bearded lieutenant colonel, with a squad of 30 burly and vigorous Russians, discussed the situation of the prisoners with Sgt. Harold Leith. The Russian then announced that he was leaving for Mukden within the hour. If the prisoners could furnish their own transportation, he would take them with him. Wainwright turned to Marui, his former captor, and asked that busses be provided for the prisoners. Marui, his demeanor much changed by the arrival of the Russian troops cradling machine guns, quickly answered, "Yes sir."[14] Wainwright enjoyed the reply. It was the first time in his captivity that any Japanese had shown him that courtesy.

The Russo-Allied convoy promptly got lost and spent three days in vehicles and several trains to travel the 100 miles to Mukden. Major Lamar was at the railroad station to meet the prisoners when they arrived and informed Wainwright that he would fly to Chungking in the morning and was invited to attend the surrender ceremony on the *Missouri*. General MacArthur had requested his presence. With that news, Wainwright seemed to move from the past memories of Corregidor into the postwar era.[15]

Gen. Jonathan Wainwright on his way home after three years in captivity. Maj. Gus Krause welcomes him to Hsian, China.

US Army

228

39

ALLIED PRISONERS IN HAINAN

On August 27, in the darkness of predawn Kunming, China, another of the OSS teams formed to rescue allied prisoners boarded a C-47 transport plane and headed for the Japanese-held island of Hainan, off the coast of South China.

There was reason to believe that the Japanese military forces on Hainan, cut off from normal communications with their headquarters, might not be aware of Japan's surrender. However, it was known that there were Allied prisoners on Hainan, and the American relief team was intent on bringing them out.

The leader of this team was Capt. John Singlaub.[1] Other members were 1Lt. Charles Walker, the intelligence officer; 1Lt. John Bradley, USMC, in charge of weapons; 1Lt. Arnold Breakey, supply; Capt. Leonard Woods, executive officer; Sgt. Tony Denneau, radioman; Cpl. Jim Healy, medic; and 1Lts. Ralph Yempuku, a nisei interpreter, and Peter Fong, a chinese interperter. Yempuku had been involved in OSS campaigns in Burma and China. He would have a crucial role in this mission.

The nine men jumped from 600 feet and landed safely, except for Yempuku, who smashed his chin on landing, and Woods, who was a bit groggy from hitting his head. Before the team could do more than gather their chutes, three trucks filled with Japanese troops came speeding down a road toward the Americans. From another direction, a huge crowd of Chinese, moving towards the team, came into view. It was crisis time.

The Japanese arrived as Singlaub's team was picking up their supplies and gathering them into a pile. The Japanese lieutenant approached the team and demanded to know who they were. Yempuku translated Singlaub's response as, "The major says, we have come to help the Allied prisoners now that the war is over. Send your soldiers to the far side of the field to protect my people and equipment from those civilians."[2]

Obviously confused, the lieutenant hesitated. The Japanese troops far outnumbered the Americans and held their rifles ready for orders. Finally, the officer spoke and his men moved across the field towards the advancing Chinese. Yempuku translated Singlaub's demand to turn the troops around to face the Chinese. The befuddled lieutenant, having lost the initiative, did so. "Bring a truck over here to help load up the supplies," continued Singlaub.[3] Again, Yempuku spoke to the Japanese officer and the truck moved forward. Through bravado and timing, Singlaub had won the first round.

The team and their supplies were taken to the POW camp which housed 356 Allied soldiers and sailors. Once there, Singlaub refused to discuss anything with the lieutenant, demanding instead to speak with the senior officer in charge. Since the colonel in overall command could not arrive until the following day, the team was housed in the camp messhall.

About noon on August 28, a procession of cars arrived at the gate, and the Japanese colonel stepped out and led the way to a long table where they sat down. The colonel looked at the young major and said that he had just learned about the ending of the war. The suspense was over. Singlaub asked that the senior-ranking prisoner be brought to the conference. Reluctantly, the colonel agreed.

When Australian Lt. Col. William J. R. Scott arrived, Singlaub, with Yempuku translating, told the senior Japanese colonel to move and make room for Scott. The Japanese colonel stiffened and remained seated. Singlaub repeated the order in a harsh voice. This time the Japanese colonel moved aside and Scott sat down as his equal.[4]

The OSS POW rescue team has just landed on Hainan Island. Singlaub (on right) has refused to negotiate with the Japanese lieutentant in charge of the troops who were sent to capture Singlaub's team. Lt. Ralph Yempuku has his back to the camera.

US Army

Scott quickly explained the situation. Food was critical, men were starving to death. Medicine could come later. Scott also passed to Singlaub his diary of his years in captivity which would later be used to indict some of his keepers. The Japanese had experimented with the Hainan prisoners, not only by maltreating them, but by a systematic procedure of bringing them to the edge of starvation and then giving them just enough food to keep them working. To test their theories of nutrition, the Japanese stripped the prisoners food of all vitamins so that they gained no strength from the diet. The prisoners who survived did so by trapping and eating rats and other rodents.[5] The prisoners' cadaverous bodies testified to their years of starvation.

The prisoners were Australian, Indian, and Dutch who had been

231

captured more than three years earlier when the Japanese overran Java and the Dutch East Indies. For some, rescue came too late as they continued to die despite the efforts of the rescue team. For the others, the OSS team saved them from certain death from starvation. The huge graveyard behind the prison testified to all those who had gone before. Of the total of 263 Australians in the camp, only 177 were alive when their rescue came.

Colonel Scott would later disclose that of 50,000 Chinese laborers sent to work in the nearby iron ore mines, 45,000 died.[6] When he returned to Hong Kong, Singlaub provided details of how nine American airmen, shot down over Hainan, were bound with wires piercing their arms, paraded through the streets, and then butchered.[7]

Prisoners were also being liberated in the Japanese home islands. In Nagoya, 287 ex-POWs bought the bull that had hauled away their daily excrement, slaughtered, cooked, and ate it. The men gorged themselves for days. At Kobe, the POWs refused to obey their former wardens and walked away from the camp. At most POW camps, the surviving skeletons waited anxiously for the arrival of Americans at the camp gates.

Australian prisoners of war at POW camp on Hainan.

Ralph Yempuku

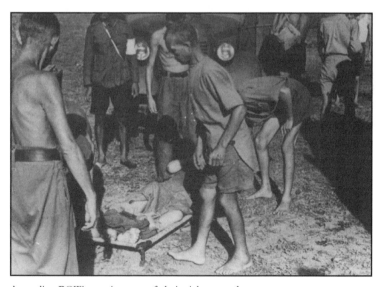

Australian POWs moving one of their sick comrades.

Ralph Yempuku

Japanese troops on Hainan Island. These men were not aware that
the war had ended.

Ralph Yempuku

Lt. Ralph Yempuku with Japanese officer on Hainan Island shortly
after the OSS team landed.

US Army

234

40

Independent Forces and Unnecessary Battles

As a nation, Australia put a larger percentage of its population in military uniform and fought for a longer period of time in World War II than did the United States.[1] Yet, most Americans know little of the sacrifices of the Australians. This chapter introduces some of the Australian campaigns and controversy associated with them.

Middle East

When Italy turned North Africa into a battlefield in 1940, the Sixth Division of the Second Australian Imperial Force (AIF) was already in Palestine. The Sixth Division, supported by British tanks and guns, defeated Italy in the first desert campaign and cost Italy 100,000 troops. The Sixth also fought in Crete, Libya, and Greece, where, in April, the Germans drove the ANZAC Corps, (Australian-New Zealand Corps) under Gen. Sir Thomas Blamey, out of the Greek mainland, killing 200 Australians and capturing 2,000. This was the last time that Australian and New Zealand forces fought as a corps-size organization.[2] The Ninth Division held Tobruk while the Sixth and Seventh Divisions joined to destroy the Vichy army in Syria. The Australian Eighth Division was sent to Malaya to help defend Singapore and was captured when Gen. Arthur Percival surrendered Singapore on February 15, 1942. Many of the Australian POWs were forced to work and die on the railways in Thailand and the Death Railway in Thailand-Burma.

Following the loss of the British battleship, HMS *Prince of Wales* and cruiser HMS *Repulse* off the coast of Malaya on December 11, 1941, the Australian War Cabinet began to question the ability of the Commonwealth to protect Australia. Accordingly, a request was made to return the First Australian Corps (Sixth and Seventh Divisions) to Australia. The request became a demand after the fall of Malaya and Singapore, and the bombing of Darwin on February 19, 1942. Prime Minister Churchill argued in vain for the divisions to be sent to Burma, but the Australian cabinet held firm. The two divisions, less 3,440 troops aboard the personnel carrier, *Orcades,* which had stopped in Java, were returned to Australia. The men aboard *Orcades* were captured by the Japanese.[3]

More than 8,000 Australians were taken prisoner in the European theater and 22,000 in the Pacific. Of the Pacific prisoners, 7,685 (35 percent) did not survive their captivity.[4]

New Guinea

The New Guinea campaign was essentially an Australian war. On March 8, 1942, Japanese troops captured Lae and Salamaua, on the north shore of the territory of Papua New Guinea, which was administered by Australia. By June, there were 369,000 Australian army and militia on the south side of Papua New Guinea, plus 38,000 Americans, mostly members of the U.S. Army Air Force, with P-38 fighter aircraft.

Frustrated by their inability to land forces near Port Moresby, the territorial capital, Admiral Isoroku Yamamoto, commander-in-chief Japanese Combined Fleet, and Maj. Gen. Tomitaro Horii, conqueror of Rabaul, decided on a two-pronged attack which would land troops on the northern coast of New Guinea near Buna, secure Buna and Gona, and then march over the Owen Stanley Mountain Range on a narrow trail called the Kokoda Track to attack Port Moresby. The second prong would be an amphibious assault on the southern coast in Milne Bay, to outflank the Australian defenders of Port Moresby.

The first prong was executed on the evening of July 21-22, when Col. Yosuke Yokoyama and 2,000 troops landed near Buna with orders to secure the Gona-Buna area and prepare the approach route to the Kokoda trail for General Horii's army.

Colonel Yokoyama established the main Japanese base at Sanananda, midway between Gona and Buna, sent his infantry rapidly up the approach to the track, and, in securing the area, murdered Australian plantation managers, mission priests, sisters, lay-workers, and even a six-year-old boy. Another group, consisting of five Australian soldiers, five American airmen, and two Australian mission sisters, which were trying to escape the Japanese advance, were similarly murdered. Sisters Mavis Parkinson and May Haymon were bayoneted to death and thrown into hastily dug trenches.[5]

The 150-mile long Kokoda Track deserves more than a passing comment, as do the Japanese and Australians who fought and died there. The Track is a two-to-three-foot wide path that creeps through thick rain forests that shut out sunlight and hide the undergrowth of vines and creepers that prohibit passage. On the Port Moresby, or southern, side, there is an area of dryness, but in the mountains and on the Buna, or northern, side, it rains constantly. The area is inhospitable and loaded with tropical diseases.

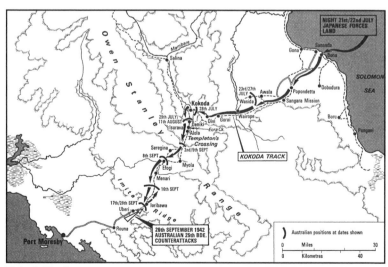

Kokoda Track

Australian War Memorial

Starting from the southern approach, the Track is a series of ridges, each higher than the next, which rise to 7,000 feet. Steps for the Track were fashioned with small logs that were held in place by stakes. Many of the logs would work loose and cause the soldier, with his 45-pound pack and weapon, to trip and fall backward onto the person behind him or into the mud on the trail. From Port Moresby, it took twelve hours to complete nine miles which brought one to the 1,200-foot level.[6] The Track then dropped 1,000 feet before another climb of 2,000 feet. Much of the final portion was nearly vertical and required one to crawl in order to reach the top. Over most of the Track, the constant rain made the ground a mass of moving mud which hid the roots and vines that entangled your legs and arms when you fell. There were mosquitoes, mites, chiggers, and leeches in abundance. Steam from persistently wet clothes would fill the air as the temperature rose during the day and men would drop beside the Track suffering from malaria, dengue fever, dysentery, jungle rot, dehydration, and fatigue.

More mountain ranges followed until a center ridge permitted the troops to follow it to Templeton's crossing. From there, the Track went up and down for another ten miles until one reached Kokoda, the mid-point of the trek to Buna. The distance from Kokoda to Buna was 40 miles, and was not quite as rough as the uphill portion. It did include rotting swamps, scorpions, crocodiles, ants, and centipedes[7]

In June, 1942, the Australians organized a force called Maroubra which consisted of the 39th Australian Militia Battalion and local Papuan militia. On July 7, Maroubra Force assembled at the foothills of the Kokoda Track, 30 miles north of Port Moresby, and began the overland crossing to Buna.[8] They were the first military force to attempt a crossing of the Owen Stanley Mountain Range and were doing so to implement General MacArthur's directive to establish a defensive force at Buna by August 10. General Horii disrupted MacArthur's timetable by landing troops near Buna on July 21 and pushed the local militia forces back to Kokoda. The Japanese advance was so swift that anyone who was wounded, left behind, or captured was never seen again. The bleached bones of unknown soldiers became a common sight alongside the Track.

The Australians and local militia destroyed rope bridges across rivers as they fell back, but the Japanese, veterans of Rabaul, Guam, and Malaya, quickly bridged the rivers, outflanked the defensive positions and drove the defenders up the trail. A brief stand was made at Kokoda, but, by August 29, the defenders were an army in retreat.[9]

By September 17, the Australians were pushed back to Imita Ridge which was too close to Port Moresby for General MacArthur's comfort level. Brig. Gen. Kenneth W. Eather, who had just arrived on the Track with the 25th Brigade, was told, "There won't be any withdrawal from the Imita position. You'll die there if necessary. You understand?" Eather understood.[10] While General Eather was given his do-or-die ultimatum, General Horii's troops received their first glimpse of the sea past Port Moresby. They wept for joy and threw themselves into each other's arms. Their weariness from wave after wave of endless mountain ridges suddenly vanished as they looked down at their objective, Port Moresby. Horii decided to fortify a defensive position, rest his weary troops, and wait for additional reinforcements before renewing the attack.

On the night of September 24, a message was received from Rabaul ordering Horii to withdraw back over the Owen Stanley Range. General Horrii's emaciated face blanched as he read the message. Then he turned to Lt. Col. Toyanari Tanaka, his chief staff officer, and exploded, "I'm not going back, not a step! How can we abandon this position after all the blood the soldiers have shed and the hardships they have endured? I cannot give such an order."[11] Another message was received. This one directed Horii to move to the coast near Buna. Before he could digest the meaning of the message, a message arrived from Imperial General Headquarters in Tokyo explaining that Horii's forces were needed to defeat MacArthur's anticipated assault of Buna. He was to leave immediately. All night in a soft, cold drizzle, Horii's troops prepared to leave their positions. The mountain guns which would have launched projectiles on Port Moresby were the first to be withdrawn.

Horii sent a battalion of engineers and artillery ahead to establish a defensive position guarding a steep ravine beyond Myola, the most difficult spot to traverse on the entire Track. Eora creek roared through the ravine and the huge rocks made passage most difficult.

The Australian 25th Brigade pursued Horii's retreating army but paused to bury hundreds of bodies in various stages of decay. Besides the rotting, maggot-infested corpses, there were many skeletons, uniforms already rotted away, and flesh picked clean by the legions of huge ants and other insects. The Australians were also slowed by the narrowness of the trail between steep cliff walls which forced the troops to move single file and often crawl on hands and knees, clinging to vines and roots in order to advance two miles a day.[12] Many of the men were affected by diarrhea and dysentery, some so severely that they cut away the seats of their trousers.

When the Australians were forced back from Buna, their supply line from Port Moresby became shorter. Just the opposite happened to the Japanese who had to receive supplies from Buna. The Japanese had been forced to scrounge for food from native gardens for some time. Now the Australians found numerous indications that the Japanese were starving. Emaciated Japanese corpses had no wounds, and there were signs of grass, leaves, and wood being ripped out and eaten. Although General Horii had successfully driven the Australian defenders over the Track, the number of casualties favored the Australians, who lost 314 killed and 367 wounded. Horii lost 1,000 killed and 1,500 wounded, many of which would prove impossible to evacuate back down the track.

The Australian 16th Brigade, led by Maj. Gen. C. E. M. Lloyd, relieved the 25th Brigade and reached Eora Creek on October 21. General Horii gave orders for his commander to hold Eora Creek until October 28, while he prepared his next defensive position at

Oivi, on the Track between Kokoda and Buna. The battle for Eora Creek lasted for seven days, exactly the amount of time specified by the Japanese general.

The Australians, clinging like leeches to the cliffs in a cold driving rain, could make no headway against the strong Japanese fortifications until the Japanese withdrew on the morning of October 28. The Australians, with both Eather's 25th Brigade and Lloyd's 16th Brigade, encountered the Japanese defensive positions at Oivi on November 5. The Australians divided their forces with Eather's Brigade following a jungle trail to outflank the Japanese at Gorari. Horii anticipated such a tactic and threw back the Australians on November 9, with heavy casualties. The fighting surged both ways until Eather's forces captured Gorari on the 10th.

General Horii and about 900 of his men were outflanked and forced to conduct a difficult night withdrawal through the jungle over a little-used trail to the Kumusi River where a track led to Buna. Horii and four men from his headquarters, impatient at the delay in fording the river, pushed a log raft into the swift current of the Kumusi. The raft overturned, the general and his men were swept away and never seen again.[13]

About 1,200 men of Horii's army reached the Buna coast where they found six Japanese warships unloading reinforcements (1,000 troops), equipment, and supplies. Port Moresby had been saved by the Australians, but the battles for Buna, Gona, and Sanananda were yet to begin.

While General Horii's troops were driving Maroubra Force over the Owen Stanley Range, Gen. Harukichi Hyakutake, commander of the 17th Army on Rabaul, implemented the second prong of the Japanese attack which was to land Japanese marines at Milne Bay to outflank the Australian forces at Port Moresby. Hyakutake was forced to reduce the number of troops because of the successful landing of the First Marine Division on Guadalcanal. He had to further modify his assault plans because Milne Bay was already occupied by the Australians.

Hyakutake landed 1,900 troops in Milne Bay on August 26. The Milne Bay battle was nip-and-tuck for two weeks, but, on September 6, the Japanese evacuated 1,300 survivors. Australian casualties were 161. This Australian victory was the first Allied ground success over Japan since the war began.

Independent Forces

On the day following the Japanese attack on Pearl Harbor, an Australian force was landed on Dutch Timor in accordance with an agreement between the Australian and Dutch governments. The agreement stipulated that Australia would deploy forces to certain strategic locations to defend against the anticipated Japanese invasion. A number of these forces were referred to as Independent Companies due to their composition, training, equipment, and ability to operate independently for extended periods. Some of the units, such as the company that was sent to Ambon, trained together for 16 months prior to their deployment.[14] The 2/1st Independent Company was spread from the Admiralties to New Hebrides.[15] The 2/2nd was sent to Timor, 2/3rd was on New Caladonia, 2/4th was in the Northern Territories, and 2/5th was sent to Port Moresby. During these early battles, a high proportion of the Australian forces were quickly overcome by the Japanese advance and became prisoners until the end of the war, or until a merciful death claimed them.

Portuguese and Dutch Timor

In December, 1941, while the Allies were suffering one defeat after another in the Pacific, a small group of Australian volunteers took the first offensive action of the war. Embarking from Darwin, Australia, "Sparrow Force," the 2/40th Bn. landed in Koepang on the western tip of Dutch Timor followed by the 2/22nd Independent Company which landed at Dili in Portuguese Timor. The landing at Koepang on December 13 was welcomed by the

Dutch who had signed an agreement with the government of Australia in early 1941, whereby Australia would reinforce Ambon and Timor if war with Japan seemed imminent.

The landing of troops on December 17 at Dili, the capital of Portuguese Timor, was not so well-received. The Portuguese governor, Manuel d'Abreu ferreira de Carvelho, who had not been consulted beforehand, refused to agree to the Allied plan for defense of Portuguese Timor, and promised to oppose the landing with all the forces he had. After consultation with Mr. David Ross, the British consulate general in Dili, the governor agreed to the landing if it did not take place in Dili harbor.

Following the landing of troops some distance from Dili, Consul Ross gained permission for the old Dutch troopship, *Sourabaya,* to offload the Australian equipment and supplies in the harbor. Within a short time, the troops and equipment were in position around the airfield.

The Australians had a month to reconnoiter and prepare defensive positions before the Japanese arrived. Adm. Chuichi Nagumo, commanding the same naval task force that attacked Pearl Harbor, attacked Darwin, Australia on February 19, destroying 10 Allied ships, 23 aircraft, and killing 288 Australians. The attack ensured that the Allies would not be able to interfere with the Japanese landings on Portuguese and Dutch Timor.[16] On the same day, 5,000 Japanese troops were landed in Koepang and 1,000 at Dili. Singapore had surrendered on February 15, which permitted Japan to deploy an additional 15,000 men of the experienced 48th Division from Malaya to the Pacific island territories. Additional troops followed including a regiment of Japanese marines and elements of the 38th Division which captured Hong Kong on Christmas day.

Col. Bill Leggatt's 2/40th Bn. was forced to surrender after three days of fighting during which they suffered 84 killed and 132 wounded. Though they were unable to contest the Japanese landings and occupation of Dili, over the next 13 months the Second AIF Company on Portuguese Timor killed 1,500 Japanese while suffering only 40 casualties. Perhaps the greatest contribution of the Independent Company on Timor was tying up some 20,000 Japanese forces which could have been committed to the campaigns in Burma, Guadalcanal, or Papua New Guinea.

Rabaul

As war with Japan became obvious, a battalion of the Eighth Division's 23rd Brigade was sent to Rabaul, on the northern tip of New Britain, to protect the airfield which was on the approach route to the Philippines. The Japanese began bombing Rabaul on January 4, 1942, and, on the 23rd, the Australian garrison of 1,400 men was overwhelmed by a Japanese force of 5,300 under command of Maj. Gen. Tomitaro Horii.[17] Many of the Australian prisoners were tied to the trunks of coconut palms and bayoneted to death. Some, perhaps less fortunate, were sent back to Japan to do forced labor.

Most of the expatriates, administration officials, and the native police force managed to escape before the Japanese arrived and made their way to Port Moresby, Papua New Guinea. Authors White and Lindstom reported that the natives who remained in the Rabaul area were not abused by the Japanese military.[18] Such was not the situation for POWs who remained on Rabaul. Of the 80 prisoners who remained, only 18 survived the war. During July, more than 1,000 Australians (840 POWs and the rest civilians) died when their unmarked prison ship, *Montevideo Maru*, which was taking them to Japan, was torpedoed off Luzon by an American submarine.[19]

The 23rd Brigade had a disastrous record in the war. Besides the battalion decimated at Rabaul, other battalions that were deployed independently from the brigade were destroyed on Ambon and Timor.[20] The Australian Joint Chiefs of Staff understood the vulnerability of these forward-deployed forces but, as Lt. Gen. Sir

Sidney F. Rowell, who became chairman of that group, observed after the battalions were decimated, "It's not the first time that a few thousand men have been thrown away and it won't be the last."[21]

Ambon

Australia sent 1,150 men of Gull Force, as the 2/21st Battalion of the 23rd Regiment was called, to Ambon in December 1941, as part of the Australian/ Dutch agreement. Ambon is a small island in the Moluccas group, better known to the world for its spices-nutmeg and cloves-than for its superb deep-water harbor. But the navies of the world were well aware of the anchorage, protected on each side by peninsulas which allowed ships to steam directly to the wharves with complete protection from the elements. As such, Ambon became a strategic facility desired by both Japan and the Allies.

Japanese forces landed on four separate locations on the evening of January 30-31, 1942, and quickly overran the Dutch positions. Within 24 hours, the Dutch commander surrendered his 2,600 troops. The Australians continued to conduct guerrilla warfare into February but were reduced to increasingly smaller areas of operations and forced to surrender. In addition to the Australian battle casualties, the Japanese executed more than 200 Australian prisoners who defended an airstrip at Laha on the northern end of the Island. Thirty-six Australians escaped before they were taken prisoner and 13 more escaped very early during their captivity. A total of 795 Australians were imprisoned on Ambon.

During October, 263 of the prisoners were shipped to the inhospitable island of Hainan. When the war ended, only 123 of the 532 prisoners left on Ambon remained alive.[22] The death rate of Australian prisoners who were retained on Ambon was 77 percent. For those prisoners moved to Hainan, the rate was 31 percent. Only the Australians doing forced labor on the Death Railway (39.3 percent) and those held prisoner in North Borneo

(99 percent) suffered higher death rates.[23]

Prisoners died from a number of causes, chief among them disease, due to a near complete lack of medicine, exhaustion from prolonged heavy labor, beatings, starvation, and executions. In addition to the physical stress and exhaustion, the Ambon prisoners must have suffered from extreme mental anguish since they had no contact with the outside world during their captivity. Most Allied prisoners were moved once or twice during their captivity and had an opportunity to talk to natives, locals, or other prisoners who could bring them somewhat up to date on the condition of the war. The Australians on Ambon, as well as the Dutch and a handful of Americans, were completely isolated from the rest of the world for the duration of the war.[24]

Unnecessary Battles

From October 1944 until August 1945, Australian forces fought six controversial island campaigns in the Pacific that produced 6,000 Australian casualties. These campaigns were fought with negligible publicity, insufficient equipment, and under some of the most grueling conditions imaginable.

Most of the soldiers who fought in these campaigns knew that the battles had no strategic import towards the defeat of Japan. The campaigns were launched against Japanese who had been bypassed on Pacific islands and who were already defeated; incapable of being supplied, reinforced, or evacuated; and reluctant to fight. Most of the effort being expended by the Japanese was finding or growing enough food to survive. The only reason the Japanese fought was because the Australians forced them to do so.

Historians disagree on why Australia fought these campaigns. Gen. Douglas MacArthur stated that the Australian mop-up operations on Bougainville, New Britain, and Papua New Guinea were unnecessary, inadvisable, and did not have his approval. Gen.

Sir Thomas Blamey, commander-in-chief of all Australian troops, argued that, since MacArthur's staff provided landing craft for the Aitape-Wewak, New Guinea campaign, he did, in fact, approve the operation. Blamey also defended his offensive with the statement that ". . . if Australian troops did not take the offensive, their skills would deteriorate."[25] While Prime Minister John Curtin and his cabinet fiddled, General Blamey went to war. Much later and very reluctantly, the War Cabinet gave their retroactive approval.

Bougainville

Bougainville was relatively unknown to the Australians in 1944. It was not one of the mandated territories administered by Australia, such as Papua New Guinea. The U.S. Third Marine Division defeated the Japanese on Bougainville in two attacks in November 1943. Since then, the estimated 12,000 bypassed Japanese had been contained in three small enclaves. Only 20 percent of the Japanese forces manned defensive positions, the rest were either sick or involved with food production or other survival duties. The senior Japanese officer, Lt. Gen. Harukichi Hyakutake, who commanded the 17th Army at Rabaul and was defeated at Guadalcanal, had his headquarters in the southern enclave near Buin. He had no desire to expand his defensive perimeter.

The Australian forces completed their relief of the Americans on Bougainville in mid-December 1944. They began vigorous patrolling immediately. Whereas the Americans and Japanese had coexisted in outposts as close to one another as 50 meters, the Australians began pushing the Japanese back. The cease-fire was over for the Japanese.

On December 23, Lt. Gen. Sir Stanley Savige, the corps commander, issued orders to ". . . take the war to the Japanese and destroy them."[26] Over the next eight months, Australian forces attacked the Japanese with success. One such attack involved an Australian force of less than 100 men attacking a Japanese position defended by 900 Japanese. The Australians prevailed, not so much because of their prowess as the fact that the Japanese had little ammunition, less food, and no medicine to combat the tropical diseases. When the emperor announced Japan's surrender on August 15, Australian casualties were 516 killed and 1,512 wounded. Japanese dead were estimated at 8,500, with another 9,800 dying of illness or starvation.

Papua New Guinea

During August 1944, General Blamey ordered the Australian Imperial Force (AIF) 6th Division to prepare to land at Aitape and Wewak in New Guinea to relieve the American forces there. The Australian relief was completed on December 7. Once again, the Australians criticized the Americans' lack of aggressiveness, sloppy camp hygiene, and luxury accommodations. The Australians compared the unsanitary camp area to the Italian camps after the battles around Sidi Barrani in the European theater.[27]

The Japanese army on New Guinea was estimated at 35,000 men in three understrength divisions Their situation was much the same as the Japanese on Bougainville. Most of their forces were occupied in foraging for food and many were ineffective due to starvation or disease.

The AIF 6th Division, according to Blamey, "Australia's First and Finest,"[28] landed at Aitape in November 1944, relieved the Americans and immediately began long-range patrolling. Patrols reported finding many dead Japanese in deserted camps, apparently dead from starvation, and many obvious examples of cannibalism being practiced by the Japanese in an effort to stay alive.

By May 1945, the Japanese were driven away from the coast and into a small position in the mountains. The final assault on Japanese positions was made in July. In the ten months prior to the emperor's surrender, the 6th Division suffered 442 killed and 1,141 wounded. Another 16,000 were admitted to hospitals for malaria, scrub typhus, dengue, and dysentery. Japanese dead were estimated at more than 9,000.

New Britain

The AIF 5th Division followed a different course of action on New Britain in the Bismark Sea. The Japanese had used Rabaul, at the northeast end of New Britain, and Gloucester, in the southwest corner, as major staging bases for all operations in the northwest Pacific since they defeated an Australian force there in January 1942.

The U.S. First Marine Division seized Gloucester in late 1943, and was relieved by the U.S. Army 40th Infantry Division in April 1944. By August 1944, the Army had its forces divided between the Talsec-Cape Hoskins area, Arawe, and Cape Gloucester. Japanese strength was estimated at 38,000 men.[29] In December 1944, two captured Korean laborers reported Japanese strength as more than 110,000. The report was deemed unreliable but, in actuality, was much closer to the real figure.[30] When the war ended, a much smaller Australian force had pushed the Japanese into the Rabaul-Gazelle peninsula area where the Japanese were planning a major breakout and offensive against the smaller Australian force. Australian casualties were 53 killed and 140 wounded.

No reports of the Bougainville, New Guinea, or New Britain campaigns appeared in the Australian newspapers during 1944. There are several reasons for this censorship, none of which seems justifiable. First, General MacArthur had a penchant for releasing only information which made him appear to be the commander in the field. Since he was not involved in the campaigns, he adopted a strict censorship on the results. Second, General Blamey had a well-known distrust of the press and disregard of the Australian newsmen who followed the campaigns. Blamey made little, if any, attempt to have MacArthur relax his censorship restrictions. When news of the island campaigns did reach the newspapers, it had to compete with the surrender of Germany, the firebombing of Japan, the invasion of the Philippines and Okinawa, and the two atomic bombs. These were events of much greater significance and more dramatic success. Finally, even the reporters and newspapers showed little interest in reporting the local campaigns.

Borneo

During April 1945, MacArthur was directed by the Joint Chiefs of Staff to plan for the occupation of Borneo using Australian forces. Plans were developed to invade Tarakan, Brunei Bay, and Balikpapan. The rationale for the capture of Borneo at such a late date was to secure a base for the British to support the invasion of Japan. The British wanted no part of Borneo. They rightly pointed out that it was too far from Japan, facilities were in bad repair after the Japanese occupation, and Subic Bay in the Philippines would be a far better facility for the purpose. Neither MacArthur or Adm. Chester Nimitz, commander-in-chief Pacific, wanted the British navy at Subic Bay so plans went forward for the invasion of Borneo.

The war in Europe ended on May 7. There remained no strategic or tactical reasons for invading Borneo. At Balikpapan, the Japanese occupied a refinery that the Dutch destroyed when they were overrun and which the allies kept inoperable by bombing. Brunei Bay and Tarakan offered no military or political rationale for occupation save freeing the natives, which had not been a major issue before in the Pacific. A possible rationale has been advanced that Australia wanted to invade and hold Borneo in order to exchange Borneo for Dutch New Guinea or Dutch Timor after the war. Regardless of rationale, or lack of it, the Australian First Corps was directed to conduct the Borneo campaign. The AIF 7th Division was to capture Balikpapan, the 9th Division would land at Brunei Bay, and the reinforced 26th Brigade would land at Tarakan with 12,000 troops.

The landing at Tarakan on May 1 was successful and troops rapidly moved inland to seize key objectives. Japanese strength was estimated as 4,000 men, of which half were civilians or engineers who operated the oilfields. Fighting continued until Japan surrendered. Australian losses were 235 dead and 669 wounded. Japanese losses were 1540 killed while more than 200 surrendered.

On June 10, the remainder of the 9th Division landed at Brunei Bay, opposite the island of Tarakan. Troops moved rapidly ashore with only scattered resistance. When Japan surrendered, Australian losses were 114 killed and 221 wounded. Japanese losses were 1,500 killed.

The most contested landing on Borneo was at Balikpapan. The 7th division was opposed by 4,000 Japanese troops in well-fortified positions. In this campaign, MacArthur supplied all the naval gunfire and air support the ground commanders requested. The total air and naval supremacy permitted a relatively easy landing. Less than three hours after the first landing craft touched the shore, General MacArthur made his appearance at Balikpapan. This campaign made the newspapers. When the war ended two weeks later, 229 Australians were dead and 634 were wounded. Japanese casualties were estimated as 2,000 killed and 63 prisoners.

Balikpapan was the site of the last amphibious operation in World War II. It was also the one of the last recorded examples of Japanese atrocities towards prisoners and civilians. As the Australians moved through the deserted villages, they found the bodies of mutilated Indonesian men and decapitated bodies of teenage girls.

The courage of the Australian soldiers in these final campaigns was superb. So were the tactics employed and the leadership of the commanders in the field. The troops fought well, even though they knew that the battles would have no effect upon the resolution of the war. For reasons as to why these battles were fought, one must look towards the senior military leadership, Gen. Sir Thomas Blamey, and to the political leadership, Prime Minister John Curtin and his secretary of the Advisory War council, Sir Frederick Sheddon. Sheddon also held the positions of secretary of the War Cabinet and secretary of Department of Defence Coordination.[31]

History tells us that Sheddon provided little in the way of advice or options to Curtin or his cabinet. Curtin, for his part, simply turned the war over to MacArthur and Blamey, although he did write MacArthur as early as 1943 "That Australia had a special interest in seeing its own forces employed to clear New Guinea."[32] MacArthur did not object to Blamey's offensive spirit in Bougainville, New Britain, and Papua New Guinea. When Curtain abdicated his political responsibility, Blamey seized the opportunity to punish a foe which had humiliated Australia in Malaya and Singapore, and on many of the Pacific islands at the start of the war. Deprived of participation in the campaigns for the recapture of the Philippines and Okinawa, perhaps Blamey saw these island campaigns as an opportunity for the Australian military, and, therefore, himself to gain some measure of respect which they surely deserved. Respect was hard to come by. Most of the surviving troops wanted out rather than respect. Many Australians had put the war behind them well before Blamey began his offensive operations on the bypassed islands. They now held him personally responsible for the needless death and maiming of husbands, fathers, and sons. Investigations and debates over who was to blame for the needless campaigns occupied the newspapers. General Blamey, who survived as commander-in-chief, was abruptly dismissed following the war.

On June 8, 1949, Sir Robert Gordon Menzies, the elected prime minister, restored Blamey to the active list so that he might be promoted to the grade of field marshall, the only Australian to be so honored. The ceremony was conducted on September 16, with Blamey in a wheel chair due to failing health. It was an appropriate recognition for the role played by the old soldier, who wanted little more than an opportunity to command Australian forces in battle against the enemy, an opportunity MacArthur never gave him. Instead, Blamey was forced to provide Australian troops to MacArthur whenever tasked, and to function for the entire war without guidance or much support from his own government. Blamey died of a stroke on May 27 1951.[33]

41

THE SURRENDER CEREMONY: SEPTEMBER 2, 1945

Sunday, September 2, 1945, the day Japan would officially surrender to the Allies, dawned cool under a heavy overcast that caused a grayishness over Tokyo Bay and the surrounding shoreline.[1]

At 7:30 A.M., the Japanese officials boarded the destroyer USS *Lansdowne* for the 16-mile trip to the USS *Missouri*. The *Lansdowne* proved to be another source of embarrassment to the Japanese since they discovered late the evening before that there was not a single Japanese vessel nearby that was seaworthy enough to take the dignitaries to the ceremony.

Although there were 258 Allied warships in the bay,[2] all attention was focused on Adm. William "Bull" Halsey's flagship, *Missouri*. The choice of the ship had not been easy. Back in Washington, D.C., the rivalry between the army and navy concerning involvement in the ceremony had been intense.

The navy wanted Adm. Chester Nimitz, commander of the U.S. Pacific Fleet, to represent the Allied powers. The army wanted Gen. Douglas MacArthur in his position as supreme Allied commander to represent the Allies. The army won. As a fallback position, the navy then argued that the ceremony should be conducted on a combatant ship. President Harry Truman was from *Missouri* and could not resist the suggestion to use the battleship *Missouri* for the ceremony.

Halsey was designated as host for the event and was thoroughly enjoying the part. Halsey had fought in the war since the first day.

His task force had delivered aircraft to Wake Island just before the attack on Pearl Harbor. He had been a ferocious adversary, salty, profane, and loved by his troops. He now stood by the gangplank greeting the arriving dignitaries.

Two of the first to arrive were Gen. Jonathan Wainwright, who had surrendered Corregidor, and Gen. Arthur Percival, who had surrendered Singapore. Both generals had just been rescued from the prison camp in Sian, China, and hurried to Tokyo to participate in the ceremony, skeletons though they were.

The Japanese armed forces were represented by Gen. Yoshijiro Umezu, army chief of staff. The foreign office was represented by Mamoru Shigemitsu, former foreign minister. The selection of the Japanese representatives had been difficult. Emperor Hirohito insisted that no member of the Imperial family sign the surrender

Japanese representatives on board the USS *Missouri* in Tokyo Bay. They are from left to right: Foreign Minister Mamoru Shigemitsu and Gen. Yoshijiro Umezu.

National Archives

document. Several of the senior army officers threatened to commit suicide if asked to attend the ceremony. Chief of Staff Umezu was finally persuaded to represent the military. Shigemitsu was most uncomfortable by the time he reached the ship due to the rough roads en route and the need to climb the boarding ladder. Shigemitsu had lost his left leg to a terrorist bomb in China in 1932, and, due in large part to a clumsy and ill-fitting stump, lived in constant pain.[3]

The timing for the Japanese arrival and subsequent ceremony was crucial since General MacArthur had directed that the Japanese remain on board for the briefest possible time. The actual ceremony took only 22 minutes, testimony to the planning and rehearsals conducted by Capt. Stuart S. Murray, commander of the *Missouri*.[4]

In front of the dignitaries was a faded American flag, vintage 1853, that had been flown by Matthew Perry when he entered Tokyo Bay 92 years earlier. Halsey had asked the Naval Academy at Annapolis to deliver the relic, and Lt. John Breymer personally carried the precious colors to the *Missouri*.[5]

A moment of near panic had ensued about 15 minutes earlier when it was discovered that the beautiful polished mahogany table furnished by the British for the signing ceremony was too narrow for the official documents. Captain Murray quickly requisitioned a worn table from the crew's galley, along with a coffee-stained green tablecloth, and put it in the place of honor.[6]

The British delegation wore shorts and white knee stockings. The Russians were resplendent in red epauletted uniforms. The elaborate uniforms of the Chinese, French, and Canadians contrasted sharply with the American khaki undress uniforms with no ties. The Japanese wore their appropriate military uniforms, and Shigemitsu was dressed in formal wear with top hat, cutaway coat, and striped trousers.

At 9:00 A.M., General MacArthur, followed by Admirals Nimitz and Halsey, faced the Japanese. MacArthur, standing in front of the old mess table, read, "We are gathered here . . . to conclude a solemn agreement whereby peace may be restored . . . ." The General stepped back and motioned for the Japanese to sign. Shigemitsu, then Umezu signed. MacArthur then signed as supreme commander of the Allies and Nimitz for the United States. Gen. Hsu Yung signed for China, Adm. Sir Bruce Fraser for Britain, Lt. Gen. Kozma Derevyanko for Russia, Gen. Sir Thomas Blamey for Australia, Col. Moore Cosgrove for Canada, Gen. Jacques Leclerc for France, Lt. Gen. L.H. Van Oyen for the Netherlands, and Air Vice Marshall L.M. Isitt for New Zealand.[7]

After the signatures were affixed, MacArthur gave one of the pens used for the signing to General Wainwright and another to General Percival.[8] He then stepped forward and solemnly declared, "Let us pray that peace be now restored to the world and that God's will preserve it always. These proceedings are closed."[9]

Following the ceremony, Captain Murray was relaxing in his cabin with some of the ships' officers when someone suggested that the old mess table used for the signing of the surrender might be a future museum piece. Murray rushed to the deck of the ship only to find that the table was gone. After a short search, he located it back in the crew's galley where it was being set for the next meal. Murray did some fast talking to the chief, rescued the table, and locked it in his cabin.[10]

The Allies had laid down the terms of surrender at Potsdam. The atomic bombs and the emperor of Japan had enforced them. Vengeance seemed not to be much of a factor. The dead at Hiroshima and Nagasaki had, in some way, offset the hundreds of thousands killed at Nanking. The hundreds of thousands killed in the firebombings had offset the Allied war prisoners and civilians who had been starved, beaten, and worked to death in the numerous Japanese concentration camps. The survivors did not want vengeance, they wanted and deserved peace.

The official surrender ceremonies aboard the USS *Missouri* on September 2, 1945. The Japanese delegation is at lower center of photograph, facing the camera.

US Army / US Naval Academy

Corsairs over Japan (above). Aircraft from Marine Air Group-31 fly over Mount Fuji during the occupation of Japan. Return to Tentsin (below). Troops of the 1st Marine Division arrive in North China in 1945 and receive a warm welcome.

US Marine Corps

42

THE "OTHER" SURRENDER CEREMONIES

During August and September 1995, the 50th anniversary of the end of World War II was celebrated in Honolulu, Hawaii. The event gained international attention and drew thousands of veterans from around the world, including a large delegation from Japan.

Pictures, films, articles, and speeches recalled the surrender ceremonies aboard USS *Missouri* in Tokyo Bay on September 2, 1945. Few Americans are aware that the ceremony aboard *Missouri* was neither the first nor last surrender ceremony of Japanese forces in the Pacific.

Surrender ceremonies were conducted at other locations for several reasons, foremost being to put the Japanese military in the role of prisoner, rather than their accustomed role as conqueror. The Allies also needed to seize the weapons of the Japanese to preclude continued resistance, to send a clear signal to everyone that the war was over, and to provide humanitarian assistance and reparation of Japanese civilians and military as rapidly as possible.

These "other" surrender ceremonies were every bit as important to the civilian and military personnel involved as was the *Missouri* ceremony for their governments. Until these ceremonies took place, there was uncertainty as to how the forces in the field would react to the Japanese government's decision to surrender. Many of the ceremonies, such as those conducted by the British and Australians, were only slightly less spectacular than the ceremony aboard *Missouri*.

The Marshall Islands

Not all Allied assaults and occupation of territory held by the Japanese resulted in surrender ceremonies. Sometimes there was no one left to surrender. Occasionally the Allies simply bypassed the Japanese strongpoints and waited until the war was over to occupy them.

Occupation of various atolls in the Marshall Islands began on March 8, 1945, when 350 marines from the 1st Battalion, 22nd Marine Regiment landed, unopposed, on Wotho Atoll. There were 12 Japanese on the island, crewmen of a plane that had recently crash-landed on the reef. All 12 crewmen committed suicide rather than surrender.

Two days later, the same marines landed on Ujae, where they discovered six Japanese operating a weather station. Five of the Japanese committed suicide but the sixth was taken prisoner. On March 13, marines landed on Lae Atoll but found no Japanese. The same was true of Lib Island southwest of Lae.

One week later, 650 marines from the 3rd Battalion, 22nd Marines, landed on Ailinglap Atoll, southeast of Kwajalein. About 40 Japanese were found in prepared defensive positions which had to be assaulted. Two Japanese were captured, 37 killed, and two or three escaped. The marines suffered three wounded.

Next, the marines landed on Namu Atoll. They found a total of seven Japanese, including a woman and four children, all of whom surrendered. Namorik was searched on March 26, but no Japanese were found there. A detachment of the 2nd Battalion, 22nd Marines landed on Bikini, northwest of Kwajalein on March 28. The five Japanese on the atoll committed suicide.[1]

A search of Rongelap Atoll on March 31, found no Japanese, although their presence had been reported. The same was true of Ailuk Atoll. A few Japanese stragglers were found on the Mejit

Islands and Likiep and Utrik Atolls, all of whom surrendered. Company I of the 111th Army Infantry Regiment landed on Ujelang Atoll, 140 miles southwest of Eniwetok, on April 22. They discovered and killed 18 Japanese.

Mili Atoll, Marshall Islands: August 22, 1945

In November, 1943, American planes started their bombardment of the Marshall Islands to destroy Japanese aircraft prior to the Allied invasion. The airfields at Taroa on Maloelap and Mili on Mili Atoll were the primary targets. By late January 1944, Taroa and Mili were destroyed and the force of the American bombing raids fell on Roi on Kwajalein, Wotje, and Eniwetok. The first island seized in the Marshalls was Majuro, an atoll 265 miles southeast of Kwajalein. On the night of January 30, an American destroyer landed troops who captured the only Japanese military person on the atoll without firing a shot (a warrant officer that had been left behind as custodian of Japanese property on Majuro.)

As soon as Majuro was secure, Naval Construction Battalion personnel, "Seabees," landed on Dalap island and constructed a 4,800-by-445-foot runway that was used for raids against Mili, Wotje, Maloelap, and Jaluit. Two marine dive-bomber squadrons and part of a patrol squadron were established on the island, and space was provided for temporary operation of an army fighter group based on Makin.

Following the loss of Majuro, Adm. Monzo Akiyama, commander of Japanese forces in the Marshalls, shifted many of his forces from Kwajalein to Mili to meet the anticipated next Allied attack. Unfortunately for Admiral Akiyama, the Americans next struck the northern and southern ends of Kwajalein Atoll. On January 31, Roi, twin island of Roi-Namur on the northern approach, was quickly overrun, but the naval forces on Namur fought to the last man. U. S. marine losses were 195 killed and 545 wounded. Japanese losses were 3,472 killed or committed suicide, and 91 prisoners, of which 40 were Korean laborers. The 121st Seabee Battalion landed two days later to begin construction of a major airfield on Roi. The Seabees suffered 157 casualties from Japanese aerial attacks on February 12, when Japanese bombers from Ponape bombed the large ammunition dump and turned the island into an exploding inferno. Work on the airfield continued despite the casualties and it was fit for operations a short time later. Roi-Namur became a major base for air operations against Truk and the other bypassed Islands.

Japanese defense of Kwajalein was tenacious. The Japanese fought without air cover, naval support, armor, or artillery, and with no possibility of reinforcement or resupply. Theirs was truly a "forlorn hope," but one they did not abandon. Their defeat on February 5 resulted in the total annihilation of all 3,600 defenders.

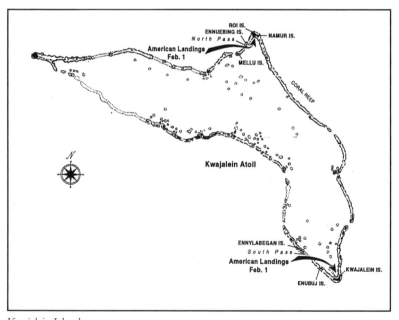

Kwajalein Island.

HPU graphic

In March, two Seabee battalions built a 6,300-foot runway with two taxiways and 102 hardstands for heavy bombers. Next, Ebeye Island on the southeastern side of the atoll was assaulted despite heavy Japanese fire. Seven Americans were killed and all 450 Japanese defenders died. All the western and southern islands that make up the Kwajalein Atoll were investigated by U. S. Army units. Total army casualties were 142 killed and 845 wounded. Japanese losses were 4,938 killed and 200 prisoners, of which 127 were Korean laborers.[2]

The Japanese defense of the Marshalls was fanatic and consistent with the hallowed military term of *gyokusai* or crushed jewel. *Gyokusai* meant that death in battle was the most honorable way to represent their country. Surrender was impossible. Entire battalions, regiments, and even divisions chose mass annihilation before surrender.[3] Japanese casualties in the Marshalls were 11,910 killed. Only 363 Okinawan and Korean laborers surrendered.[4]

On February 19, the American offensive reached Eniwetok, the most northwesterly atoll in the Marshalls. Eniwetok had a force of 2,500 men under the command of Maj. Gen. Yashima Nishida, and 10 fighter aircraft based on Engebi Island. Engebi fell on the 19th, Eniwetok on the 20th, and Parry Island, which guarded the entrance to the lagoon, on the 21st.

The Americans now resorted to their strategy of bypassing islands which posed no threat to the Allied advance. The Japanese garrisons on Wotje, Jaluit, Mili, and Maloelap in the Marshalls were left to rot in the sun. For the Japanese on these islands, the situation was far more serious than just being bypassed. They were isolated and left to die of starvation and disease. They had no ships, aircraft, or effective communications with higher headquarters or even among themselves. They were cut off from all resupply, unable to evacuate themselves, their dead, or their dying. Although bypassed, they were subject to frequent aerial bombardment, whenever the Americans had a few bombs to spare. By April 1945, the Japanese flag no longer flew over any of the Marshall Islands.

The garrison on Wotje learned of the Japanese surrender from an Australian radio broadcast. By then, the force was so depleted from starvation and disease that only 1,000 of the 3,000-man garrison survived the surrender and repatriation to Japan. Similarly, on Maloelap, slightly more than 1,000 men of the original 3,000 survived the situation. The forces on Jaluit learned of the surrender when a B-24 bomber dropped copies of the surrender document.

On August 22, 11 days before the government of Japan signed the documents of surrender, 2,395 starving soldiers and civilians on Mili earned the distasteful distinction of being the first Japanese Pacific Command to surrender to the Allies. Of the original garrison of 4,700, 900 were killed by American bombings, and the remainder died from starvation and disease. The surrender ceremony was held on destroyer escort *Levy* with Capt. H. B. Grow, USN, accepting the surrender on behalf of the commander of the Gilberts-Marshalls Area. Americans occupied Mili on August 28 and evacuated all but 12 officers on a Japanese merchant ship for Japan. The 12 officers were retained pending investigation of the deaths of five American airmen who bailed out over Mili and were known to have been captured. The investigation revealed that the airmen had been tortured and decapitated. The Japanese officer in charge accepted responsibility for the atrocity and committed suicide. The remainder of the Marshall Island garrisons surrendered two weeks later at Truk.

The difficulties encountered by the 7,000-man Woleia Atoll detachment in the Carolines probably serves as an example of what being bypassed meant to the men in these situations. Woleia, sometimes called Mariaon by the Japanese, was about halfway between Palau and Truk. Prior to the war, there had been about 300 Micronesians on the atoll who collected copra for shipment to Japan, and survived by eating coconuts, breadfruit, and fish. In 1942, the Japanese navy built a small airstrip on one of the 20 islands which made up the atoll, and, in 1944, Maj. Gen. Katsuzo Kitamura's 15th Independent Mixed Brigade arrived to strengthen the atoll's defenses.

By mid-June, American carrier air had destroyed all Japanese aircraft on the island, sunk all transports used to bring in food and supplies, and destroyed all the facilities on the ground. General Kitamura's men went to a daily ration of 500 grams of rice. Throughout the summer, the mortality from disease, usually dysentery, climbed at an unbelievable rate. During August, B-24 bombers attacked the insignificant atoll daily. The daily ration dropped to 200 grams. The shelter for the sick and wounded consisted of an open concrete trench where the men lingered without medicine until they died. In October, the daily ration fell to 100 grams of food per man.

General Kitamura did everything he could to maintain the morale of his unit. He visited his men daily, encouraged the singing of a garrison anthem, organized the troops into labor battalions for vegetable production, and, finally, asked higher headquarters to ship his unit to the front so they could die in battle rather than starve to death on Woleai. Unfortunately, there were no ships left to resupply or evacuate the dwindling force.

During October 1944, a single submarine arrived and delivered 70 tons of food and medical supplies. For a brief period, the mortality rate slowed but, by March 1945, the garrison's strength had dropped to 2,500 men. By this time, everyone remaining alive was so feeble that they were unable to bury their dead or work in the vegetable gardens. In August, when General Kitamura received information that Japan had surrendered, only 2,000 of the original 7,000 men were alive. On September 19, the 1,600 survivors were evacuated aboard *Takasago Maru* and taken to Beppu for medical care and rehabilitation.[5]

Roku Roshi POW Camp: August 22

Roku Roshi POW camp was located in a suburb northwest of Osaka, Japan. Four-hundred POWs from the Philippines, survivors of the Bataan Death March, Cabanatuan POW camp, and the Death Ships, were moved there on November 26, 1942. By July

31, 1943, 87 of the POWs had died and 30 were so sick they could not work or be moved to another camp. Two years later, none of the men were fit to work.

Most of the men succumbed to malnutrition and diet deficiencies. The most common diseases and sicknesses were beri-beri, edema, dysentery, pellagra, pneumonia, malaria, and influenza.

The work assigned the POWs was heavy labor in a factory, carrying heavy loads, stoking blast furnaces, and working in extreme heat. The POWs were not provided with any safety equipment, medical supplies, medicines, or doctors.

A 50-pound weight loss was not uncommon for the prisoners. The POWs were weighed each Sunday, but were forced to stand backward on the scale so that they could not see their weight. Of course, the next POW in line would note the weight of the man in front of him and pass the information along so that the amount of weight loss was no secret.

On August 22, 1945, Sergeant Tanaka, the camp commandant visited the POW barracks. He went directly to the cot of the senior officer, Colonel Unrhue, and read a statement that said, as a result of a peace conference held in Manila, the war was over. Tanaka announced that he would keep his guards in place to ensure the safety of the POWs.

Colonel Unrhue interrupted Tanaka and directed him to have all arms and ammunition stacked near the flag pole in 30 minutes. Tanaka objected, saying he was responsible for the safety of the prisoners, and besides, his new samurai sword was a part of his uniform and he could not be separated from it.[6] After some additional discussion, Tanaka responded, "Yes Sir," and departed.

Colonel Unrhue moved quickly. The day of liberation had finally come and he was not about to lose control of the situation. He notified the other prisoners that the war was over and that the

Japanese had surrendered. He then issued orders to other officers to arrange a surrender ceremony to take place near the flag pole in 45 minutes. Two platoons were quickly organized, one was assigned to remove all of the boards which the Japanese had nailed to the front door and windows of the barracks to limit POW information about the Allied bombing raids. The other platoon was designated to take custody of all the Japanese weapons and ammunition that were being deposited near the flagpole.

At the designated time, Unrhue called "attention," and the two platoons snapped-to. POWs who could stand only with assistance a short time before, now stood proudly at attention. A sobbing Sergeant Tanaka was called forward and surrendered his precious sword to Colonel Unrhue. The POW color guard lowered the Japanese flag from the flagpole and hoisted a small silk American flag that had been secreted into the camp from the Philippines and protected for the past three years.

All of the POWs saluted from the time the flag was tied to the rope until it waved majestically at the top of the 60-foot flagpole. Every eye was on the tiny American flag and tears streamed down the faces of the Americans.[7]

Tanaka then made a gift of some cigarettes and a small jigger of sake to each of the prisoners. After a humble evening meal, the men gathered for a service of prayer and thanksgiving. They sang the national anthem, other patriotic songs, and stayed up most of the night talking about wives, families, and loved ones.

The following day, the former prisoners had the best dinner they could recall at the Roku Roshi camp. Dinner consisted of fresh bread and one pound of meat for every 20 men. The evening formation and report was done for the first time in the English language.

Later, the former prisoners went into the village of Roku Roshi and confiscated a radio from the mayor's office. That night they heard General MacArthur broadcasting to the various POW camps and learned that an airborne food drop would take place at the Roku Roshi POW camp at 11:00 A.M., on August 28. Shortly after the broadcast, the mayor who was now aware that the POWs were free, arrived with 300 pounds of cucumbers, 400 pounds of grapes, and some small watermelons. Several of the townspeople also arrived with cookies made from barley flour and mashed beans. The POWs caloric ration made an immediate increase from 1,200 calories to 3,100.

While the men waited for the airdrop and their subsequent liberation, they compiled a report which documented the beatings that had taken place daily at the camp. They listed the unsafe conditions under which they were forced to work, and the details involving the death of their fellow prisoners.

On September 8, the first American soldiers arrived at the camp. Evacuation of the POWs began the next day. They were first taken to Fukui by truck. The POWs remembered the city with a population of one million people when they arrived in Japan. Now, Fukui was in ruins, burned to the ground.

Tents were erected to provide shelter for the POWs while they waited for the train that took them to Yokohama. General MacArthur met the train and visited the men in the coaches. A band played and the men were taken to a nearby hospital ship where they feasted on hot cakes, bacon, and coffee, along with all the fresh fruit they wanted. The POWs went by ship to Manila, and then to Seattle.

Morotai: August 26

On the morning of August 26, 16 motor torpedo boats (PTs), commanded by Lt. Cmdr. Theodore R. Stansbury, USNR, arrived at Halmahera, northwest of Netherlands, New Guinea, to meet and deliver the senior Japanese officials to Morotai for the surrender ceremony. With Stansbury was Maj. Gen. Harry Johnson, commander of the Morotai-based 93rd Infantry Division. Much to the Americans' surprise, the senior Japanese officials were not at the rendezvous point. They sent their staff members in their place. General Johnson was furious and gave explicit instructions to the Japanese staff to have their army and navy senior commanders present the following morning.

The next day, Johnson sent Brig. Gen. Warren H. McNaught with six PT boats to fetch the Japanese. This time, Lt. Gen. Ishii, commanding general, and captain Fujita, naval commander, were waiting for the torpedo boats. The surrender party was transported to Morotai where Maj. Gen. Johnson, USA, commanding the 93rd Division on Morotai, accepted the surrender of 41,700 Japanese military and civilians in the Halmahera group. Also surrendered were 19,000 rifles, 900 cannons, and, 600 machineguns.

Kerama Retto: August 22-29

Many of the small garrisons in the Okinawa chain began surrendering to 10th Army representatives in late August. The ceremony usually involved the senior Japanese officer or officers being brought to the American warship and piped aboard. The Japanese official then surrendered his ceremonial sword and signed the documents which confirmed their surrender. The garrison commander on Aka Shima surrendered on August 22, and Japanese forces on Tokashiki Shima surrendered the next day. On August 29, Japanese forces on Kerama Rhetto surrendered. Maj. Gen. Toshiro Noumi surrendered the forces on Saki Shima, and Brig. Gen. Toshisada Takada surrendered forces on Amami Oshima.

Yokosuka Naval Base and Marcus Island: August 30 and 31

On August 30, Brig. Gen. William T. Clement, USMC, received the surrender of the Yokosuka Naval Base Area from Vice Adm. Michitara Totsuka (also spelled Tozuka), commandant of the First Naval District and the Yokusuka Naval Base. Rear Adm. Robert B. Carney, USN, accepted the surrender of the First Naval District from Vice Admiral Totsuka shortly thereafter aboard USS *San Diego,* which tied up at the Yokosuka dock. On the 31st, 2,542 starving troops on Marcus Island surrendered to Rear Adm. F. E. M. Whiting aboard USS *Bagley.* Marcus Island lies midway between Wake and the Bonins.

Truk Island "Gibraltar of the Pacific": September 2

Early in February 1944, Japan's Combined Fleet realized that Truk, with its 800 square miles of sheltered lagoons and strong defensive capability, had become vulnerable to Allied attacks and moved most of its warships to safer anchorages in the Palaus. Left at Truk were hundreds of freighters and transports, the 52nd Division with more than 8,000 men, 350 combat aircraft, and antiaircraft and coastal defense guns. Vice Adm. Chuichi Hara, commander, Fourth Fleet, was expected to uphold the reputation of Truk as "the impregnable bastion of the Pacific," when the Americans arrived. The Americans had other ideas. Occupation of Truk was not necessary for the Allied advance on Japan. In Washington, the decision was made to neutralize and bypass Truk, another step in a series of bypassing Japanese strong-points.

Carrier aircraft from Adm. Marc Mitscher's Task Force-58 attacked Truk at first light on February 17. Thirty of the Japanese aircraft that managed to get airborne were quickly shot down, and then the Americans turned their attention to the ships and aircraft on the ground. The attack continued during the remainder of the day, that night, and through noon on the 18th.

The Japanese losses were catastrophic. Truk was a smoking shambles, never again to pose a threat to the Allies. A total of 31 ships (137,000 tons) were sunk including ten warships (two cruisers and three destroyers). Two-hundred-seventy aircraft were destroyed, and 600 military personnel were killed, not including those lost with their ships. Two-thousand tons of food and 17,000 tons of fuel were destroyed, along with hangars, barracks, warehouses, and ammunition dumps. Although the Japanese flew in replacement aircraft to Truk, Allied aircraft continued to pound the runway and aircraft throughout the spring, finishing with a carrier aircraft sweep on April 28-29 that destroyed another 93 aircraft.

By fall 1944, Vice Admiral Hara's forces on Truk had become so isolated and ineffective that starvation and disease became the enemy rather than the continuous air attacks. Growing vegetables and fishing the lagoons became the major activities. On Kusaie, more than 300 men died from starvation. On Truk, 38,000 men scratched the soil to raise small amounts of taro, sweet potatoes, and vegetables. On Babelthuap, Lt. Gen. Sadae Inoue's 59th Infantry Division ate grass, palm leaves, lizards, rats, and crabs to stay alive. By the time Vice Admiral Hara surrendered these forces, more than 2,000 had died of starvation.

The arrangements for the surrender of Japanese forces in Micronesia were concluded in the wardroom of destroyer USS *Stack,* offshore Truk on August 30. Two days later, on September 2, aboard cruiser USS *Portland,* Vice Adm. George D. Murray, USN, commander of the Marianas, accepted the surrender of Lt. Gen. Sunzaburo Mugikura, commanding general 31st Army on Truk, and Vice Admiral Hara. The Japanese forces surrendered included all forces on Truk, Wake, the Palaus, Nomoi, Mili, Ponape, Kusaie, Jaluit, Maloelap, Wotje, Puluwat, Woleai, Rota, Pagan, Nomoluk, Nauru, and Ocean.[8] The 9,000 civilians on Truk and other islands under his jurisdiction were surrendered by Rear Adm. Aritaka Aihara, Imperial Japanese Navy (Retired). Aihara was in charge of the Eastern Branch of the South Seas Government, a Japanese government organization.[9]

Rota Island and Palau: September 2

On September 2, the commander of Japanese forces on Rota surrendered his 2,651-man force to Col. Howard N. Stent, USMC, representing the Guam Island Naval Command. Also on that date, Lt. Gen. Sadae Inoue, commander of Japanese forces in the Palau group and Yap, surrendered 45,000 of his forces to Brig. Gen. Ford O. Rogers, USMC, Pelelieu Island commander.[10]

Like numerous other atolls and islands, Palau was isolated by the Allied advance in 1944. Approximately 50,000 Japanese and 5,000 Palauans were reduced to farming and fishing in an effort to survive.[8] After a year of starvation and famine, the Palauans were forced into the jungle to live like animals, foraging for food and living in shelters and holes. Koror, the capital of Palau, was reduced to rubble by the American bombings, and the islands of Pelelieu and Anguar were denuded of all vegetation during the Allied invasion.

Ogasawara Gunto (Bonin Islands): September 3

On September 3, Lt. Gen. Yosio Tachibana, senior commander, surrendered his forces on Ogasawara Gunto to Commodore John H. Magruder, Jr. aboard USS *Dunlap,* outside the harbor of Chichi Jima.[11] Tachibana, who succeeded Lt. Gen. Tadamichi Kuribayashi upon Kuribayashi's death, surrendered 22,941 military and civilians on Chichi and Haha Jimas. Col. Presley M. Rixey, USMC, and a battalion of marines landed on Chichi Jima on September 13 to occupy the island, and to investigate the reports of inhumane and barbaric treatment of Allied POWs at the hands of their Japanese captors. During the investigation, it was learned that two U.S. naval aviators were captured in 1944, tortured, and bayoneted to death at General Tachibana's orders. Five more American airmen were captured when they bailed out of their disabled aircraft. Three were beheaded, one was beaten to death, and one was killed by bayoneting. The Japanese resorted to cannibalism and ate the flesh of the five airmen.

The war crimes trials of 21 Chichi Jima officers and men were held on Guam during the fall of 1946. One of the accused was acquitted because he was not aware that the flesh he ate was human. The other 20 were found guilty and received sentences ranging from death by hanging to life imprisonment. One of the guilty members was hung in June. General Tachibana and three other officers were executed on Guam on September 24, 1947.[12]

Marshalls and Gilberts Area: September 4

Rear Adm. Shigematsu Sakibara surrendered Wake Island to Brig. Gen. Lawson H. M. Sanderson, USMC, representing the commander Marshalls-Gilberts area, on September 4, aboard destroyer escort USS *Levy*.[13] Wake Island was designated as a Naval Air Facility on the same day. Sakibara surrendered 1,262 army and navy personnel on Wake, but that was a small number of the Japanese that were isolated when Wake was bypassed. American shelling and bombing killed 600 Japanese, 1,208 died of malnutrition and disease, and 974 had been evacuated to the home islands of Japan. Of the 1,262 that surrendered, 405 were so ill that they had to be given emergency treatment before they could be evacuated. All Japanese except Admiral Sakibara and 16 officers were repatriated by November 1, 1945. The admiral and other officers were detained pending an investigation into the murder of American civilian workers on Wake Island.[14]

New Britain: September 6

Following the surrender ceremony on board USS *Missouri*, General Sir Thomas Blamey, commander-in-chief Australian forces, quickly planned similar ceremonies for those areas where Australian forces had responsibility. The first such ceremony was conducted on September 6 aboard the British aircraft carrier HMS *Glory* anchored in St. Georges channel between New Britain and New Ireland.[15]

Lt. Gen. Hitoshi Imamura, commanding general Eighth Army, and Vice Adm. Jinichi Kusaka, commander South East Area Fleet, surrendered 139,000 Japanese troops to Lt. Gen. Vernon A. H. Sturdee, commander First Australian Army. The Japanese forces were located on New Britain, New Ireland, New Guinea, the Solomons, and adjacent islands.

As the Japanese delegation arrived at the gangplank of HMS *Glory*, all but Lieutenant General Imamura were disarmed. The Japanese were then directed to move forward facing a table flanked by a guard of Royal Marines. Lieutenant General Sturdee moved

Lieutenant General Sturdee is to the right of the table standing on the white line. Lieutenant General Imamura is saluting Sturdee prior to moving forward and placing his sword on the table.

Australian War Memorial

forward to the table and Imamura was told to move forward, halt, and place his sword on the table.

The terms of surrender, other orders, and instructions were then read and translated. Imamura signed three copies of the surrender documents for the Japanese Eighth Army, and Kusaka signed for the navy. Following Sturdee's signature, one copy was given to Imamura's aide.

Imamura then made a brief speech in which he stated his appreciation for the consideration that had been shown them and his intent to comply immediately with the orders of Lieutenant General Sturdee.

Lieutenant General Imamura signs the document of surrender aboard HMS *Glory*.

Royal New Zealand Air Force

Okinawa and the Ryukyus: September 7

On Okinawa, Gen. Joseph W. Stilwell, U.S. Army, accepted the surrender of Rear Adm. Tadao Kato, the senior surviving Japanese officer of the Japanese Ryukyus garrison, at Tenth Army headquarters (now Kadena AFB) on September 7, 1945. Japanese casualties during the battle for Okinawa numbered 110,000. Only

7,400 Japanese were taken prisoner.[16] The latest casualty figures for Okinawan civilians is 150,000.[17]

Balikpapan: September 8

On September 8, near the mouth of the Mahakam river delta, 50 miles north of Balikpapan, Dutch East Indies, the Australian frigate HMAS *Burdekin,* became the site for the surrender of Japanese forces in Dutch Borneo.

The Japanese delegation, headed by Vice Adm. Michiaki Kamada, commander of the Special Naval Base Force in Balikpapan, were delivered to the surrender site in seven motor torpedo boats under the command of Lt. Cmdr. Henry S. Taylor, USNR. The delegation arrived at *Burdekin,* climbed the boarding ladder, and passed between the rows of Australian guards. Then they waited nervously for the arrival of Maj. Gen. E. J. Milford, commanding general Australian 7th Division. Milford purposely kept the Japanese delegation waiting at attention for several minutes and then, accompanied by the commander of *Burdekin,* walked quickly to the prepared table and returned the salutes of his own staff officers.

Milford then faced the Japanese delegation who remained at rigid attention. He did not return Vice Admiral Kamada's salute. Kamada was instructed to sign the surrender documents and to place his sheathed sword on the table. He did so, obviously in great misery, as he surrendered all Japanese forces in Dutch Borneo.

Overhead, Australian aircraft were less formal, doing rolls, climbs, and zooms, until their low-fuel state caused them to depart.

Following the signing, Vice Admiral Kamada made a plea for speedy Australian occupation of Dutch Borneo because anti-Japanese feelings were high among both Chinese and native peoples.

Nanking: September 9

More than one million Japanese troops laid down their arms in the China theater on September 9. The surrender was signed by General Yasuji Okamura, commander-in-chief of all Japanese forces in China, including Formosa and French Indo-China north of latitude 16. Gen. Ho Ying-ching, commander-in-chief of Chinese forces, accepted the surrender on behalf of Generalissimo Chiang Kai-shek. Representatives from Australia, Great Britain, the Netherlands, Russia, and the United States attended the ceremony which was conducted in the walled city of Nanking.

There was total silence as the Japanese delegation entered the room. The silence continued until the clock struck the hour, the cue for General Okamura to present his credentials. Okamura then scrawled his signature on the surrender document, using a Chinese brush made especially for the occasion. Following the signing, General Ho Ying-ching broadcast a victory message to the Chinese people. Most of the Japanese were repatriated on American ships between October 1945 and June 1946.

Korea: September 9

The first Russian troops entered Korea in early August and moved rapidly southward. The United States had not planned to occupy Korea and was unprepared for the Soviet advance. The only troops immediately available to counter the Soviets were the U. S. Army XXIV Corps in Okinawa. The Corps, under Lt. Gen. John R. Hodge, was ordered to Korea to accept the surrender of Japanese forces south of the 38th parallel. Hodge and three divisions, consisting of 72,000 troops, arrived in Korea on September 8, almost a month after the first Soviet troops occupied North Korea.[18]

The surrender of all Japanese forces in South Korea took place on September 9, in the governor-general's palace in Keijo, (the Japanese name for Seoul). Admiral Thomas Kincaid and Lt. General

Hodge signed the surrender document for the United States after General Abe Nobuyuki, the governor-general of South Korea, signed and surrendered his 360,000 men.[19] Following the signing, the Japanese flag was lowered and the Stars and Stripes raised in its place.

The end of the war hit the Koreans like a bombshell. All hope of freedom had nearly disappeared and, due to the strict censorship, isolation, and propaganda efforts, there was little forewarning of the event. Following the surrender, the Koreans started treating the Japanese as foreigners, which, to the Japanese, was unbearable. The previous Japanese masters now bowed to Koreans when they came face to face on the streets, but mostly the Japanese stayed home, kept out of sight, and wished for a speedy reparation to Japan. Although the Japanese were fearful of revenge, few of the "foreigners" were molested.

Morotai, Dutch East Indies: September 9

On Morotai Island, headquarters of the Australian forces in the Dutch East Indies, General Sir Thomas Blamey, commander-in-chief of all Australian forces, accepted the oath of surrender from Lt. Gen. Fusataro Teshima, commander of the Japanese 2nd Army, in front of 10,000 assembled Allied forces. Lt. Gen. Teshima surrendered 126,000 Japanese forces in the eastern half of the Dutch East Indies. Teshima and his chief of staff, Lt. Gen. Shikao Fujitsuka, would later be interrogated concerning the execution of Allied war prisoners at Idore in 1944.[20]

General Blamey read the terms of surrender which were then translated. General Teshima saluted, laid his unsheathed sword on the table, and signed the documents of surrender. Signatures were also affixed to the document by Japanese naval officers, Capt. Toru Oyama and Capt. Miroru Toyama.

Following his signing of the document, General Blamey made a passionate speech in which he stated that he did not recognize

Lt. Gen. Fusataro Teshima is being escorted to the area where the surrender documents were to be signed on Morotai Island, Dutch East Indies. More than 10,000 Allied soldiers attended the ceremony.

Royal New Zealand Air Force

the Japanese present at the ceremony as honorable or gallant foes.[21] Blamey recalled the treacherous attacks on the British Empire and the United States in December 1941, and the atrocities committed by the Japanese military. He warned that any Japanese found in possession of arms or in violation of the surrender agreement would be dealt with severely.[22]

British Borneo (North Borneo and Sarawak): September 10

In a 12-minute ceremony at Labuan, British Borneo on September 10, Lt. Gen. Baba Masao surrendered the Japanese 37th Army to Maj. Gen. G. F. Wootten, commanding general of the Australian 9th Army.

Following the signature of the Japanese commander and surrender of Masao's sword, Wootten ordered a victory salute of 101 guns. On order, the salute was fired in each Australian-occupied sector of British Borneo.

The surrender of Japanese forces on Sarawak was scheduled for 2:00 P.M. on September 10. The ceremony was to take place aboard HMAS *Kapunda* which had proceeded up the Sarawak River to Pending (junction of the Kuap and Sarawak Rivers) where the Japanese were supposed to board *Kapunda*.

The Japanese surrender party failed to arrive at the scheduled time so a boat was dispatched at 2:30 P.M. to bring Major General Yamamura, the senior Japanese commander, to the ship. The Australian boat returned without Yamamura and with a message that he was otherwise indisposed. Brigadier T. C. Estrick, the senior Australian officer, ordered the boat to return for Yamamura and to bring him back regardless of his disposition. A penitent Yamamura and two staff officers arrived at *Kapunda* at 3:00 P.M.

After a discussion concerning the expected conduct of the Japanese forces and the conditions of surrender, Yamamura and Estrick signed the surrender document. The Japanese delegation departed *Kapunda* at 4:00 P.M. Shortly thereafter, US motor torpedo boats landed the first Australian re-occupation forces in Kuching, the capital of Sarawak.[23]

Dutch Timor: September 11

Col. Kaida Tatsuichi surrendered his sword to Brig. Gen. Lewis Dyke and signed the document that surrendered the forces on Dutch Timor on September 11. Brigadier General Dyke commanded the Australian forces sent to reinforce Dutch Timor early in the war. Like Lt. Gen. Arthur Percival at Singapore, his forces had been defeated by the Japanese. Colonel Kaida Tatsuichi surrendered the Japanese forces aboard HMAS *Moresby* in Koepang Harbor. The surrender document was signed by Colonel Tatsuichi, who surrendered his sword after the signing.

Guam: September 11

The loss of Guam to the Japanese on December 10, 1941,

was the first loss of American territory to an enemy in World War II. Liberation Day for Guam was July 21, 1944. During the ensuing two-and-one-half years of Japanese occupation, the Guamanians (hereafter referred to as Chamorros), suffered all the terror, indignity, and brutalization that characterized Japanese occupations throughout Asia.

Defense of Guam was short-lived. Warned of probable attack by Japanese aircraft bombings on the 8th of July, messages from Pearl Harbor, and capture of Saipanese spies, the 80-man all-Chamorro Guam Insular Force drew weapons and ammunition at 2:00 A.M. on the 10th. By 5:45, defense of Guam ended when Capt. George J. McMillin, USN, naval governor of Guam, surrendered to Maj. Gen. Tomitaro Horii.[24] To add insult to the surrender, the Japanese forced Capt. McMillin to remove his trousers and sign the surrender document in his underwear. The surrender was made before the Japanese approached the U.S. Marine positions on the Orote Peninsula, though the final outcome would have been no different had the marines been involved.[25] Captain McMillin spent the rest of the war as a prisoner in the Mukden, China POW camp.

Japan moved quickly to assimilate the Chamorro people into the Greater East Asia Co-Prosperity Sphere. The name of Guam was changed to Omiyajima (the Great Shrine Island). Agana, the capital city, was changed to Akashi (the Red City), in honor of the rising sun on the Japanese flag. All able-bodied men, 16 years of age and older, were conscripted to work on defensive installations. Those men, women, and children not able to do heavy labor were put to work in the rice fields to feed the Japanese military. Instead of pay, the Chamorros were given an occasional cup of uncooked rice and punched, kicked, slapped, and often beheaded for their effort.

Japanese atrocities on Guam are well-documented and include the execution, usually by beheading, of 684 Chamorros. Prominent civilians like Father Jesus Baza Duenas, a Chamorro catholic priest, his nephew, Eduardo Duenas, a retired U.S. navy enlisted man, Juan N. Pangelinan, and another unidentified civilian were tortured and beheaded.

Murder, beatings, and rapes of Chamorros were commonplace on Guam. This should not be surprising, since the Japanese troops were led by the same type of men who supervised the Bataan Death March, the Rape of Nanking, and the Death Railway.

The Manengon Death March on Guam began on July 12, 1944, when Chamorros were evicted from Yigo and Santa Rosa in the north, and forced to march to Barrigda, Mangilao, and the Manengan valley, where they were told to build their own camp. The march was done over several days in the summer rains. People fell and were beaten, clubbed, and bayoneted if they fell behind.[26] Mrs. Hannah Chance Tores, while carrying her baby daughter, was beaten to death for not moving fast enough. Matilde Flores Sablan buried her grandmother and another lady during the march.

The first night at Manengan, the Japanese took 40 men from the camp to carry equipment for them. When the men finished, their hands were tied behind their backs, they were tied to trees, and all were beheaded.[27]

In all, 15,000 of the 20,000 Chamorro people on Guam were moved to concentration camp sites. Taicho Takebana, the senior police officer of the Fina district of Agat village, ordered 50 girls, ages 16 to 19, to remain behind when their families were forced to move. On July 19, Takebana had the girls moved to several caves near Fina, where they were slapped, beaten, and raped repeatedly throughout the night by Japanese soldiers. In the morning, the Japanese threw grenades into the caves, killing and wounding many of the girls. As the survivors fled from the caves, they were shot by Japanese snipers.[28] Eight of the girls who fled into another cave for protection, found 30 dead Chamorro men, including family members that had been murdered by grenades.

On July 15, the 800 residents of Merizo were rounded up and marched to the Geus River valley. There, 25 men and five women, representing the leadership of the village, were taken to a cave near Tinta, where they were shot, grenaded, and slashed with swords. Only a few, like Joaquina Concepcion, survived by playing dead and hiding under dead bodies. The next day, the Japanese took another group of 30 Merizo Chamorros to a cave near Faha, where all 30 were murdered.[29]

The remaining 740 Merizo villagers were marched for two days to a valley near Atate, where they were told to dig a hole large enough to accommodate all of them. Recognizing that the hole was to become their grave, the villagers, behind such men as Jose Reyes, turned against the Japanese, captured their weapons, and killed all but one guard who managed to escape. The Chamorros then dispersed into the jungle to await the arrival of the Americans.[30]

As the Americans advanced, the Chamorros broke free of their concentration camp sites and ran to meet them. All of their years of frustration, fatigue, hate, fear, and humiliation at the hands of the Japanese burst from their hearts, and they began to cry, laugh, and express thanks for their liberation. They often tried to bow to the Americans (as the Japanese had forced them to do), shake hands, hug, and kiss their liberators, all at the same time.[31]

Maj. Gen. Roy S. Geiger, USMC, commander of the III Amphibious Corps, announced at 11:31 A.M., on August 10, 1944, that all organized resistance on Guam had ended. There was no formal surrender ceremony on Guam since all of the senior Japanese officers died in the battle or committed suicide. However, unlike their countrymen on Tarawa, where no Japanese soldiers surrendered, 1,200 Japanese soldiers on Guam broke with their *bushido* code and surrendered.

The hunt for Japanese stragglers on Guam continued for many years. As late as November 1944, Lt. Col Hideyuki Takeda in northern Guam and Major Sato in the south, had 100 Japanese soldiers under their control. Major Sato surrendered himself and 34 soldiers on June 10, 1945.[32] Takeda with 67 men, surrendered on September 4, 1945. Lt. Col. Takeda was later instumental in convincing 46 more Japanese stragglers to surrender. Takeda has the distinction of surrendering the last organized Japanese unit on Guam.

On Christmas Day 1946, a Guam Police Combat Patrol surprised two Japanese stragglers who were preparing their breakfast in a jungle bivouac area. Tokujiro Miyazawa was killed when he attempted to flee, but Sergeant Shoichi Itoh was able to escape. Itoh, and two other stragglers, Bunzo Minegawa, and a soldier named Unno, survived in the jungle for another eight years until Unno became sick and died in 1954. During May 1960, Minegawa was captured and on May 23, 15 years after the end of the war, Tadeshi Ito emerged from the jungle and surrendered. Ito would not be the last Japanese straggler. On January 24, 1972, 58-year-old Sergeant Shoichi Yokoi, was captured while setting his shrimp nets. Yokoi had evaded capture for 28 years.[33]

Long before the Japanese stragglers on Guam surrendered, the War Crimes Commission on Guam was trying alleged war criminals. A total of 139 Japanese and Japanese sympathizers were charged with war crimes. Only two of the sympathizers were from Guam; 12 were Saipanese, two were from Rota, and one from Palau. No Japanese military personnel from Guam survived to be charged with war crimes. Twenty-five Japanese military personnel from other locations were found guilty of war crimes and sentenced to death.

Perhaps the most famous Japanese to be tried on Guam was Vice Adm. Kose Abe, commander of forces on Kwajelein in the Marshall Islands. Vice Admiral Abe ordered the execution of nine U.S. Marines that had been captured on Makin Island on August 17, 1942. The marines were executed on October 16, 1942. Abe was convicted of murder by the War Crimes Commission and hung on June 19, 1947. Capt. Yoshio Obara, Kwajalein Island commander, who arranged the executions of the marines, was sentenced to ten years imprisonment.[34]

A U.S. Army officer attached to the Marine Barracks Guam was the official hangman and executed 11 of the criminals. Marines executed the last two war criminals following the army officers' departure.[35] Guamanians became American citizens on August 1, 1950, and gained the right to self-government.

Ponape: September 11

Ponape is a high, volcanic island in the Carolines of Micronesia. It is one of the largest islands in the chain, as well as the wettest and most fertile. Ponape was ruled by the colonial governments of Spain, Germany, and, from 1914, Japan.

The people of Ponape fared reasonably well under Japanese rule until February 1944, when B-24 "Liberator" bombers began to bomb the two small airstrips, communication and radar facilities, and gun emplacements. During May, six U. S. warships shelled the island for 70 minutes, destroying all worthwhile targets and 75 percent of all buildings on the island. More than 250 airstrikes during the next 18 months ensured that the damage was not repaired.

All shipping to Ponape was blockaded, and the island was bypassed by the Allies. Self-sufficiency for both the native people and the Japanese became the major concern.

At first, the Ponapeans were given breadfruit and coconuts to eat. As conditions worsened, the diet became swamp taro. Finally, potato and potato leaves were consumed to stay alive. Many people died of starvation, including the Japanese, who took the best food that could be cultivated, as well as the fish and other protein that were harvested.

The Ponapeans were warned that they would not be allowed to be taken prisoner. If the Americans invaded, the Japanese would kill everyone on the island and fight to the death themselves. In the end, following the emperor's decree, the surrender of Ponape was done peacefully.

Lt. Gen. Masao Watanabe surrendered Ponape to Cdr. Ben H. Wyatt, U. S. Navy, aboard the USS *Hyman* on September 11. Capt. Albert Momm, division commander of the *Hyman*, became the new military governor of Ponape the next day.

Singapore: September 12

The reoccupation of Singapore by British forces began on Wednesday, September 7, thus ending the period of Japanese occupation that began on February 16, 1942, when Lt. Gen. Arthur Percival surrendered to Lt. Gen. Tomoyuki Yamashita.

First to land, following entrance of the warships, was a vanguard of more than 100 press correspondents representing news agencies from over the world. Their way was cleared and roads kept open by Japanese soldiers, estimated to number 60,000 in Singapore alone. The British forces were led by Admiral Lord Louis Mountbatten, supreme commander of Southeast Asia forces. The British forces were from the 15th Indian Corps, recently returned from long and heavy fighting in Burma. The first act of the British was to liberate 34,000 Allied prisoners from their captivity in Singapore.

The surrender was received in the municipal building in the presence of British naval, air, and army commanders-in-chief, and representatives of Australia, China, France, Holland, India, and the United States.

General Seishiro Itagaki, Japanese Army commander, received a fiercely hostile reception from the dense crowd when he arrived at the Padang (parade field) with other Japanese officials to sign the documents of surrender. When General Itagaki informed his troops that he had been told to surrender his forces under orders from the emperor, 300 Japanese officers committed suicide by blowing themselves up with hand grenades. A platoon of troops did the same. Field Marshall Count Hisaichi Terauchi, commander-in-chief of the Southern Regions, was to have surrendered the Japanese forces but could not due to residual paralysis from a stroke suffered in April.

British marines lined the streets as the huge Singapore crowd flocked to the Padang which had been leveled and filled for the occasion by hundreds of Japanese prisoners. All vantage points were crowded and nearby roofs were filled with Chinese, Malay, and Indian youngsters anxious to see the historic ceremony.

The guards of honor included detachments from the 5th Indian Division, Commandos, Dogras, Gurkhas, Punjabis, Australian paratroops, French sailors from battleship *Richelieu,* and detachments from HMS *Sussex.* Flanking the steps of the Municipal Offices were Royal marines from HMS *Cleopatra*, and, just inside the building, was a file of men from the Chinese Resistance Army. Slick and determined, the men carried Tommy and Stenn guns, wore khaki uniforms, and peaked khaki caps with their insignia of three red stars.

As Admiral Mountbatten approached, the command "Present, Arms," rang out. The royal salute was given and the national anthem was played. Following the command "Order, Arms," Lord Mountbatten inspected the parade. Meanwhile, Mosquito bombers, Sunderland flying boats, and Dakota transports flew overhead.

The arrival of the Japanese delegation was announced by hoots and jeers from the crowds. The Japanese stepped out of their cars, lined up one behind the other, and were marched into the Municipal Office. The Japanese, faces pale and expressionless, looked neither right nor left as they marched, under escort, to the ceremony site. They walked up the steps into the building, past the soldiers from the Chinese Resistance Army, and to a room where they were told to wait until they were summoned for the ceremony.

Seated in the audience was the sultan of Johore, Sir Ibrahim, the bishop of Singapore, the Right Rev. J. L. Wilson, a victim of Japanese imprisonment and torture. Also present was Mr. L. Rayman, former president of the Singapore Municipality, and Justice N. A. Worley, another victim of torture at the hands of Japanese military police. Many other former leaders of the community were also in attendance.

Exactly on cue, a door opened and the seven Japanese delegates, headed by General Itagaki, moved forward and took their places before the table. Lt. Gen. Numata, chief of staff to field marshall Terauchi, opened a black dispatch case and extracted Lt. General Itagaki's credentials as Count Terauichi's official representative. Next, Lord Mountbatten entered the room and took his seat between General William J. Slim, who directed the defense of India and liberated central Burma, and Lt. Gen. Raymond A. Wheeler, U. S. Army, Southeast Asia command.

Lord Mountbatten announced that "I have come here today to receive the formal surrender of all the Japanese forces within the British South-East-Asia Command."[36] Mountbatten's voice was stern as he looked directly at the Japanese delegates and added, "I wish to make this plain: the surrender today is no negotiated surrender. The Japanese are surrendering to superior force, now massed here in this port of Singapore."[37] Mountbatten then examined the credentials of General Itagaki and read the instrument of surrender. When he finished, Major General Fenny placed 11 copies of the document in front of General Itagaki to sign. Itagaki signed the documents, which surrendered 700,000 Japanese forces, and affixed both his personal and the official Japanese Army seals. Admiral Mountbatten then signed the documents, and the Japanese were told to leave. They bowed, and shuffled out under escort. The signing took nine minutes.

Lord Mountbatten then addressed the crowd from the top of the steps in front of the municipal offices. The national anthem was played and the Union Jack, the same flag that flew when the

Japanese captured Singapore, was raised. There was much emotion, eyes were misted and many throats choked as the Union Jack flew proudly where the red emblem of Japan, with its signal of oppression and persecution, had flown for the past three-and-one-half years. General Seishiro Itagaki would later be tried and hung as a war criminal.

Wom: September 13

Lt. Gen. Hatazo Adachi, commander Japanese 18th Army, surrendered his forces to Maj. Gen. H.C.H. Robertson, commanding general Australian 6th Division, on September 13, on the Wom airstrip. The Japanese delegation arrived in jeeps and drove to within 20 yards of the table where General Robertson was seated. The surrender document was read by the interpreter, at which time Adachi signed the document and relinquished his sword.

Burma: September 13

On September 13 (September 14, Tokyo time), in Rangoon, Lt. Gen. Heitaro Kimura, commander of Burma Area Army, handed his personal Samurai sword to Field Marshall Sir William Slim and, in doing so, surrendered all Japanese troops in Burma.[38] The ceremony, so full of meaning for the defeated Japanese, was the final act to the terrible end of Japan's conquest in Burma. Japan's Burma Area Army had been defeated and destroyed. The remnants of Japan's army that survived the slaughter of the final month of the war were demoralized and more than ready to quit. Unfortunately, it took a long time to repatriate the Japanese prisoners of war. Their presence in Burma was a constant reminder of their despised occupation policies and practices.

Nauru: September 13

The surrender of Nauru took place on the quarterdeck of HMAS *Diamantina,* off Nauru on September 13. Capt. Hisayuki

Soeda, commander of Japanese forces on Nauru, surrendered his forces to Brig. Gen. J. R. Stevenson, commander Australian 11th Brigade. A few weeks later on October 1, Stevenson accepted the surrender of the Japanese forces on Ocean Island in the Ellice Islands (Ocean was also called Banaba) from Lt. Cdr. Nahoomi Suzuki.

China: September 14

Formal surrender of Japanese forces in the Kiukiang-Nanwang area was accomplished when Lt. Gen. Yukio Kasahara, commander of the 11th Army in South China, handed his sword to Chinese General Lu Tao-yan in Nanso, China. The Japanese troops were permitted to keep their weapons until the Chinese government could take over administrative and police functions.

Throughout China, Japanese senior officers followed the lead of Lt. Gen. Kasahara. In Beijing, Maj. Gen. Hiroshi Nemoto represented Japan at the surrender ceremony. At Shantung, it was Maj. Gen. Tadayasu Hoisokawa. In Shansi province, Maj. Gen. Raishiro Sumida surrendered his sword. In Honan province, Maj. Gen. Takashi Takamori, commander 13th Army, surrendered his forces. Maj. Gen. Jiro Sagawa, commander of the Japanese 6th Army, surrendered Japanese forces in Anhwei province. Maj. Gen. Takuro Matsui surrendered the Japanese 13th Army in Shanghai. In Nanking, Kiangsu province, Maj. Gen. Jiro Sagawa, joined by Maj. Gen. Haruki Isayama from Formosa (Taiwan), surrendered Japanese forces. The surrender at Wuhan-Hankow, Hupeh province, was made by Gen. Naosaburo Okabe. Japanese forces in Hunan province were surrendered at Changsha by Maj. Gen. Ichiryo Banzai and Brig. Gen. Naosuki Tomita. Japanese forces in the Canton area, Kwantung province and Hong Kong were surrendered by Maj. Gen. Hisakazu Tanaka, commander Japanese 23rd Army. [39]

Wolei Atoll: September 19

Lt. Col. Parker R. Colmer, representing the island commander

290

of Guam, accepted the surrender of the Wolei Atoll from Major General Katsuzo Kitamura on September 19.[40]

Banaba (Ocean Island): October 1

Australian, British, and New Zealand officials arrived on Banaba Island on October 1, 1945, to accept the Japanese surrender. After the Allied officials had been there a short time, they expressed surprise that there were no native islanders present. They were told that all civilians had earlier been evacuated to other islands to protect them from the Allied bombings.

The truth was that the Bonabanese, Gilbertese, and Ellice Islanders were forced to labor for the Japanese and then executed on August 20, after the emperor's announcement of surrender. The execution of prisoners and forced laborers following Japan's surrender was not unusual. The local commanders had good reason to fear a revolution by the captives if they were set free, or, perhaps, more to the point, the captives could testify against their captors concerning the many Japanese atrocities.

Only one native survivor was found, a Gilbertese named Kabunare who hid in a cave and eluded the Japanese until the war ended. Kabunare's testimony was largely responsible for the trial of the garrison commander, Lt. Cdr. Nahoomi Suzuki. Suzuki was later convicted as a war criminal, found guilty, and hanged.[41] Other Ellice Islanders who had been forced to labor for the Japanese were found in Kusaie (now Kosrae), Nauru, and Tarawa. All were returned home by December 1945.

Taiwan Province, Formosa: October 25

The ceremony for the surrender of Japanese forces on Taiwan province was held at the Chungshan Hall in Taipei on October 25. The chief of staff of Japanese forces in China surrendered to Ho Ying-chin, representing the commander-in-chief of the China theater.

The Japanese surrender of Taiwan was held at the Chungshan Hall in Taipei on October 25, 1945 (above). In the bottom photograph, General Asaburo Kobayashi (left), chief of staff of Japanese forces in China, surrenders his forces to Ho Ying-chin, representing the commander-in-chief of the China theater.

Kuomintaug Historical Commission

43

THE SEVEN SAMURAI

The impressive stone monument to the "Seven Samurai," located at the Matsui family's "Shrine of Remorse," memorializes seven political and military leaders of Japan's wartime government. The Seven Samurai were sentenced to death following the conclusion of the International Military Tribunal for the Far East, known also as the "Tokyo Trial." The trial began on May 3, 1946, and lasted for two-and-one-half years. Judges from 11 Allied nations listened to testimony or otherwise participated in the process for 818 court days.[1] The verdicts were read on November 4, 1948. The judges, one from each country, were appointed by Australia, Canada, China, France, Great Britain, India, the Netherlands, New Zealand, the Philippines, the Soviet Union, and the United States.

The justices pose on opening day. Front (left to right): Patrick (G.B.), Higgins (U.S.), Webb (Australia), Mei (China), Zaryanov (U.S.S.R.). Back (left to right): McDougall (Canada), Röling (Netherlands), Bernard (France), Northcroft (New Zealand). Still to arrive are Justices Jaranilla (Philippines) and Pal (India).

US Army

A total of 28 defendants were tried in the Tokyo Trial. None of the defendants were personally accused of committing an atrocity. Other military tribunals throughout Asia tried 5,700 Japanese officers and enlisted defendants who were accused of committing atrocities, and passed judgement and sentences.[2] Of those so tried, 920 were executed, including General Tomoyuki Yamashita who was hanged, and General Masaharu Homma who was executed by a firing squad.

The judges in the Tokyo Trial heard evidence that, for many years prior to 1928, Japan had claimed a place among civilized nations of the world and voluntarily assumed treaty obligations designed to further the cause of peace and to outlaw aggressive war. They heard testimony that, from 1928, Japan launched aggressive war against her neighbors and freely practiced torture, murder, rape, and other inhumane cruelties. The judges found such testimony to be conclusive. The questions remaining for the tribunal were: why did such aggression happen, and who was responsible?

The defendants stand as the justices enter the courtroom

US Army

At the end of the proceedings, the tribunal found that the actual planning, preparation, and waging of the wars of aggression were not the work of one man but of many of Japan's leaders acting together with a common plan to achieve a common purpose. Of the 28 defendants, seven (the Seven Samurai) were sentenced to death, 16 were sentenced to life imprisonment, one to 20 years imprisonment, and one to seven years imprisonment. One defendant, Dr. Shumei Okawa, was deemed mentally unfit for trial, and two defendants, Yosuke Matsuoka, foreign minister (1940-41), and Osami Nagano, naval minister and chief of the naval general staff (1941-44), died during the proceedings. None of the defendants were acquitted.

Why were seven men sentenced to death by the tribunal? Who were the "Seven Samurai," and what was their crime?

Gen. Kenji Doihara (1883-1948)

General Doihara graduated from the Army Academy in 1904 and the Army War College in 1912. In 1913, as a first lieutenant, he was posted to China and was promoted rapidly. As a colonel, he became chief of the Special Affairs Section, the Kwantung Army's political espionage activity in Mukden.

Doihara was one of the emperor's "Eleven Reliables" and was intimate with Chinese warlords, malcontents, and out-of-power Manchu princes in China.[3] He knew well the power of women, bombs, and opium in the espionage business, and his trafficking earned him the nickname, "Lawrence of Manchuria."

When the Mukden railway incident was engineered on the evening of September, 17, 1931, Colonel Doihara, having already done his work, was in Mukden politicking with his Chinese friends so as to become "mayor of Mukden" the following day.[4] Doihara did become mayor and engineered the riots, threats, and, finally, the abduction that caused Henry Pu'Yi to serve as the puppet ruler of Japanese-occupied Manchukuo.

Kenj Doihara was the premier Japanese intelligence officer in Manchuria. His presence was always the precursor of trouble. He organized a network of brothels and opium dens which provided him with information and agents for his "incidents."
Asahi Shimbun

In 1935, Doihara concluded the Doihara-Ch'in Agreement, whereby Chinese troops withdrew from North China. This and other agreements were made with local Chinese authorities rather than with Chiang Kai-shek. Later, as the army commander in Singapore, Doihara was held responsible for the brutalities conducted upon POWs and internees in camps in Malaya, Sumatra, Java, and Borneo.

Doihara was found guilty of eight of the 10 possible counts against him. He was hung on December 23, 1948, and was the first "Samurai" to be declared dead.

Gen. Hideki Tojo (1884-1948)

General Tojo was one of the most recognized of the defendants due to his position of importance during the war and his attempted

296

suicide at war's end. His suicide attempt was well covered by the press and included graphic pictures in every paper.

Tojo was the son of a samurai and followed the military profession naturally. He was the military attaché in Switzerland and Germany from 1919 to 1922. He taught at the Army War College and was assigned to the army ministry before commanding a regiment in 1929.

Defendant Tojo testifies.

US Army

In 1933, he was promoted to major general, but, because of his relationship with an army group not in favor at the time, was relegated to obscure posts. Following his assignment to military police headquarters, he became responsible for the arrest of many army mutineers following the February 26, 1936, incident whereby the Army First Division assassinated cabinet members and occupied the center of Tokyo for three days before surrendering.[5]

In May 1938, Tojo became army vice minister and demonstrated the abilities that earned him the nickname "razor" or "razor sharp." Tojo supported expansion of the China war and wanted a firm date for a decision as to when war would be conducted against the Allied nations. Following the resignation of the Konoye cabinet, Tojo became prime minister and led Japan in its war against the Allies.

The early years were kind to Tojo, but as Japanese losses began to mount, he was blamed and removed from office in July 1944. Tojo was a stubborn militarist, a brilliant tactician and strategist, and a loyal servant to his emperor. He took total responsibility for all actions of his government and the military during the war.

Tojo was convicted of seven of the 10 possible counts against him and was hung on December 23, 1948. He was the second "Samurai" to be declared dead.

Gen. Akira Muto (1892-1948)

General Muto was vice chief of staff of the Kwantung Army in 1937, army commander in Sumatra in 1942-43, and army chief of staff in the Philippines in 1944-1945. Troops under Muto's command participated in both the rape of Nanking in 1937 and the rape of Manila in 1945. Muto also had overall direction of POW camps in Sumatra, where the civilian population was terrorized and used as slave labor.[6]

Muto was found guilty of seven of the possible 10 counts against him. He was hung on December 23, 1948, and was the third "Samurai" to be declared dead.

Gen. Iwane Matsui (1878-1948)

Emperor Hirohito summoned reserve general Iwane Matsui to the Imperial Palace on August 15, 1937, and asked him to lead a relief force of two divisions to assist the Japanese garrison in Shanghai. Matsui, highly honored, agreed. Hirohito proclaimed him commander-in-chief of all Japanese forces in central China and sent him on his way.

Following his brief audience with the emperor, Matsui was given specific instructions by Prince Konoye, counselor to the emperor, as to what the emperor really wanted. What the emperor wanted Matsui to do was to break the will of Chiang Kai-shek, and the way to do it was to capture Nanking, the Chinese capital, and terrorize the population.

Eight days later, Matsui landed in China with 35,000 fresh troops and began a protracted siege of street fighting in Shanghai. Matsui's slow pace with nearly five divisions frustrated Hirohito. By September, Maj. Gen. Kanji Ishiwara was sent to "assist" Matsui. Ishiwara was provided additional assistants such as: Sadamu Shimomura, who had drafted the plan for the attack on Nanking at the behest of the emperor; Kazumoto Machijiri, favorite aide-de-camp to the emperor; Maj. Gen. Suzuki Tei-Ichi, who was attached to the 16th Division and tasked with the actual conduct of the rape; secret police (*kempei tai*) chief Lt. Gen. Kesago Nakajima, also responsible to the emperor to "get it right," and Col. Akira Muto, another member of the Imperial cabal.

Muto disregarded Matsui's orders for the troops to remain outside the city walls of Nanking. Instead, he invited all four divisions to enter town and bed down where they wished. Finally, Hirohito sent a member of the Imperial family, Prince Asaka, to also ensure that the job was done right. Responsibility for the resulting Rape of Nanking was laid at the feet of Matsui who was then recalled, decorated by the emperor, and placed on the reserve list.

Matsui was convicted of only one of the 10 possible counts against him, but it was the big one. He "deliberately and recklessly disregarded his duty to take adequate steps to prevent atrocities."

When General Matsui, age 70, went to his death, he raised a call of defiance as he approached the gallows. "Banzai! Banzai! Banzai!," he shouted. His cry was echoed by Gen. Kenji Doihara, Gen. Hideki Tojo, and Gen. Akira Muto, who were also walking unassisted up the 13 steps to the gallows platform. When the men reached the platform, they faced the witnesses, black hoods were adjusted over their heads, and at one-and-one-half minutes after midnight, the traps were sprung.

Matsui was hung on December 23, 1948. He was the fourth "Samurai" to be declared dead.

Gen. Seishiro Itagakai (1885-1948)

General Itagaki graduated from the Army Academy in 1904 and from the Army War College in 1916. He was another of the "Eleven Reliables." He was a tough, back-slapping, Chinese intelligence specialist who was posted to China in 1929, where he assisted Kanji Ishiwara to plan the Kwantung Army seizure of Manchuria.

From 1932 to 1937, he was chief advisor to the army chief of staff for Manchukuoan affairs, and worked closely with Kenji Doihara to exploit the new Japanese colony. He was commander of the Fifth Division at the outbreak of the Sino-Japanese war in July 1937, but was recalled to Tokyo to serve as army minister in the cabinet. As war minister in 1938 to 1939, he presided over the disastrous Lake Khasan and Nomonhan battles with Russia.

He became chief of the general staff of the Kwantung Army in 1939 and was promoted to general in 1941. He served as an army commander in China, Korea, and Malaya, and was found to be responsible for prison camp conditions in Java, Sumatra, and Borneo. Itagaki was also charged by the Soviet prosecutor as being the chief instigator of all anti-Soviet aggression on the Asian continent.

He was found guilty of eight of the possible 10 counts against him and was hung on December 24, 1948; the fifth "Samurai" to be declared dead.

Baron Koki Hirota (1878-1948)

Baron Hirota became one of Prince Fumimaro Konoye's informants within the Black Dragon Society as early as 1921. As a result of his close contact with Konoye, who was a confidante and friend of the emperor, Hirota was appointed ambassador to the Soviet Union from 1928 to 1931, foreign minister from 1933 to 1936, and prime minister from 1936 to January 1937.

As foreign minister, he negotiated the purchase of the strategic Chinese eastern railway in Manchuria, and, in October 1935, he announced his three principles *"Hirota sangensoku"*: the establishment of the Japan-China-Manchukuo association, the suppression of anti-Japanese activities in China, and the organization of a Sino-Japanese front against communism.

Hirota became a substitute prime minister in 1936, when Prince Konoye asked to be relieved from the position due to the prime minister's responsibility to conduct the emperor's purge of the army "Strike-North" faction. Hirota increased the military budget and pushed for associated war-related heavy industry. On January 23, 1937, he was forced to resign his entire cabinet due to his confrontation with Gen. Count Terauchi, who became the next war minister.

Hirota was foreign minister on July 7, 1937, during the "Marco Polo Bridge" incident, and did nothing to oppose the army's plan for all-out war in China. The same is true of his lack of action a month later during the Rape of Nanking. As prime minister, he was a leader in the planning for the invasions of Southeast Asia and the Pacific islands. As Japan's military position deteriorated, Hirota, as a senior statesman, sought to arrange a peace through Soviet Ambassador I.A. Malik, but failed.

Hirota was found guilty of three of the possible 10 counts against him. He was hung on December 24, 1948; the sixth "Samurai" to be declared dead.

Gen. Heitaro Kimura (1888-1948)

Genaral Kimura was chief of staff of the Kwantung Army from 1940 to 1941, vice minister of war under Prime Minister Tojo

(1941 to 1943,) and army commander in Burma 1944-1945. He assisted in the planning of the wars of aggression and explicitly approved the use of native and POW slave labor to build the "Death Railway." He was found to have detailed knowledge of the conditions on the railway and was especially brutal in his treatment of Burmese civilians.[5]

Kimura was found guilty of seven of the 10 possible counts against him. He was hung on December 24, 1948; the last "Samurai" to be declared dead.

The wooden coffins of the "Seven Samurai" were loaded onto an army truck and taken to the Kuboyama Crematorium in Yokohama. Most of the ashes were put in small black boxes, taken away, and scattered to the winds. A small amount of the cremation ashes were allegedly obtained by a Japanese trial lawyer and presented to the families of the "Seven Samurai" on April 22, 1965.[7] The ashes were later interred at the Shrine of Remorse near Atami. The reverse side of the cenotaph lists the names of the "Samurai" while the front of the marker has the Chinese ideographs *"Shichishi no Haka"* (Grave of the Seven Gentlemen). Please refer to chapter three for additional information on the Shrine of Remorse.

Emperor Hirohito, the supreme ruler of Japan, reviews troops in 1940.
US Navy

44

PRISONER OF WAR

In the preface, I stated my purpose for writing this book. Lest the reader think otherwise, I should state that I am not so naive as to think that peace will invade the earth because of this or any other book that may be read. We seem to read history in a detached mode, as if war, starvation, rape, torture, and execution have no real meaning for us. We visit shrines where atrocities took place and museums documenting them but learn little of lasting value. If we cannot stop wars, perhaps we can, through books, slowly modify man's inhumanity towards his fellow man.

In this book, most of the chapters have described the horror of war as seen through the eyes of an American. The following story, as told by a Japanese prisoner of war, expresses so well all that is wrong with war. It is a fitting way to remind the younger generation what war is really like.

In August 1945, the Soviet Union invaded Manchuria, overwhelming the Japanese military and civilian occupants. Estimates of Japanese casualties inflicted by the Soviets range as high as 500,000 with as many as 700,000 taken to harsh labor camps in Siberia. There has never been a full accounting of these prisoners, although, in 1990, the Soviets announced that approximately 62,000 died in captivity.

Tominaga Shozo is one of the Japanese who survived to tell his story. I believe you will find his story interesting, and, when considered in the context of loneliness, confusion, pain, suffering, and guilt—those traits associated with prisoners in any war—you may also share my belief that this is the type of story that needs to be retold.

Shozo graduated from Tokyo Imperial University in 1939 with a degree in agriculture. At the time, the government needed settlers for the territory of Manchukuo (formerly Manchuria) in China. Manchukuo was seen as a new world to be settled and developed. The area's coal and iron deposits, plus its great potential for agriculture, required that Japan establish homes and businesses there. Men were needed to oversee the Chinese who were used as laborers. Families were also needed to fully occupy and develop the annexed territory. Shozo took his professor's advice and went to Manchukuo where he worked for a company in charge of grain distribution throughout the territory.[1]

In 1940, Shozo was drafted into the Imperial Japanese Army and trained as an officer. In the summer of 1941, he was sent to central China and stationed at the most advanced part of the Japanese front line. Shozo has never forgotten his first meeting with the men of his platoon. He recalls that the men had evil eyes, the eyes of leopards or tigers.[2] The men had been at war for a long time, had fought in many battles, and killed many Chinese. They looked at Shozo with no respect because of his lack of such experience. The day after his arrival at the front, Shozo, along with 21 other new replacements, were taken to a field where a group of blindfolded, emaciated Chinese prisoners were squatting with their hands tied behind them. After one demonstration of how to force a prisoner to his knees and chop off his head with one stroke of the long sword, each of the new officers was required to perform the ritual until he got it right.

Shozo recalls that he was horrified and could hardly breathe.[3] When his turn came, he took a deep breath, steadied himself, and swung the sword with all his strength. He passed the test on the first try. At that moment something changed inside him. He was no longer self-conscious in front of his men. Their eyes seemed normal. He had become one of them.

Shozo was indistinguishable from hundreds of other officers recently drafted, hurriedly trained, and shipped to China to replace casualties from the conflict which had been ongoing since 1931. Like the others, Shozo would later admit that he killed prisoners, forced new conscripts to execute prisoners, and ordered his men to shoot Chinese soldiers who surrendered. He also ordered the burning of civilian homes and the massacre of the occupants.

By August 1945, there were about 1,125,000 Japanese troops in China with an additional 365,000 troops and 300,000 civilians in Manchukuo. The United States dropped the second atomic bomb on August 9. A few hours before the thunderclap was heard, a different terror engulfed Japan as the Soviet Union entered the war and overran Manchuria. Tens of thousands of Japanese died fighting the Soviets, others died by mass suicide, and still others were killed by the Chinese Communist Army and by bandits who ran wild and killed, raped, and plundered. The people of Manchukuo turned against their tormentors and took their full measure of revenge against the Japanese settlers who had conquered them. Many families were torn apart forever.

Shozo was captured and taken through a succession of harsh Siberian camps where he met Germans, Rumanians, Hungarians, and Czechs. He finally arrived at Prison Camp Number 8, which became his home for the next five years.[4] He and his fellow prisoners were forced to work in the mines for 10 to 12 hours per day, six days per week.

In 1949, the investigation of war criminals began. According to Shozo, this was the first time that he heard that murder, rape, and setting fires to homes was wrong. It had always seemed to him to be just an unavoidable and perfectly acceptable act of war. Some of the prisoners were shown the full text of the Potsdam Declaration, particularly Article Ten, which said that all war criminals will be severely punished, especially those who treated prisoners cruelly.[5] Shozo felt certain that he would never be allowed to return to Japan or to see his wife and daughter again.

After the prisoners were questioned, many were put on trains that departed regularly. The assumption among the remaining prisoners was that those who had left were being sent home. Shozo was only asked to confirm his name and was kept at the camp until 1950. In early spring, he and the few remaining Japanese prisoners were put on a train and sent to Khabarovsk. Some other prisoners from Vladivostok joined the group, and they all performed hard labor at Khabarovsk until June 1950, when they were told that they were being sent to China.

The men were put into freight cars covered with barbed wire. Shozo remembers thinking of the train as being a long section of baskets for criminals.[6] Once loaded into the "baskets," there was total panic. The prisoners were certain that they were being taken to China to be executed for their war crimes. Most of the men would have welcomed this fate in 1945 but believed that five years of hard labor in the harsh prison camps of Siberia should have merited a better fate. There were about 960 prisoners, including, perhaps, 100 former policemen, military police, and secret police.[7] The remainder were soldiers like Shozo. When the train arrived at Fushun, China, the prisoners were marched through streets lined with armed soldiers. Japanese machine guns were now manned by Chinese soldiers and aimed at the prisoners. The men were taken to Fushun Prison, which had been built by the Japanese to hold Chinese prisoners.[8] The former Japanese warden of the prison was now one of the prisoners.

It had been 10 years since Shozo arrived in China as a new officer, and ten years since he had seen his wife and daughter. Would he ever see them again? His reveries were broken by the arrival of his first meal in the prison. He was served Chinese broccoli, a soup of pork and radishes, and white bread.[9] It was delicious, especially the bread, since the prisoners had seen only black bread for five years in Siberia. Perhaps they were being treated so well to throw them off guard and make it easier for the guards to suddenly murder them.

Murder was not what the Chinese communists had in mind. Their purpose was to reeducate these wrongdoers and to win their hearts and minds for the communist cause. Only then would they be permitted to return to their country and work for the party.

Shozo was a slow learner. He read the books by Mao, Marx, and Engels, appeared before numerous panels, and, after months of self examination, was required to write long accounts of his past. It was never good enough. He was always found not to be truly repentant. To help him concentrate, Shozo was put into a deep underground cell and told to keep writing.[10] He was kept in the dungeon for a month. Next came the oral confessions in front of groups of fellow prisoners. These "confessions" continued for months, until most prisoners "got it right." Some couldn't and committed suicide. Others died of disease, and some lost their minds.

In June 1956, the trials began. Of the approximately 1,000 men tried, 45 were indicted.[11] The others were given reprieves and allowed to return to Japan. Shozo was one of those indicted for crimes against the Chinese people. Later, he was told that there was ample evidence for his conviction, but, because he had showed clear signs of repentance and admitted his guilt, he would be allowed to return to his country. A major factor in the court's decision not to prosecute, he was told, was because Japan was no longer a militaristic nation.

After two nights aboard a ship and more than 16 years since he had left, Shozo arrived back in Japan. He was a sick and weary 43-year-old man wearing Chinese worker's clothing and was completely confused by the excitement, sights, and sounds of the dock area. He walked past the crowd until he saw what he thought was his wife's face. "I'm back," he said. "Welcome home," his wife replied.[12] Shozo thought she looked much older. Then his wife introduced the tall girl standing behind her. "This is Yumi, your daughter," she said.

After maintaining his composure in the most horrible conditions imaginable for more than 16 years, Shozo began to sob uncontrollably. This young woman standing behind his wife could scarcely walk when he last saw her. Now she was nearly grown. The reality of what he had missed and what his family had endured triggered the release of emotions that his enemies had never been able to reach. Still sobbing, Shozo, supported by his wife and daughter, began to walk to the end of the pier and home.

Supreme Commander General Douglas MacArthur and Emperor Hirohito meet in the American Embassy on September 27, 1945.

US Army

NOTES

Chapter 1 Japanese Colonialism: 1874-1931

1. Hsu 1983, pp. 315-317.
2. Russell 1958, p. 1.
3. Bergamini 1972, p. 1172.

Chapter 2 Japanese Expansion In China: 1931-1937

1. Fujimoto 1975, p. 74.
2. Bergamini 1972, p. 720.

Chapter 3 The Rape of Nanking: December 1937

1. Bergamini 1972, pp. 1-3.
2. Costello 1981, p. 56; Harries and Harries 1991, pp. 221-227. See also Timberley 1938, pp. 15-33.
3. Bergamini 1972, p. 24.
4. Bergamini 1972, p. 24.
5. Lord Russel 1958, p. 44.

Chapter 4 The Attack on Pearl Harbor: The *Iai*, December 7, 1941

1. Morley 1980, p. 78.
2. Bergamini 1972, p. 805.
3. Hoyt 1990, p. 140.
4. Prange 1981, p. 285.
5. Toland 1970, p. 168.
6. De Virgilio 1991, p. 61.
7. Prange 1981, p. 313.

Chapter 5 The Attack on Hong Kong

1. Costello 1981, p. 144.
2. Costello 1981, p. 215.
3. Costello 1981, p. 216.
4. Russell 1958, p. 56.

Chapter 6 Wake Island

1. Cressman 1972, p. 7.
2. Bergamini 1972, p. 921.
3. Daws 1994, p.42.
4. Bergamini 1972, p. 921.
5. Cressman 1972, A Magnificent Fight, p. 36.
6. Daws 1994, p. 46.
7. Daws 1994, p. 49.

Chapter 7 Death March: Bataan, April 1942

1. Knox 1981, p. xii.
2. Taylor 1981, p. 75.
3. Bradley 1984, p. 83; Spector 1985, p. 397.
4. Knox 1981, p. 121.
5. Knox 1981, p.128.
6. Knox 1981, p. 131.
7. Knox 1981, p. 131.
8. Knox 1981, pp. 133-134.
9. Knox 1981, p. 136.
10. Knox 1981, p. 145.
11. Stewart 1956, p. 58.
12. MacArthur 1964, p. 146.

Chapter 8 Death March: Camp O'Donnell

1. Knox 1981, p. 150.
2. Moret 1993, p. 62.
3. Knox 1981, p. 157.
4. Knox 1981, p. 159.
5. Knox 1981, p. 168.
6. Knox 1981, p. 169.
7. Knox 1981, pp. 182-183.
8. Knox 1981, p. 199.
9. Berry 1993, pp. 90-109.
10. Berry 1993, p. 149.
11. Berry 1993, p. 174.

Chapter 9 The Hell Ships

1. Knox 1981, p. 350.
2. Knox 1981, p. 350.
3. Stewart 1956, p. 121.
4. Knox 1981, p. 357.

Chapter 10 The Burma and Ledo Roads

1. Romanus and Sunderland 1987, pp. 76-77.
2. Romanus and Sunderland 1987, p.77.
3. Romanus and Sunderland 1978, p. 143.
4. Romanus and Sunderland 1978, p. 94.
5. Stilwell, ed by White 1962, pp. 85-92.
6. Romanus and Sunderland 1987, p. 306.
7. Buchanan and McDowell n.d., p. 55.
8. Romanus and Sunderland 1990, p. 364.

Chapter 11 The Fall of Singapore: February 15, 1942

1. Tsuji 1960, p. 3.
2. Tsuji 1960, p. 4; Banking and Monetary Statistics: 1941-1970, p. 1040.
3. Tsuji 1960, p. 10.
4. Tsuji 1960, p. 12.
5. Technically, *Repulse* was a battle cruiser not a battleship. She had been

rebuilt in the 1930s and now carried 15-inch guns, could make a speed of 29 knots, and had an anti-aircraft battery equal to *Prince of Wales*. *Repulse* was 55 feet longer, slimmer, and more maneuverable than *Prince of Wales*: Bergamini 1972, p. 905.
6. Tsuji 1960, p. 33.
7. Harries and Harries 1991, p. 306.
8. Bergamini 1972, p. 913.
9. Tsuji 1960, p. 106.
10. Bergamini 1972, p. 944.
11. Allen 1985, p. 182.
12. Manning 1986, p. 65.
13. Allen 1985, p. 14.

Chapter 12 The Raid on Tokyo: April 18, 1942

1. Doolittle 1991, p. 213.
2. Spector 1985, p. 154. See also: Doolittle 1991, p. 217.
3. Romanus and Sunderland 1987, p. 162.
4. Doolittle 1991, p. 215.
5. Doolittle 1991, p. 213.
6. Spector 1985, p. 153.
7. Spector 1985, p. 154.
8. Doolittle 1991, p. 254.
9. Doolittle 1991, p. 8.
10. Spector 1985, p. 155.
11. Doolittle 1991, p. 260.
12. Doolittle 1991, p. 262.
13. Doolittle 1991, p. 262.
14. Romanus and Sunderland 1987, p. 163.
15. Spector 1985, p. 155.

Chapter 13 The Coral Sea Battle: May 6, 1942

1. Fuchida and Okumiya 1955, p. 101.
2. Lundstrom 1984, pp. 200-202.
3. Fuchida and Okumiya 1955, p. 104.
4. Fuchida and Okumiya 1955, p. 106.
5. Costello 1981, p. 280.

Chapter 14 The Battle of Midway: June 4, 1942

1. Fuchida and Okumiya 1955, p. 115.
2. Spector 1985, p. 169.
3. Fuchida and Okumiya, p. 131.
4. Spector 1985, p. 170.
5. Fuchida and Okumiya, p. 136.
6. Spector 1985, p. 172.
7. Spector 1985, p. 173.
8. Fuchida and Okumiya, p. 163.
9. Lundstrom 1984, pp. 341-345.
10. Fuchida and Okumiya 1985, pp. 177-179; Lundstrom 1984, pp. 360-362.

Chapter 15 The Light Cruiser *Juneau*

1. Heyn 1944, p. 5.
2. Kurzman 1994, p. 131.
3. O'Neill 1943, p. 4. See also Kurzman 1994, p. 138.
4. Kurzman 1994, p. 140.
5. Kurzman 1994, p. 145.
6. Kurzman 1994, p. 169.
7. Kurzman 1994, p. 175.
8. Kurzman 1994, p. 179.
9. Kurzman 1994, p. 181.
10. O'Neill 1943, p. 9.
11. Kurzman 1994, p. 191.
12. Kurzman 1994, p. 191.
13. Heyn 1944, p. 12.
14. Kurzman 1994, p. 207.
15. Kurzman 1994, p. 214.
16. Kurzman 1994, p. 227.
17. Kurzman 1994, p. 229.
18. Kurzman 1994, p. 223.
19. Kurzman 1994, p. 235.
20. Zook 1943, p. 8.

Chapter 16 The Death of Admiral Yamamoto

1. Hoyt 1990, p. 321.
2. Spector 1985, pp. 453-454.
3. Bergamini 1972, p. 1033.
4. Chandler 1987, pp. 1-8.
5. Chandler 1987, pp. 1-8.
6. Bergamini 1972, p. 1035.

Chapter 17 The Death Railway

1. Kinvig 1973, p. 6.
2. Kinvig 1973, p. 6.
3. Kinvig 1973, p. 6.
4. Kinvig 1973, p. 32.
5. Daws 1994, p. 195.
6. Kinvig 1973, p. 86.
7. Costello 1981, p. 397.
8. Kinvig 1973, p. 86.
9. Costello 1981, p. 397.
10 Kinvig 1973, p. 127. Kinvig spells *Ryuku Maru* as *Rokyo Maru*.
11. Kinvig 1973, p. 134.
12. Kinvig 1973, p. 134.
13. Kinvig 1973, p. 142.

Chapter 18 The Kamikazes

1. Kuwahara and Allred 1957, p. 101.
2. Toland 1970, p. 568.
3. Hoyt 1983, p. 39.
4. Rossabi 1987, pp. 208-209.
5. Rossabi 1987, pp. 208-212.
6. The escort or jeep carriers had a maximum complement of 28 aircraft and

a top speed of 19 knots. They were intended for use where surface or air attack against them was minimal.

7. Toland 1970, p. 568.
8. Toland 1970, p. 567.
9. Craig 1967, pp. 3-4.
10. Hoyt 1983, p. 175.
11. Morison 1960, pp. 53-54.
12. Morison 1960, p. 55.
13. Morison 1960, p. 55.
14. Hoyt 1983, p. 10.
15. Morison 1960, pp. 94-100.
16. Toland 1970, p. 700.
17. Hoyt 1983, pp. 239-241.
18. Morison 1960, p. 177.
19. Morison 1960, p. 179.
20. Morison 1960, p. 180.
21. Morison 1960, p. 185.
22. Morison 1960, p. 185.
23. Craig 1967, p. 7.
24. Morison 1960, p. 188.
25. Craig 1967, p. 8.
26. Craig 1967, p. 8.
27. Craig 1967, p. 9.
28. Toland 1970, p. 700.
29. Werstein 1968, p. 168.
30. Hoyt 1993, p. 209.

Chapter 19 Lord James Blears: March 1945

1. This chapter is based upon Lord James Blears' presentation to the Hawaii Pacific University class, History 398k, War in the Pacific, 19 Aug. 1995. The spelling of Mrs. Britain's name was also provided by Mr. Blears.
2. Testimony of Jiro Nakahara to the War Crimes Tribunal, Tokyo, Japan, 23 Jan. 1948.
3. On 9 and 16 Sept. 1942, an aircraft piloted by Nobuo Fujita was launched from a submarine similar to the I-8. Fujita's mission was to drop fire bombs over Oregon's forest. The mission was not successful, due primarily to recent rainfall, but the dropping of bombs did cause panic on the West Coast. Sullivan 1983, pp. 21-23. See also Obituary, "Nobuo Fujita, Pilot who bombed US.," *Honolulu Advertiser*, 2 Oct. 1997, p. B2.

Chapter 20 Firebombing: March 1945

1. Edoin 1987, p. 44.
2. Craig 1967, p. 20.
3. Morrison 1979, pp. 18-24.
4. Craig 1967, p. 20.
5. Craig 1967, p. 22.
6. Craig 1967, p. 24.
7. Edoin 1987, p. 62.
8. Craig 1967, p. 26.
9. Craig 1967, p. 25.

10. Edoin 1987, p. 185.

Chapter 21 The Battleship *Yamato*: April 6, 1945

1. Spurr 1981, p. 24
2. Spurr 1981, p. 25.
3. Spurr 1981, p. 28.
4. Spurr 1981, p. 109.
5. Morison 1960, p. 200.
6. Spurr 1981, p. 235.
7. Spurr 1981, p. 262.
8. Spurr 1981, p. 279.
9. Spurr 1981, pp. 291-292.
10. Spurr 1981, p. 320.

Chapter 22 The USS *Indianapolis*

1. This story is based upon U.S. Navy Department news releases dated 23 Feb. 1946, and correspondence with the Naval Historical Center of 21 Apr. 1995. Readers who desire to know more about the disaster may refer to one or more of the following books in the bibliography: Helm 1963; Kurzman 1990; Lech 1982; Newcomb 1976.

Chapter 23 The Battle for Okinawa

1. Associated Press photographer Joe Rosenthal took the celebrated photograph that became the model for the U.S. Marine Corps War Memorial at Arlington, Virginia. The picture was also used on postage stamps commemorating the Iwo Jima victory. Secretary of the Navy James Forrestal, viewing the battle with the marine's commanding general, "Howlin Mad" Smith, told Smith, "That flag means a Marine Corps for the next 500 years." Moody Jr. 1994, p. 149.
2. Appleman, Burns, Gugeler and Stevens 1948 , p. 473.
3. Appleman, Burns, Gugeler and Stevens 1948, pp. 475-482.
4. Frank 1978, p. 106.
5. Manchester 1982, pp. 412-413.
6. Manchester 1982, p. 412.
7. Marriott 1986, pp. 20-21.
8. Feifer 1992, p. 309.
9. Sledge 1983, p. 248.
10. Sledge 1983, p. 253.
11. Sledge 1983, p. 253.
12. Boardman n.d., p. 4.
13. Manchester 1982, p. 418.
14. Frank 1978, p. 130.
15. Toland 1970, p. 723.
16. Ienaga 1978, p. 199.
17. Toland 1970, p. 723.
18. "Okinawa Memorial Marks final Battle": *Honolulu Advertiser*, 23 June 1995, A12.
19. Fifer 1992, p. 573.

Chapter 24 Hiroshima: The First Atomic Bomb, August 6, 1945

1. This chapter was written in 1980. Reference material was in the public domain by that time.

Chapter 25 The Lie of Marcus McDilda

1. Craig 1979, p. 73.
2. Craig 1979, p. 73.
3. Craig 1979, p. 74.
4. Craig 1979, p. 74.
5. Craig 1979, p. 74.
6. Craig 1979, p. 74.
7. Craig 1979, p. 134.
8. Craig 1979, p. 297.
9. Craig 1979, p. 297.

Chapter 26 The Second Atomic Bomb

1. Toland 1970, pp. 789-801.
2. Craig 1979, p. 84.
3. Toland 1970, p. 801.
4. Craig 1979, p. 86.
5. Craig 1979, p. 86.
6. Craig 1979, p. 91.
7. Toland 1970, p. 802.

Chapter 27 Nagasaki: August 9, 1945

1. Craig 1979, p. 89.
2. Toland 1970, p. 802.
3. Craig 1979, p. 94.
4. Craig 1979, p. 95.
5. Craig 1979, p. 100.
6. Oe 1985, p.186.
7. Craig 1979, p. 101.
8. Craig 1979, p. 95.
9. Ienaga 1978, pp. 236-239; Daws 1994, p. 334.
10. Ienaga 1978, p. 236.

Chapter 28 Japan Conditionally Surrenders: August 10, 1945

1. The Pacific War Research Society 1968, pp. 31-32.
2. Brooks 1968, p. 85.
3. Craig 1979, p. 105.
4. Toland 1970, p. 811.
5. Craig 1979, p. 105.
6. Brooks 1968, p. 161.
7. Pacific War Research Society 1968, p. 16.
8. Pacific War Research Society 1968, p. 16.
9. Pacific War Research Society 1968, p. 18.
10 Bergamini 1972, p. 845.
11. Pacific War Research Society 1968, p. 33.
12. Craig 1979, p. 109.
13. Toland 1970, p. 807.
14. Toland 1970, p. 807.

15. Craig 1979, p. 110.
16. Pacific War Research Society 1968, pp. 111-112.
17. Craig 1979, p. 111-112.
18. Toland 1970, p. 811.
19. Craig 1979, p. 115.
20. Toland 1970, p. 812.
21. Brooks 1968, p. 85.
22. Brooks 1968, p. 85.
23. Toland 1970, p. 812.
24. Pacific War Research Society 1968, p. 33.
25. Craig 1979, p. 119.
26. Craig 1979, p. 120.

Chapter 29 The Allied Response

1. Toland 1970, p. 816.
2. Toland 1970, p. 816.
3. Craig 1979, p. 124.
4. Craig 1979, p. 125.
5. Craig 1979, p. 125.
6. Craig 1979, p. 125.
7. Toland 1970, p. 817.
8. Pacific War Research Society 1968, p. 41.
9. Craig 1979, p. 127.

Chapter 30 Retribution: August 11, 1945

1. Daws 1994, p. 321.
2. Daws 1994, p. 328.
3. Daws 1994, p. 322.
4. Craig 1979, p. 141.
5. Craig 1979, p. 142.
6. Craig 1979, p. 142.
7. Craig 1979, p. 142.
8. Craig 1979, p. 143.
9. Craig 1979, p. 143.
10 Daws 1994, p. 336.

Chapter 31 Day of Crisis: August 12, 1945

1. Toland 1970, p. 821.
2. Craig 1979, p. 146.
3. Toland 1970, p. 821.
4. Pacific War Research Society 1968, p. 49.
5. Craig 1979, p. 148.
6. Craig 1979, p. 149.
7. Toland 1970, p. 821.
8. Craig 1979, p. 150.
9. Pacific War Research Society 1968, p. 50.
10. Craig 1979, p. 153.

Chapter 32 The Coup Develops

1. Pacific War Research Society 1968, p. 51.

2. Toland 1970, p. 824.
3. Craig 1979, p. 158.
4. Pacific War Research Society 1968, p. 73.
5. Craig 1979, pp. 162-163.
6. Pacific War Research Society 1968, p. 75.
7. Craig 1979, p. 163.

Chapter 33 The Emperor's Decree: August 14, 1945

1. Craig 1979, p. 167.
2. Craig 1979, p. 168.
3. Toland 1970, p. 829.
4. Pacific War Research Society 1968, pp. 76-77.
5. Craig 1979, p. 170.
6. Craig 1979, p. 171.
7. Toland 1970, p. 831.
8. Craig 1979, p. 171.
9. Craig 1979, p. 172.
10. Pacific War Research Society 1968, p. 89.
11.Toland 1970, p. 831.
12. Toland 1970, p. 831.
13. Craig 1979, p. 91.
14. Costello 1981, p. 595.
15. Bergamini 1972, p. 1105.

Chapter 34 Collapse of the Coup

1. Pacific War Research Society 1968, p. 106.
2. Craig 1979, p. 184.
3. Toland 1970, p. 835.
4. Pacific War Research Society 1968, p. 208.
5. Toland 1970, p. 837.
6. Bergamini 1972, p. 110.
7. Bergamini 1972, pp. 109-110.
8. Pacific War Research Society 1968, pp. 221-225.
9. Craig 1979, p. 190.
10 Costello 1981, p. 594; Morison, p. 350.
11. Craig 1979, p. 190.
12. Pacific War Research Society 1968, p. 281.
13. Craig 1979, p. 194.
14. Bergamini 1972, states that these attempted assassinations plus certain
other activity at the Palace was part of a plot designed by the emperor to gain
sympathy for his decision to surrender. If true, there may have been two coups
in operation simultaneously: Hatanaka's coup, which never gained support of
the Army; and the emperor's, which had limited objectives and was designed
for propaganda purposes.
15. Craig 1979, p. 197.
16. Craig 1979, p. 198.
17. Craig 1979, p. 201.

Chapter 35 The Emperor Speaks

1. Toland 1970, p. 850.
2. Craig 1979, p. 212.

3. Toland 1970,p. 852.
4. Morison 1960, p. 353.
5. Hoyt 1993, p. 209.
6. Daws 1994, p. 336.
7. Craig 1979, p. 214-215.
8. Daws 1994, p. 336.
9. Daws 1994, p. 336.
10 Craig 1979, p. 213.
11. Bergamini 1972, p. 120.
12. Toland 1970, p. 850.
13. Craig 1979, p. 213.

Chapter 36 Allied Prisoners in China

1. Craig 1979, p. 128.
2. Craig 1979, p. 143.
3. Craig 1979, p. 154.
4. Craig 1979, p. 221.
5. Craig 1979, p. 221.
6. Craig 1979, p. 224.
7. Craig 1979, p. 226.
8. Craig 1979, p. 226.
9. Craig 1979, p. 228.
10 Craig 1979, pp. 233-234.
11. Craig 1979, p. 234.
12. Craig 1979, p. 235.
13. Craig 1979, p. 235.

Chapter 37 The Doolittle POWs

1. Glines 1990, p. 37.
2. Glines 1990, p. 43.
3. Glines 1990, p. 47.
4. Glines 1990, p. 104.
5. Glines 1990, p. 102.
6. Glines 1990, p. 121.
7. Glines 1990, p. 123.
8. Glines 1990, p. 148.
9. Glines 1990, p. 165.

Chapter 38 The Sian Prison Camp

1. Craig 1979, p. 219.
2. Craig 1979, p. 219.
3. Daws 1994, p. 107.
4. Craig 1979, p. 274.
5. Craig 1979, pp. 274-275.
6. Craig 1979, p. 275.
7. Craig 1979, p. 275.
8. Craig 1979, p. 276.
9. Craig 1979, p. 276.
10 Craig 1979, p. 276.

11. Craig 1979, p. 276.
12. Craig 1979, p. 277.
13. Daws 1994, p. 342.
14. Craig 1979, p. 278.
15. Craig 1979, p. 278.

Chapter 39 Allied Prisoners in Hainan

1. Singlaub was promoted to the temporary grade of major for the mission in the belief that the Japanese would have more respect for a field grade officer. Singlaub 1991, p. 84.
2. Craig 1979. p. 279.
3. Craig 1979, p. 281.
4. Craig 1979, p. 283.
5. Craig 1979, p.283.
6. *South China Mail*, Late Evening Edition, 14 Sept. 1945, p. 1.
7. *South China Mail*, 18 Sept. 1945, p. 1.

Chapter 40 Independent Forces and Unnecessary Battles

1. Charleton 1983, p. 3.
2. Vader 1971, p. 44.
3. Horner 1996, p. 108.
4. Nelson 1985, p. 4.
5. Mayo 1974, p. 5.
6. Vader 1971, p. 67.
7. Vader 1971, p. 68.
8. Mayo 1974, p. 23.
9. Mayo 1974, p. 57.
10. Vader 1971, p. 78.
11. Mayo 1974, p. 75.
12. Mayo 1974, p. 85.
13. Mayo 1974, p. 97.
14. Beaumont 1988, p. 12.
15. Vader 1971, p. 50.
16. Vader 1971, p. 28.
17. Morison 1962, p. 259.
18. Leckie 1987, p. 459.
19. White and Lindstrom 1989, p. 195.
20. Daws 1994, p. 285.
21. Horner 1978, p. 39.
22. Horner 1978, p. 36.
23. Beaumont 1988, p. 6.
24. Beaumont 1988, p. 4.
25. Beaumont 1988, p. 14.
26. Charlton 1983, p. 132.
27. Charlton 1983, p. 4.
28. Charlton 1983, p. 64.
29. Charlton 1983, p. 66.
30. Charlton 1968, p. 91.
31. Morison 1963, p. 91.
32. Horner 1996, p. 22.
33. Charlton 1983, p. 164.

Chapter 41 The Surrender Ceremony: September 2, 1945

1. William B. Dickinson. "Mute Officials Sign Documents Of Surrender," *Honolulu Advertiser*, 3 Sept. 1945, p. A-1.
2. Mason Jr. 1986, p. 344.
3 Craig 1979, p. 302.
4. Mason Jr. 1986, p. 353.
5. Craig 1979, p. 302.
6. Mason Jr. 1986, p. 354.
7. Dickinson 1945, p. A-1.
8. Mason Jr. 1986, p. 357.
9. Craig 1979, p. 304.
10. Mason Jr. 1986, p. 358.

Chapter 42 The "Other" Surrender Ceremonies

1. Crowl 1955, p. 367.
2. O'Brien 1974, p. 18.
3. Peattie 1945, p. 274.
4. Hinz 1995, p. 36.
5. Peattie 1945, p. 309.
6. Coleman 1978, p. 172.
7. Coleman 1978, 174.
8. Frank 1968, p. 459.
9. Frank 1968, p. 455.
10. Frank 1968, p. 453.
11. Frank 1968, p. 460.
12. Frank 1968, p. 462.
13. Frank 1968, p. 457.
14. Frank 1968, p. 459.
15. Kneale 1945, p. 186.
16. Appleman 1948, p. 473.
17. Feifer 1962, p. 578.
18. Cho 1967, p. 63.
19. Henderson 1968, p.113.
20. Mackay 1996, p. 226
21. Kneale 1945, p. 189.
22. Kneale 1945, p. 190.
23. Bulkley 1962, p. 444.
24. Farrell 1944, p. 10.
25. Gailey 1988, p. 26.
26. Farrell 1944, p. 65.
27. Farrell 1944, p. 38.
28. Farrell 1944, p. 43.
29. Palomo 1984, p.185.
30. Farrell 1944, p. 53.
31. Farrell 1944, p. 127.
32. Gailey 1988, p. 197.
33. Gailey 1988, p. 198.
34. Frank 1968, p. 465.
35. Aquilina "Who Was Left Behind On Makin?": *Fortitudine,* Summer 1989, p. 23.
36. *Straits Times,* Thursday, 13 Sept. 1945, p. 1.
37. *Straits Times,* Thursday, 13 Sept. 1945, p. 3.

38. Smith 1979, p. 164.
39. Yuzi Nakao, Japanese National Institute for Defense Studies, letter to author, May 21, 1997.
40. Frank 1968, p. 462.
41. *Pacific Islands Monthly*, Sept. 1955, p. 35-37.

Chapter 43 The Seven Samurai

1. Brackman 1987, pp. 63-71.
2. For example, General Tomoyuki Yamashita "The Tiger Of Malaya," was tried and convicted in Manila for his role in the Rape of Manila and sentenced to death. General Yamashita was hanged outside Manila on February 23, 1946. General Masaharu Homma was tried and convicted for his responsibility for the Bataan Death March. He was sentenced to death and was shot by a firing squad on April 3, 1946.
3. The "Eleven Reliables" were a group of 11 junior army officers who were thought to be sufficiently trustworthy to serve in advisory and secret agent capacities to the emperor: Bergamini 1972, p. 1152.
4. Bergamini 1972, pp. 343-344.
5. Bergamini 1972, pp. 665-659.
6. Harries and Harries 1991, p. 465.
7. Brackman 1987, p. 343.
8. Brackman 1987, p. 254.
9. Fujimoto 1975, p. 242.

Chapter 44 Prisoner of War

1. Cook and Cook 1992, p. 40.
2. Cook and Cook 1992, p. 40.
3. Cook and Cook 1992, p. 41.
4. Cook and Cook 1992, p. 462.
5. Cook and Cook 1992, p. 462.
6. Cook and Cook 1992, p. 463.
7. Cook and Cook 1992, p. 463.
8. Cook and Cook 1992, p. 464.
9. Cook and Cook 1992, p. 464.
10. Cook and Cook 1992, p. 466.
11. Cook and Cook 1992, p. 467.
12. Cook and Cook 1992, p. 468.

BIBLIOGRAPHY

Akizuki, Tatsuichiro. *Nagasaki 1945*. London: Quartet Books, 1981.

Alexander, Joseph H. *The Final Campaign: Marines in the Victory on Okinawa*. Washington: Marine Corps History and Museums Division, 1996.

Alexander, Joseph H. *Across The Reef: The Marine Assault on Tarawa*. Washington: Marine Corps History and Museums Division, 1993.

Allen, Lewis. *British View of the Defeat of Singapore, 1941-1942*. (n.p.) 1985.

Appleman, Ray E. *Okinawa: The Last Battle*. Washington: GPO, 1984.

Aquilina, Robert V. "World War II Chronology January-March 1945: Marine Corps Aviation in the Philippines." *Fortitudine* XIII, 4 (1944): 21-23.

———. "World War II Chronology July-September 1945: Surrender of Japanese Forces in the Pacific." *Fortitudine* XV, 1 (1985): 20-23.

———. "World War II Chronology August-December 1942: Guadacanal." *Fortitudine* XXII, 1 (1992): 21-23.

———. "World War II Chronology June-August 1944: Capture of Saipan, Guam and Tinian." *Fortitudine* XXIII, 2 (1993): 30-31.

———. "World War II Chronology September-December 1944: Capture of Palau." *Fortitudine* XXIII, 3 (1993-1994): 21-23.

———. "World War II Chronology April-May 1944: Assault on the Mariana Islands." *Fortitudine* XXIII, 1 (1993): 31.

———. "World War II Chronology January-June 1943: Victory on Guadacanal." *Fortitudine* XXII, 2 (1992): 22-23.

———. "World War II Chronology July-December 1943: Assault on Tarawa." *Fortitudine* XXII, 3 (1992-1993): 23.

———. "World War II Chronology October-December 1945: Occupation Duty in China and Japan." Fortitudine XXIV, 3 (1994-1995): 22-23.

———. "World War II Chronology April-June 1945: Campaign for Okinawa." *Fortitudine* XXIV, 1 (1994): 20-21.

———. "Marine Corps Logistics in World War II." *Fortitudine* XVI, 4 (1987): 3-9.

———. "Who Was Left Behind On Makin?" *Fortitudine* XIX, 1 (1989): 22-23.

Ballendorf, Dirk Anthony. "Earl Hancock Ellis: A Final Assessment." *Marine Corps Gazette* 74, 11 (1980): 78-87.

Battle of Midway / To the Shores of Iwo Jima. 1945. Produced by the U. S. Navy. Dir. John Ford. 41 min., Viking Video Classics, videocassette.

Beaumont, Joan. *Gull Force: Survivorship and Leadership in Capitulation*. Wellington: Allen and Unwin, 1988.

———. "Gull Force Comes Home: The Aftermath of Captivity." *Journal of the Australian War Memorial* 14 (1989): 43-52.

Behr, Edward. *The Last Emperor*. New York: Bantam, 1987.

Bergamini, David. *The Imperial Conspiracy*. New York: Simon and Schuster, 1972.

Berry, William A. *Prisoner of the Rising Sun*. Norman, OK: University of Oklahoma Press, 1993.

Blair, Joan and Clay Blair, Jr. *Return From the River Kwai*. New York: Simon, 1979.

Blanch, John. "Bougainville Surrender." *Chin Up* Autumn Issue (March 1996): 14-17.

Boardman, Bob. *Unforgettable Men In Unforgettable Times*. Pamphlet. Seattle: n.d.

Bobrick, Benson. *East of the Sun*. New York: Henry Holt, 1992.

Brackman, Arnold C. *The Other Nuremberg*. New York: William Morrow, 1987.

Breuer, William B. *The Great Raid On Cabanatuan*. New York: John Wiley, 1994.

Brooks, Janice Young. *Guests of the Emperor*. New York: Ballantine, 1990.

Brooks, Lester. *Behind Japan's Surrender*. New York: McGraw, 1968.

Brown, Cecil. *Suez To Singapore*. New York: Random House, 1942.

Browne, Courtney. *The Last Banzai*. New York: Paperback Library, 1967.

Bryan, J. III and Phillip G. Reed, *Mission Beyond Darkness*. New York: Duell, Sloan and Pearce, 1945.

Buchanan, C.M. and John R. McDowell. *Stillwell Road: Story of the Ledo Lifeline*. Burma: Office of Public Relations, USF, 1BT, n.d.

Bulkley, Robert J. Jr. *At Close Quarters: PT Boats in the United States Navy*. Washington: Government Printing Office, 1962.

Burlingame, Burl. *Advance Force Pearl Harbor*. Kailua, HI: Pacific Monograph, 1992.

Burris, Jerry, ed. "Enola Gay: Two Ways to Recall a Great, Sad Story." *Honolulu Advertiser*. 4 Sept. 1994: B:1.

Callinan, Bernard. *Independent Company: The Australian Army in Portuguese Timor, 1941-1943*. Richmond, Australia: William Heinemann, 1953.

Campbell, John. ed. *The Experience of World War II*. London: Grange, 1989.

Cannadine, David, ed. *The Speeches of Winston Churchill*. Boston: Houghton Mifflin Co., 1989.

Cannon, M. Hamlin. *The Return to the Philippines*. Washington: GPO, 1973.

Carl, Marion C. *Pushing the Envelope*. Annapolis: Naval Institute Press, 1944.

Carlyon, Norman D. *I Remember Blamey*. South Melbourne: MacMillan, 1980.

Cates, Clifton B. Jr. *War History of the U.S.S. Pennsylvania*. Ship's Welfare Fund, 1946.

Chapin, John C. *Breaching The Marianas: The Battle For Saipan*. Washington: Marine Corps Historical Center, 1994.

——. *Breaking The Outer Ring: Marine Landings In The Marshall Islands*. Washington: Marine Corps Historical Center, 1994.

Charles, H. Robert. *Last Man Out*. Austin, TX: Eakin, 1988.

Charleton, Peter. *The Unnecessary War*. Brisbane: MacMillan, 1983.

Cho, Soon Sung. *Korea in World Politics: 1940-1950*. Berkeley: University of California Press, 1967.

Churchill, Winston S. *The Hinge Of Fate*. Boston: Houghton Mifflin Co., 1950.

Cohen, Stanley. *East Wind Rain*. Missoula, MT: Pictorial Histories, 1987.

——. *The Forgotten War: The Aleutians*. Missoula, MT: Pictorial Histories, 1993.

Coleman, John S., Jr. *Bataan and Beyond: Memories of an American POW.* College Station: Texas A and M University Press, 1978.

Connel, Brian. *Return of the Tiger.* New York: Doubleday, 1961.

Cook, Haruko Taya and Theodore F. Cook. *Japan at War: An Oral History.* New York: The New Press, 1992.

Costello, John. *The Pacific War.* New York: Rawson Wade, 1981.

Coox, Alvin D. *Nomonhan: Japan Against Russia, 1939.* 2 vols. Stanford, CA: Stanford University Press, 1985.

Craig, William. *The Fall of Japan.* New York: Penguin, 1967.

Creamer, Beverly. "Wounds of War." (Japanese Comfort Women) *Honolulu Advertiser.* 3 Feb. 1993: C:1.

Cressman, Robert J. and J. Michael Wenger. *Infamous Day: Marines at Pearl Harbor, 7 December, 1941.* Washington: Marine Corps Historical Center, 1992.

———. *A Magnificent Fight: Marines In The Battle For Wake Island.* Washington: Marine Corps Historical Center. 1992.

Crocker, Mel. *Black Cats and Dumbos: WWII's Fighting PBYs.* Blue Ridge Summit, PA: Aero, 1987.

Crowl, Philip A. and Edmund G. Love. *The War in the Pacific:Seizure of the Gilberts and Marshalls.* Washington: Office of the Chief of Military History, Department of the Army, 1955.

Daws, Gavin. *Prisoners of the Japanese.* New York; William Morrow, 1994.

Deacon, Richard. *Kempai Tai: The Japanese Secret Service. Then and Now.* Tokyo: Charlws E. Tittle, 1990.

Dickinson, William B, "Mute Officials Sign Surrender Documents," *Honolulu Advertiser.* 3 Sept. 1945. sec. A, p. 1.

Dunlop, Richard. *Behind Japanese Lines: With the OSS in Burma,* Chicago: Rand McNally, 1979.

Dunnigan, James F. and Albert A. Nofi. *Victory at Sea.* New York: William Morrow, 1995.

Doolittle, General James H. *I Could Never Be So Lucky Again.* New York: Bantam, 1992.

Dorn, Frank. *The Sino-Japanese War, 1937-41.* New York: Macmillan, 1974.

Dower, John W. *War Without Mercy: Race and Power in the Pacific.* New York: Pantheon, 1986.

Dull, Paul S. *A Battle History of the Imperial Japanese Navy (1941-1945).* Annapolis: Naval Institute Press, 1978.

Eads, Lyle W. *Survival Amidst the Ashes.* Winona, MN: Apollo, 1985.

Falk, Stanley. *Bloodiest Victory: Palaus.* New York: Ballantine,1974.

Farrell, Don A. *The Pictorial History of Guam: Liberation Day-1944.* Tamuning, Guam: Micronesian Productions, 1944.

Feifer, George. *Tennozan: The Battle of Okinawa and the Atomic Bomb.* New York: Ticknor and Fields, 1992.

Feldt, Eric A. *The Coast Watchers.* New York: Bantam, 1979.

Fishman, Jack. *Long Knives and Short Memories.* New York: Richardson and Steirman, 1986.

Fleming, V. Keith. "Lessons for Today's Marines Found in Visit to Iwo Jima." *Fortitudine* XIX, 4 (1940): 7-9.

Frank, Benis M. *Okinawa: The Great Island Battle.* New York: Elsevier-Dutton, 1978.

——, and Henry I. Shaw, Jr. *Victory and Occupation: History of U. S. Marine Corps Operations in World War II.* Vol. V. Washington: Historical Branch, G-3 Division, Headquarters, U. S. Marine Corps, 1968.

Fuchida, Mitsuo and Masatake Okumiya. *Midway: The Battle That Doomed Japan.* Annapolis: Naval Institute Press, 1955.

Fujita, Frank Jr. *Foo: A Japanese-American Prisoner of the Rising Sun.* Denton: University of North Texas Press, 1993.

Fujimoto, Hiroshi, ed. *Fifty Years Of Light And Dark: The Hirohito Era.* Tokyo: Mainichi, 1975.

Gailey, Harry. *The Liberation of Guam: 21 July-10 August.* Novato, Ca: Presidio, 1988.

Gayle, Gordon D. *Bloody Beaches: The Marines at Peleliu.* Washington: History and Museums Division, 1996.

Glines, Carroll V. *Attack on Yamato.* New York: Orion, 1990.

——. *Four Came Home.* Princeton: D. Van Nostrand, 1966.

Gullett, Henry. *Not As A Duty Only.* Carlton, Victoria: Melbourne University Press, 1976.

Goodman, Warren H. "Boyington: A Hero Remembered." *The Yellow Sheet.* Quantico, VA: (Summer 1994): 1.

Gordon, Harry. *Die Like The Carp.* North Melbourne, Victoria: Cassell Australia, 1978.

Gooding, Jennifer L. "Personal Diaries Reveal Marines' Reactions to War." *Fortitudine* XXI, 2 (1991): 18.

Green, T. N. ed., *The Guerrilla—and How To Fight Him.* New York: Praeger, 1962.

Griffith, Brig. Gen. Samuel II. *The Battle For Guadacanal.* New York: Bantam, 1980.

Griess, Thomas E., series ed. *The Second World War: Asia and the Pacific,* Wayne, NJ: Avery, 1984.

——, series ed. *Atlas for the Second World War: Asia and the Pacific,* Wayne, NJ: Avery, 1985.

Grove, Leon and Claire Grove. Unpublished manuscript of the Japanese Occupation of the Philippines. 1941-1945. Undated.

Hallas, James H. *The Devils Anvil: The Assault on Peleliu.* Westport, CT: Praeger, 1994.

Harries, Meirion and Susie Harries. *Soldiers of the Sun: The Rise and Fall of the Imperial Japanese Army.* New York: Random House, 1991.

Harrington, Joseph D. *Yankee Samurai.* Detroit: Pettigrew, 1979.

Harris, Brooklyn. *Bill: A Pilot's Story.* Klamath Falls: Graphic Press, 1995.

Harrison, Courtney T. *Ambon: Island of Mist,* North Geelong, Australia: C. W. and C.T. Harrison, 1988.

Harwood, Richard. *A Close Encounter: The Marine Landing on Tinian.* Washington: Marine Corps Historical Center, 1994.

Heine, William. *With Perry To Japan.* Honolulu: University of Hawaii Press, 1990.

Heilbrun, Otto. *Warfare in the Enemy's Rear.* New York: Praeger, 1963.

Helm, Thomas. *Ordeal By Sea: The Tragedy of the U.S.S. Indianapolis.* New York: Dodd, 1963.

Henderson, Gregory. *Korea: The Politics of the Vortex.* Cambridge: Harvard University Press, 1968.

Herman, Ronny. *In The Shadow of the Sun.* Surrey, B.C. Canada: Vanderheide, 1992.

Hersey, John. *Hiroshima.* New York: Bantam, 1979.

Higa, Tomiko. *The Girl With The White Flag.* Tokyo: Kodansha, 1991.

Hinz, Earl R. *Pacific Island Battlegrounds of World War II: Then and Now.* Honolulu: Bess Press, 1995.

Hoito, Edoin. *The Night Tokyo Burned.* New York: St. Martin's, 1987.

Honan, William H. "Sneak Attack Dastardly Only To Victim." *Honolulu Advertiser,* 21 Nov. 1991: p. 23.

Horner, David. *Inside The War Cabinet: Directing Australia's War Effort 1939-45.* St. Leonards, Australia: Allen and Unwin, 1996.

———. *Crisis of Command: Australian Generalship and the Japanese Threat, 1941-1943.* Canberra: Australian National University Press, 1978.

Hosoya, Chihiro, Isuke N. Ando, Asuaki Y. Onuma, and Richard H. Minear. *The Tokyo War Crimes Trial.* Tokyo: Kodansha, 1986.

Hoyt, Edwin P. *Raider Battalion.* Los Angeles: Pinnacle Books, 1980.

———. *Storm Over the Gilberts.* New York: Avon, 1978.

———. *The Battle of Leyte Gulf.* New York: Playboy Press, 1972.

———. *The Glory of the Solomons.* New York: Stein and Day, 1984.

———. *The Kamikazes.* New York: Arbor House, 1983.

———. The Last Kamikaze: The Story of Admiral Matome Ugaki. Westport, CT: Praeger, 1993.

———. *The Men of the Gambier Bay.* New York: Avon, 1979.

———. *Yamamoto.* New York: Warner, 1990.

Howarth, Stephen. ed., Men of War: *Great Naval Leaders of World War II.* New York: St. Martin's, 1992.

Hunt, Ray C. and Bernard Norling. *Behind Japanese Lines.* Lexington, KY: University Press of Kentucky, 1986.

Hynes, Samuel. *Flights of Passage.* Annapolis: Naval Institute Press, 1988.

Hsu, Immanuel C.Y. *The Rise of Modern China.* New York: Oxford 1983.

Ienaga, Saburo. *The Pacific War: W.W. II and the Japanese, 1931- 1945,* New York: Pantheon, 1978.

Iriye, Akira. *The Origins of the Second World War in Asia and the Pacific.* New York: Longman, 1987.

Isley, Jeter A. and Philip A. Crowl. *The U.S. Marines and Amphibious War.* Princeton: Princeton University Press, 1951.

Jaeger, Clete. *Six More Months.* Rapid City: Clete Jaeger, 1988.

John, Mike. *The Black Sheep Squadron.* New York: Bantam, 1978.

Johnson, Stanley. *Queen of the Flat-Tops.* New York: Bantam, 1979.

Kahn, David. *The Codebreakers.* New York: New American Library, 1973.

Kelly, C. Brian. *Best Little Stories from W.W. II.* Charlotte, VA: Papercraft, 1990.

Kerr, George H. Formosa. *Licensed Revolution and the Home Rule Movement, 1895-1945.* Honolulu: University of Hawaii Press, 1974.

Kurita, Isamu. *Japanese Identity.* Tokyo: Fujitsu Institute of Management, 1987.

Kinvig, Clifford. *Death Railway. Ballantine's Illustrated History of the Violent Century.* New York: Ballantine, 1973.

Kneale, R. V., E. E. Smith and R. F. O'Malley, ed., *Stand Easy.* Canberra: Australian War Memorial, 1945.

Knox, Donald. *Death March: The Survivors of Bataan.* New York: Harcourt, 1981.

Kouwahara, Yasuo. *Kamikaze.* New York: Ballantine, 1957.

Kurzman, Dan. *Fatal Voyage: The Sinking of the USS Indianapolis.* New York: Antheneum, 1990.

———. *Left To Die: The Tragedy Of The USS Juneau.* New York: Pocket, 1994.

Kyodo News Service, "Murayama Extends WWII Apology To Asia," *Honolulu Star Bulletin,* 24 Aug. 1994, sec. A, p. 13.

Layton, Edwin T. *And I Was There: The Saga of World War II.* New York: William Morrow, 1985.

Lech, Raymond B. *All The Drowned Sailors.* New York: Stein and Day, 1982.

Leckie Robert. *Delivered From Evil.* New York: Harper and Row, 1987.

Lodge, Major O.R. *The Recapture of Guam.* Washington: Marine Corps Historical Center, 1954.

Lord, Walter. *Day of Infamy.* New York: Bantam, 1980.

———. *Incredible Victory,* New York: Harper and Row, 1967.

Lowry, Thomas P. and John W.G. Wellham. *The Attack on Taranto: Blueprint for Pearl Harbor.* Mechanicsburg, Pa: Stackpole, 1975.

Lundstrom, John B. *The First Team and the Guadalcanal Campaign.* Annapolis: Naval Institute Press, 1994.

Lyons, Michael J. *World War II: A Short History.* Englewood Cliffs, NJ: Prentice Hall, 1994.

MacArthur, Douglas. *Reminiscences.* New York: McGraw-Hill, 1964.

MacDonald, Alexander. *My Footlose Newspaper Life.* Bangkok, Thailand: Post Publishing, 1990.

Machorton, Ian. *The Hundred Days of Lt. Machorton.* New York: Bantam, 1958.

Macintyre, Donald. *Aircraft Carrier: The Majestic Weapon.* New York: Ballantine, 1971.

Mackay, James. *Betrayal in High Places.* Auckland: Tasmand Books, 1996.

Manchester, William. *American Caesar: Douglas MacArthur 1880-1964.* New York: Dell, 1972.

———. *Goodbye Darkness: A Memoir of the Pacific War.* New York: Dell, 1980.

Manning, Paul. *Hirohito: The War Years.* New York: Dodd and Mead, 1986.

Maraini, Fosco. *Meeting With Japan.* New York: Viking, 1960.

Martin, Michael. "Coastwatchers of the Solomons." *The Retired Officer* XLIII, 4 (1987): 34-38.

Martin, Ralph G. *The G.I. War.* New York: Avon, 1968.

Mason, John T. Jr. *The Pacific War Remembered: An Oral History Collection.* Annapolis: Naval Institute Press, 1986.

Masters, John. *The Road Past Mandalay.* New York: Bantam, 1963.

Mayo, Lida. *Bloody Buna.* New York: Playboy Press, 1979.

McQuarie, Peter. "When Fighting Finally Stopped." *Pacific Islands Monthly.* (Sept. 1945) 35-37.

Mee, Charles L. Jr., *Meeting at Potsdam.* New York: Dell, 1976.

Melson, Charles D. *Up The Slot: Marines In The Central Solomons.* Washington: Marine Corps Historical Center, 1993.

Merrill, Edson L. "Three Thousand Meals A Day." *Marine Corps Gazette* vol. 74, 11 (Nov. 1980) 89-93.

Mersky, Peter B. *Time Of the Aces: Marine Pilots In The Solomons.* Washington: Marine Corps Historical Center, 1993.

Millett, Allan R. *Semper Fidelis: The History Of The United States Marine Corps.* New York: Macmillan, 1980.

Minear, Richard H. *Victor's Justice: The Tokyo War Crimes Tribunal.* Princeton: Princeton University Press, 1971.

Moody, Sidney C. Jr. *War Against Japan.* Novato, CA: Presidio, 1994.

Morison, Samuel Eliot. *U. S. Naval Operations in World War II,* vol. 3, *The Rising Sun in the Pacific: December 1931 to April 1942.* Boston: Atlantic-Little, Brown. Reprint of 1950 ed.

———. *Victory In The Pacific.* vol. XIV, Boston: Little, Brown, 1960.

———. *The Two Ocean War.* Boston: Little, Brown, 1963.

Morley, James William, ed., *Japan Erupts: The London Naval Conference and the Manchurian Incident, 1928-1932.* New York: Columbia, 1984.

———., ed. *The China Quagmire: Japan's Expansion on the Asian Continent, 1933-1941.* New York: Columbia University Press, 1983.

———., ed. *Japan's Advance into Southeast Asia, 1939-1941,* New York: Columbia University Press, 1980.

Morrett, John J. *Soldier Priest.* Roswell, GA: Old Rugged Cross, 1993.

Morrison, Wilbur H. *Point of No Return.* New York: Playboy Press, 1980.

Morton, Louis. *The Fall of the Philippines.* Washington: GPO, 1985.

Nalty, Bernard C. *Cape Gloucester: The Green Inferno.* Washington: Marine Corps Historical Center, 1945.

Nelson, Hank. *Prisoners Of War: Australians Under Nippon.* Adelaide: Australian Broadcasting Corporation, 1985.

Newcomb, Richard F. *Abandon Ship: Death of the U.S.S. Indianapolis.* Bloomington: Henry Holt, 1976.

———. *Iwo Jima.* New York: Bantam, 1982.

———. *Savo.* New York: Holt, Rinehart and Winston, 1961.

Nichols, David. ed. *Ernie's War.* New York: Simon and Schuster, 1986.

Nishimura, Haruo and others, *Fifty years Of Light And Dark: The Hirohito Era.* Tokyo: Mainichi Newspapers, 1975.

Numnonda, Thamsook. *Thailand and the Japanese Presence 1941-1945.* Singapore: 1977.

O'Brien, Cyril J. *Liberation: Marines in the Recapture of Guam.* Washington: Marine Corps Historical Center, 1994.

O'Brien, Robert J. *The Battles of Kwajalein and Roi-Namur.* Kwajalein: Bell Telephone Laboratories, 1974.

Oe, Kenzaburo. ed., *Fire from the Ashes.* Japan: Shueisha, 1983.

Ogawa, Tetsuro. *Terrraced Hell: A Japanese Memoir.* Portland, VT: Charles E. Tuttle, 1972.

Pacific War Research Society. *Japan's Longest Day.* Tokyo: Kodansha International Ltd., 1980.

Palomo, Tony. *An Island in Agony.* Washington, D.C.: T. Palomo. 1984.

Peattie, Mark R. *Nan'yo: The Rise and Fall of the Japanese in Micronesia, 1885-1945.* Honolulu: University of Hawaii Press, 1988.

Peers, William R. *Behind the Burma Road.* Boston: Little, Brown, 1963.

Piccigallo, Phillip R. *The Japanese on Trial.* Austin: University of Texas Press, 1979.

Pomeroy, Earl. American Policy Respecting the Carolines and Marshalls, 1898-1941. *Pacific Historical Review.* 17(2); 43-53.

Potter, E.B. *Nimitz.* Annapolis: Naval Institute Press, 1976.

Prange, Gordon W. *At Dawn We Slept.* New York: Penquin, 1981.

Quilter, Charles J. II. "Marine's Lively Photos of 1920's Peking a Rich Gift." *Fortitudine* XX, 1 (1990) 12-14.

Reischauer, Edwin O. *The United States and Japan.* New York: Viking, 1965.

Report from the Aleutians. 1986. Dir. John Huston. Viking Video Classics, 47 min. Videocassette.

Romanus, Charles F. and Riley Sunderland. *The China-Burma-India Theater: Stilwell's Mission To China.* Washington: GPO, 1987.

———. *The China-Burma-India Theater: Time Runs Out in CBI.* Washington: GPO, 1990.

Romulo, Carlos P. *I Saw The Fall of the Philippines.* New York: Doubleday, 1943.

Ross, Bill D. *Iwo Jima: Legacy of Valor.* New York: Vanguard, 1985.

Ross, Donald K. and Helen L. Ross, *"0775" The Heroes of Pearl Harbor.* Montezuma, IA: Sutherland, 1988.

Russell, Lord. *The Knights of Bushido.* New York: E.P. Dutton, 1958.

Sacrifice at Pearl Harbor. (n.d.) Narrated by Edward Herman. British Broadcasting Corporation. 47 min., videocassette.

Sakai, Saburo. *Samurai.* New York: Bantam Books, 1978.

Salisbury, Harrison E. *The Long March: The Untold Story.* New York: Harper, 1985.

Samson, Jack. *Chennault.* New York: Doubleday, 1987.

Schafer, Edward H. *Shore of Pearls.* Berkeley: University of California Press, 1970.

Schooland, Ken. *Shogun's Ghost: The Dark Side of Japanese Education.* New York: Bergin and Garvey, 1990.

Searles, John M. *Tales of Tulagi.* New York: Vantage, 1992.

Seward, Jack. *Hara-Kiri.* Rutland, VT: Charles E. Tuttle, 1968.

Shaw, Henry I. Jr. *First Offensive: The Marine Campaign For Guadalcanal.* Washington: Marine Corps Historical Center, 1992.

———. *Opening Moves: Marines Gear Up For War.* Washington: Marine Corps Historical Center, 1991.

———. *The United States Marines In The Occupation Of Japan,* Washington, Historical Branch, G-3 Division, Headquarters, U.S. Marine Corps, 1961.

———. Bernard C. Nalty, and Edwin Turnbladh. *History of U.S. Marine Corps Operations in World War II,* vol. 3, Central Pacific Drive, Washington: Historical Branch, G-3 Division, Headquarters U.S. Marine Corps, 1966.

Sherman, Admiral Frederick C. *Combat Command.* New York: Bantam, 1982.

Sherrod, Robert. *History of Marine Aviation in World War Two.* Washington: Combat Forces, 1952.

———. "Saipan: Smith versus Smith." *Fortitudine* XIX, 4 (1990): 5.

Simmons, Edwin H. "Guadalcanal 50 Years Later." *Fortitudine* XXII, 2 (1992): 3-12.

———. "Guam Redux." *Fortitudine* XXIV, 2 (1994): 3-12.

———. "Readers Always Write: More Comments On Wake Island." *Fortitudine* XXIII, 2 (1993): 10-12.

———. *The United States Marines: The First Two Hundred Years 1775-1975.* New York: Viking, 1974.

Singlaub, John K. *Hazardous Duty.* New York: Summit, 1991.

Skidmore, Ian. *Escape From Singapore—1941.* New York: Scribner's, 1973.

Sledge, E. B. *With The Old Breed: At Peleliu and Okinawa.* New York: Bantam, 1983.

Smith, E. D. *Battle For Burma.* New York: Holmes and Meier, 1979.

Smith, Robert Ross. *The Approach to the Philippines.* Washington: GPO, 1984.

———. *Triumph In The Philippines.* Washington: GPO, 1984.

Snow, Edgar. *People On Our Side.* Cleveland: World, 1945.

Spector, Ronald H. *Eagle Against The Sun.* New York: Free Press, 1985.

Spurr, Russell. *A Glorious Way To Die.* New York: Newmarket, 1981.

Stafford, Edward P. *The Big "E."* New York: Ballantine, 1962.

Stephan, John J. *Hawaii Under the Rising Sun: Japan's Plans for Conquest After Pearl Harbor.* Honolulu: University of Hawaii Press, 1984.

Stewart, Sidney. *Give Us This Day: The Bataan Death March.* New York: Popular Library, 1956.

Stewart, William H. *Saipan in Flames: The Turning Point in the Pacific War.* Saipan: J.M. and Associates, 1993.

———. *Ghost Fleet of the Truk Lagoon.* Missoula, MT: Pictoral Histories, 1991.

Strobel, John., ed. "Japan Plans Compensation." (Comfort Women) *Honolulu Advertiser* 30 Aug. 1994: A:6.

———. ed. "Wartime sex slaves to get at least $19,100." *Honolulu Advertiser,* 6

June, 1996: A:12.

Sullivan, George. *Strange But True Stories of World War II.* New York: Walker, 1983.

Swinson, Arthur. *Defeat In Malaya: The Fall Of Singapore.* New York: Ballantine, 1969.

Tan, Lily, ed. *The Japanese Occupation: Singapore 1942-1945.* Singapore: Archives and Oral History Dept., 1985.

Taylor, Lawrence. *A Trial of Generals.* South Bend: Icarus, 1981.

Terweil, B. J. *A History of Modern Thailand: 1767-1942.* London: University of Queensland Press, 1983.

The Battle of China. 1944. 67 min. International Historic Films. videocassette.

The Stilwell Road. 1986. Produced by the U.S. Army Signal Corps. Narrated by Ronald Reagan. 51 min., Viking Video Classics, videocassette.

Thompson, V. *Thailand, the New Siam.* New York: Paragon, 1967.

Timperley, Harold J. *Japanese Terror In China.* New York: Books For Libraries, 1969.

Togo, Shigehiko. "How A Japanese Diplomat Tried To Avoid War." *Honolulu Advertiser,* 1994, sec B.2.

Toland, John. *The Rising Sun: The Decline and Fall of the Japanese Empire 1936-1945.* New York: Random House, 1970.

To The Shores of Iwo Jima / Guadacanal. 1986. Produced by the U.S. Navy, 41 min., Viking Video Classics, videocassette.

Tse-Han, Lai and Ramon H. Myers. *A Tragic Beginning: The Taiwan Uprising of February 28, 1947.* Stanford: Stanford University Press, 1991.

Tsuji, Mosanobu. *Singapore: The Japanese Version.* New York: St. Martins, 1961.

Ulanoff, Stanley M., ed. *Fighter Pilot.* Garden City, New York: Doubleday, 1962.

U.S. Department of the Army, Office of the Chief of Military History. "Inner South Seas Islands Area Naval Operations, Part 2, Marshall Islands. (Dec. 1941- Feb. 1944)" *Japan Monographics, No. 173. 1945-1960b.*

Vader, John. *New Guinea: The Tide Is Stemmed.* New York: Ballantine, 1971.

Vandegrift, A.A. *Once A Marine.* New York: Norton, 1964.

Victory at Sea. 1952. Dir. M. Clay Adams. Vol. 1, Series 2 (Pearl Harbor) 22 min., Embassy Home Entertainment, videocassette.

———. 1986. Dir. M.Clay Adams. Vol. 1, Series 4 (Midway is East) 22 min., Embassy Home Entertainment, videocassette.

———. 1952. Dir. M. Clay Adams. Vol. 2, Series 6 (Guadalcanal) and 7 (Rabaul) 23 min., Embassy Home Entertainment, videocassette.

———. 1952. Dir. M. Clay Adams. Vol. 3, Series 12 (Gilberts and Marshalls) 23 min., Embassy Home Entertainment, videocassette.

———. 1952. Dir. M. Clay Adams. Vol. 4, Series 13 (New Guinea) 23 min., Embassy Home Entertainment, videocassette.

———. 1952. Dir. M. Clay Adams. Vol 5, Series 17 (Marianas Turkey Shoot) 23 min., Embassy Home Entertainment, videocassette.

———. 1952. Dir. M. Clay Adams. Vol 5, Series 18 (Peleliu and Angauer) 22 min., Embassy Home Entertainment, videocassette.

———. 1952. Dir. M. Clay Adams. Vol. 5, Series 19 (Battle for Leyte Gulf) and 20 (Liberation of the Philippines) 24 min., Embassy Home Entertainment, videocassette.

———. 1952. Dir. M. Clay Adams. Vol.6, Series 23 (Iwo Jima) 24 min., Embassy Home Entertainment, videocassette.

———. 1952. Dir. M. Clay Adams. Vol.6, Series 24 (China, Burma and India) 22 min., Embassy Home Entertainment, videocassette.

———. 1952. Dir. M. Clay Adams. Vol. 6, Series 25 (Okinawa) 25 min., Embassy Home Entertainment, videocassette.

———. 1952. Dir. M. Clay Adams. Vol. 6, Series 26 (Surrender of Japan) 23 min., Embassy Home Entertainment, videocassette.

Wa, Tsang Shuk. "Reliving War Days In Singapore." *Pacific Asia Travel News,* Mar. 1991, 30-32.

Werstein, Irving. Okinawa: The Last Ordeal. New York: Thomas Y. Crowell, 1968.

West, Rodney T. *Honolulu Prepares For Japan's Attack.* Unpublished booklet, 1992.

Wheeler, Keith. *The Road to Tokyo.* Chicago: Time Life Books, 1979.

Wheeler, Richard. A Special Valor: The U.S. Marines and the Pacific War. New York: Harper and Row, 1983.

———. *Iwo.* New York: Kensington, 1980.

White, Geoffrey M. and Lamont Lindstrom. ed. *The Pacific Theater: Island Representations of World War II.* Pacific Islands Monograph Series, No. 8. Honolulu: University of Hawaii Press, 1989.

White, Theodore H., ed. *The Stilwell Papers,* New York: MacFadden-Bartell, 1952.

Willmont, H.P. *Empires In The Balance: Japanese and Allied Strategies to April, 1942.* Annapolis: Naval Institute Press 1982.

Wilson, Dick. *When Tigers Fight: The Story of the Sino-Japanese War, 1937-1945.* New York; Penguin, 1983.

Winslow, W. G. *The Fleet the Gods Forgot.* Annapolis: Naval Institute Press, 1984.

———. *The Ghost That Died at Sundra Strait.* Annapolis: Naval Institute Press, 1984.

World War II: CBS Reports: Victory in the Pacific. 1995. 93 min., CBS News, videocassette.

World War II: The Great War. 1992. 150 min., Bridgestone Group. videocassette.

Wyatt, David K. *Thailand: A Short History.* New Haven: Yale University Press, 1982.

Wright, Michael A. *The World at Arms: Illustrated History of World War II.* New York, The Readers Digest Association, 1989.

Zangora, Donald S., ed. *Soviet Policy in East Asia.* New Haven: Yale University Press, 1982.

INDEX

335

Y

Z

Pearl Harbor Survivor

PhM2c Sterling Cale

"My God, those are Japanese planes, and we are being attacked."

Pharmacists mate Sterling Cale was assigned to the Pearl Harbor Shipyard dispensary on the morning of December 7, 1941. He saw the attacking aircraft and made the statement shown under his photograph. He was subsequently put in charge of the burial party that removed bodies from the USS *Arizona*.

Cale later served as a navy corpsman with the First Marine Division on Guadalcanal. He transferred to the U.S. Army in 1948, and served in Korea during the Korean War. He served in Vietnam from 1955 to 1974, both as an Army Sergeant Major, and a State Department civilian. Cale has an MBA degree from Chaminade University.

He retired in 2005 after 57 years of government service. He volunteers at the USS *Arizona* Memorial Visitors Center on a regular basis and shares his experiences with those that visit the memorial.